DOING QUALITATIVE
RESEARCH IN
EDUCATION
SETTINGS

DOING QUALITATIVE RESEARCH IN EDUCATION SETTINGS

J. Amos Hatch

STATE UNIVERSITY OF NEW YORK PRESS

Published by
State University of New York Press, Albany

For information, contact State University of New York Press, Albany, NY
www.sunypress.edu

Production by Christine L. Hamel
Marketing by Anne Valentine

Library of Congress Cataloging-in-Publication Data

Hatch, J. Amos.
  Doing qualitative research in education settings / by J. Amos Hatch.
    p. cm.
  Includes bibliographical references (p.) and index.
  ISBN-13: 978-0-7914-5503-6 (HC : alk. paper) —
978-0-7914-5504-3 (pbk. : alk. paper)
  ISBN 0-7914-5503-3 (HC : alk. paper) — 0-7914-5504-1 (pbk. : alk. paper)
    1. Education—Research. I. Title.

LB1028 .H36 2002
370'.7'2—dc21
                                                                2002023121

13 12 11 10

After all, for Deb

CONTENTS

Handwritten annotations: Wk 1, 1-20; Wk 2, 20-35; Wk 5, θ 38-41; Wk 4; Wk 15, θ 45-69; ← Wk 7-Chptr 3; Wk 3, θ71-91; Wk 6+8, θ131-140; Wk 9, θ116-131

vii

PREFACE

One of my responsibilities as a university professor has been to teach qualitative research methods to advanced graduate students in education, and teaching such courses has led me to see the need for a text that actually guides novice researchers through the concrete realities of planning and implementing qualitative studies. This book is a guide for *doing* qualitative research in education settings. The emphasis throughout is on learning how to do what it takes to plan, carry out, and write up a qualitative research project. My goal has been to provide enough structure and detail that novice researchers can get a handle on exactly what's required at the various stages of the research process.

Doing Qualitative Research in Education Settings is written primarily for graduate students and others new to qualitative research. I have tried to write in the same language I use when talking to bright, well-prepared students who are just learning about qualitative research. This is not "qualitative research for dummies." The complexity of qualitative work and depth of understanding needed to do it are addressed, but my approach is to be systematic about dealing with the complexity and straightforward about exploring the depth, giving new researchers a way to get into the research process without becoming overwhelmed by it.

I designed this book to be a primary text for an introductory course in qualitative research, but another audience is the large number of professors who serve on and sometimes chair the doctoral committees of students doing qualitative studies. Often these individuals have little formal training and no direct experience doing qualitative research themselves. The book is unique in that criteria for assessing the adequacy of each step of the research process are provided at the end of each chapter. This makes it possible for students and their professors to make judgments together about the quality of the work at each step along the way. An editor friend of mine reminded me that these criteria will also be helpful to individuals reviewing qualitative manuscripts for journals and book publishers.

While I admire many of the books devoted to qualitative research, most seem to be written for folks who already know a great deal about qualitative work. Even books that focus on qualitative methods leave novices wondering how to do qualitative research. I have tried to make this a methods book that speaks directly to new researchers and addresses their needs in a step-by-step fashion. I think this book contributes something different in the following ways:

- It is written in language that is accessible to graduate students (and instructors and doctoral committee members) who do not have an extensive background in qualitative research. The explicit audience is novice researchers.

- It emphasizes learning how to do qualitative work. Even the first chapter's focus on the historical and epistemological roots of qualitative research is framed within the practical reality of deciding if qualitative research is the way to go.

- Specific examples from real studies, using real data and demonstrating real analyses are provided throughout. The research process is demonstrated step-by-step.

- Each chapter includes a concluding section that provides students, instructors, and committee members with criteria for assessing the adequacy of each research element. These kinds of criteria provide useful guidance that is not found elsewhere.

- Extensive references to appropriate primary sources are included. While the book aims to be "to the point," it is well grounded in the relevant literature.

- The book is designed to guide doctoral candidates through the dissertation process. Chapters are framed around the assumption that students and committee chairs could use the book to shape and assess dissertation research from unpacking assumptions and identifying research questions through to writing the final draft.

- Alternative research paradigms are introduced, and alternative data collection strategies are explored. A taxonomy of qualitative paradigms is presented in chapter 1, and associated data collection and analysis methods are described throughout.

- Five approaches to *doing* qualitative data analysis are detailed. Many doctoral candidates get to the analysis phase of their research without a clue as to how to actually analyze their qualitative data, and these sections give novice researchers models that can be modified to fit a variety of qualitative data sets.

- Recommendations for writing up and publishing qualitative work are included in chapter 5. I use my experiences as a journal editor, dissertation examiner, and author to help students navigate the difficulties of writing and publishing qualitative studies.

The organization of the book parallels the development of a research project from beginning to end. I have been deliberately systematic as I describe the stages of the qualitative research process. From deciding if a qualitative approach is appropriate, through design, data collection, analysis, and writing up the final product, I have tried to provide enough structure to guide individuals who are working through the research endeavor for the first time. I expect that some experienced researchers will find this systematic approach stultifying. My response is that everyone needs a starting place from which to make changes. Everyone needs a framework on which to hang adaptations. Everyone needs a core set of ideas from which divergence emerges. This is not *the way* to do qualitative research. It is a starting place, a framework, a set of core ideas designed to help new researchers develop their own ways of doing qualitative research in education settings.

I would like to acknowledge everyone who has helped me learn about qualitative research, but the list is too long. I owe a special debt to the graduate students who have forced me to think through the ideas in this book, but listing all their names is impossible as well. I will name those with whom I have had the good fortune to work directly on projects related to qualitative research. In different ways, each of these individuals contributed to the thinking in this book. I am grateful for the lessons learned from colleagues Dorene Ross, Sue Kinzer, Buffy Bondy, Evelyn Freeman, Lynn Johnson, Dorothy Brice, Mary Kidwell, Mary Mason, Beverly McCarthy, Pam Browning, Marian Phillips, Gail Halliwell, Sue Grieshaber, Kerryann Walsh, and Charlotte Duncan. Special thanks to Rod Webb and Richard Wisniewski who have been mentors as well as colleagues. I also want to acknowledge the reviewers and editors who helped shape the final version of this book and thank Vicki Church, Melissa Salvaggio, Nathaly Perez, and Jennifer Gramling who assisted with the appendices, indexes, and figures.

CHAPTER ONE

_____

Deciding to Do a Qualitative Study

Should I do a qualitative study? This is a question I hear often as I meet with advanced graduate students and occasionally as I talk with academic colleagues. They come with a variety of reasons to answer yes to their own question. Some are convinced that qualitative research is more suited to their personal style. After all, educators would not be in the business unless they were interested in people and making positive social contacts with them, so the idea of treating teachers or children as subjects upon which experiments are to be done or treatments are to be tried seems off-putting for starters. Others are suspicious of the usefulness of quantitative research for making real changes in education. They have had to read a lot of traditional research as part of their training, and it's difficult for them to see how breaking the complex world of classrooms and schools into supposedly discrete dependent and independent variables then running sophisticated statistical analyses actually reveals much about what's really happening or what really needs to be done.

Others openly confess that they have never felt comfortable with math, especially statistics. They reason that their strengths are verbal and conceptual, so why not go with the best fit and take the qualitative route? Others are interested in taking action, in using their research to bring about social, political, and/or economic change. They have learned that in some qualitative approaches, engaging participants in the change process is a desirable outcome, while such an action orientation would be virtually forbidden in most quantitative work.

I am more empathetic with some reasons than others ("I am no good at math" is not my favorite). I understand that every person comes to the

1

decision about whether to go quantitative or qualitative with different understandings, feelings, and expectations. When I don't know the individuals, I usually try to find out what they know about qualitative research before I give advice. I try to give them my sense of what qualitative research can and cannot do. I emphasize the importance of receiving the appropriate "training" to do qualitative research—my rule of thumb is *at least* two formal qualitative research courses, one of which must include experience collecting real data and doing real analysis. Then I try to get them to do something that most of them have never been asked to do: unpack their ontological and epistemological beliefs.

Most students have heard the terms but have no idea what *ontology* and *epistemology* actually mean, so I ask them their beliefs about how the world is ordered and how we can come to know things about it. I try to outline my argument that their approach to thinking about research ought to grow out of their answers to the ontological and epistemological questions. I don't expect them to be able to articulate their metaphysical perspectives on the spot or to see with clarity the connections between assumptions and method, but I want to establish the importance of their being introspective about their worldviews and tying their assumptions to decision making about research (see Garrick, 1999).

Then I send them off to read. I usually recommend general texts to introduce them to the foundations and distinguishing features of qualitative work and more specific "methods" books if they have an interest in a particular methodological approach. I always suggest that the best way to find out what qualitative research is and what it can do is to read qualitative research reports in areas of scholarly interest to them. In addition, several internet sites include information about qualitative research (see appendix A for an annotated list of several such sites).

As I put this chapter together, I tried to include the kinds of information that I think beginning students of qualitative research ought to consider. I provide some foundational knowledge that prospective researchers should have before declaring that they will do a qualitative study. I present a list of characteristics that distinguish qualitative from quantitative research. I then offer a discussion of research paradigms that provides a way for novice researchers to begin to conceptualize the relationships among ontological, epistemological, and methodological issues and to come to terms with their own metaphysical assumptions. I next describe several kinds of qualitative research, including references to original sources and examples of studies done in educational settings using the approach described. I conclude the chapter with a discussion of what to call the work once one has decided to do it.

FOUNDATIONS

While direct applications of qualitative research to education settings are a fairly recent phenomenon, qualitative approaches to social research (especially in anthropology and sociology) have rich and interesting histories. The first professional qualitative researchers were probably anthropologists who wrote ethnographies describing "primitive" cultures in faraway places. Franz Boas was one of the first social scientists to spend time in natural settings and to attempt to understand a culture inductively. Working in the late 1800s, Boaz's studies were a sharp contrast to previous accounts provided by missionaries, explorers, and colonial bureaucrats who characterized the peoples they were describing in terms of their deficiencies in relation to Western culture and norms. Boaz was a cultural relativist who believed that the object of anthropological study is to describe the knowledge that members use to make sense within their own culture.

Denzin and Lincoln (1994) provide a framework of historical "moments" that is useful for thinking about the evolvement of qualitative research. From 1900 to World War II, the time Denzin and Lincoln (1994, p. 7) label the "traditional period," anthropologists such as Malinowski, Margaret Mead, and Radcliffe-Brown exemplified the model of the "lone ethnographer" (Rosaldo, 1989, p. 30), spending extended periods of time doing participant observations among natives in a distant land. They produced ethnographic accounts that are considered classics, and they developed fieldwork practices such as participant observation, interviewing, and artifact gathering that continue to be the mainstays of qualitative data collection today. While the work of these classic ethnographers is seen by many as relics that are linked to objectivism, colonialism, and imperialism (Denzin & Lincoln, 1994; Rosaldo, 1989), it provides important historical bedrock on which qualitative foundations are built.

In parallel with the development of qualitative anthropology, sociologists around the turn of the century were exploring the possibilities of qualitative research methods. Much of the activity in qualitative sociology centered on the emergence of "Chicago sociology" at the University of Chicago. Chicago sociologists utilized their city as a social laboratory and for three decades produced urban ethnographies that captured human life in the city (Vidich & Lyman, 1994). These researchers emphasized a slice-of-life approach, using the ordinary language of their participants to reveal the points of view of working-class and poor migrants. Chicago sociology was undertaken in the context of reform efforts by muckrakers, organized charities, and other social reformers, but advocating for reform was secondary to providing empirically based descriptions (Bogdan & Biklen, 1992). As in anthropology, the work of sociologists such as Redfield, Park, Thomas, and Hughes is recognized for its foundational contribution. However, contemporary scholars criticize the work as sociological stories that romanticized the subject, turning the deviant into a hero and producing the illusion that a solution to a social problem had been found (Denzin & Lincoln, 1994).

Denzin and Lincoln (1994, p. 8) characterize the period that extends from the postwar years to the mid-1970s as the "modernist phase." It was during this period that qualitative methods were formalized, and scholars became much more self-conscious about their research approaches. Qualitative researchers attempted to make a fit between positivist expectations for validity, reliability, and generalizability and constructivist models of doing research. Important books were written describing qualitative methods and alternative theoretical approaches. Glaser and Strauss published *The Discovery of Grounded Theory* (1967), and Blumer wrote *Symbolic Interactionism* (1969). In education, books by Jackson (1968), Wolcott (1973), Henry (1965), and the Spindlers (1955) pointed to the efficacy of applying qualitative methods to understanding the special social contexts of schools and schooling. New theories associated with ethnomethodology, phenomenology, critical theory, and feminism began to be recognized (Denzin & Lincoln, 1994).

The next period includes the 1970s and early 80s, the "moment of blurred genres," according to Denzin and Lincoln (1994, p. 9). The blurring was widespread. A wide range of paradigms, methods, and strategies became available, and researchers were reaching across boundaries as they designed and reported their work. Qualitative researchers in education sampled perspectives, theories, and methods from a variety of fields, challenging traditional territoriality among disciplines. Further, the boundaries between the social sciences and humanities were becoming blurred as interpretive methods such as semiotics and hermeneutics that were developed in the humanities began being adapted for use in qualitative analyses (Denzin & Lincoln, 1994).

It was during this time that qualitative work began to develop more stature as a legitimate form of educational research. The great paradigm war between quantitative and qualitative scholars raged in the pages of *The Educational Researcher* during these and subsequent years, and many more sessions at national research conferences, especially the American Educational Research Association (AERA) meetings, were given to qualitative presenters (Hatch, 1995a). A number of journals devoted to publishing qualitative studies were begun, and mainstream education journals began to publish occasional qualitative studies.

The blurring of genres has continued and the complexity of qualitative work has escalated during the years since 1985. I will try to unravel some of that complexity later in this chapter, but to wrap up this mini-history, something needs to be said about the "crisis of representation," Denzin and Lincoln's (1994, p. 9) name for the stage that takes them through the publication of their essay in 1994. Critical anthropologists of this period (e.g., Clifford, 1988; Marcus & Fischer, 1986) challenged the norms of classic ethnography, arguing that traditional methods and writing produce texts that do not and cannot represent lived experience. They contend that understandings of human experience are always processed through language, and language is inherently unstable (Denzin, 1989a). Ethnographers who claim to have captured their participants' perspectives in field notes and interviews then written these into accounts that objectively represent the cultural experience of those participants are said to be *creating culture* rather than representing reality. The crisis of representation places qualitative researchers in a bind similar to the one they created for their quantitative colleagues. Its resolution may require another paradigm shift, to include new ways of thinking about what constitutes "Truth" and ways to come to know and communicate it.

It is useful to divide this historical overview into periods following Denzin and Lincoln's moments, but it is important to remember that, as the field has evolved, the development of new perspectives and methods has not meant the abandonment of perspectives and methods that came before (for a comprehensive critique of the five moments model, see Delamont, Coffey, & Atkinson, 2000). At present, deconstructivist and poststructuralist perspectives are being taken seriously by contemporary qualitative researchers, and critical, feminist, and other transformative epistemologies are having a major impact on the field, but there are qualitative researchers who continue to do work that might be classified as "traditional" or "modernist." As Denzin and Lincoln (1994, p. 11) point out, "each of the earlier historical moments is still operating in the present, either as legacy or as a set of practices that researchers still follow or argue against." Later in this chapter, I describe an array of perspectives and methods that define the field of contemporary qualitative research. For now, I want to give more information to help potential researchers make methodological decisions by describing characteristics of qualitative research.

What is qualitative research? What about qualitative research distinguishes it from other forms of inquiry? What kinds of knowledge are foundational for understanding qualitative research? What are the kinds of research that count as qualitative? What should I call my research? These are questions novice qualitative researchers should struggle with as they consider doing qualitative work. When I make students confront these questions, I don't tell them they have to find *the answer* to each question because I don't believe a single correct answer exists. I do tell them that they have to find *an*

answer, that they must be able to articulate *their answer* in a rational and consistent manner, and that I will force them to defend their answer at every step of the research process.

Qualitative researchers have attempted to define their work in many different ways. The literature contains a variety of approaches to defining what qualitative research is and is not (see Potter, 1996). Definitions range from straightforward attempts such as "any kind of research that produces findings that are not arrived at by means of statistical procedures or other means of quantification" (Strauss & Corbin, 1990, p. 17) to more descriptive formulations such as "a research paradigm which emphasizes inductive, interpretive methods applied to the everyday world which is seen as subjective and socially created" (Anderson, 1987, p. 384), to more product-oriented statements, for example, "research procedures which produce descriptive data: people's own written or spoken words and observable behavior. [It] directs itself at settings and the individuals within those settings holistically; that is, the subject of the study, be it an organization or an individual, is not reduced to an isolated variable or to an hypothesis, but is viewed instead as part of a whole" (Bogdan & Taylor, 1975, p. 2). Coming up with a dictionary definition is not essential, but thinking about and exploring the definitions of others is useful because it forces researchers to consider the boundaries of what they are doing. I ask students to write descriptions of what they think qualitative research is. Their responses may be a sentence, paragraph, or short essay. The form matters less than the act of organizing one's thoughts and establishing some conceptual boundaries.

CHARACTERISTICS

Many attempts have been made to characterize qualities that distinguish qualitative work from other research approaches. I have reviewed several widely cited sources to synthesize the following list of characteristics. The goal is not to provide a definitive list against which all qualitative work ought to be measured. Different research approaches within the qualitative domain emphasize certain characteristics, ignore others, and generate alternatives. The intent here is to give novice researchers a starting place for understanding the dimensions of qualitative work. Descriptions are brief, and readers are invited to search out original sources for a more comprehensive discussion (see also Hatch, 1998).

Natural Settings

For qualitative researchers, the lived experiences of real people in real settings are the objects of study. Understanding how individuals make sense of their everyday lives is the stuff of this type of inquiry. When research settings are controlled or contrived or manipulated, as in traditional research, the outcomes are studies that tell us little more than how individuals act in narrowly defined and inherently artificial contexts. In qualitative work, the intent is to explore human behaviors within the contexts of their natural occurrence (Bogdan & Biklen, 1992; Erickson, 1986; Hammersley & Atkinson, 1983; Jacob, 1988; Lincoln & Guba, 1985).

Participant Perspectives

Qualitative research seeks to understand the world from the perspectives of those living in it. It is axiomatic in this view that individuals act on the world based not on some supposed objective reality but on their perceptions of the realities that surround them. Qualitative studies try to capture the perspectives that actors use as a basis for their actions in specific social settings. Erickson (1986) identifies the key questions that qualitative researchers ask as: "What is happening here, specifically? What do these happenings mean to the people engaged in them?" (p. 124). The perspectives or voices of participants ought to be prominent in any qualitative report (Bogdan & Biklen, 1992; Hammersley & Atkinson, 1983; Jacob, 1988; Lincoln & Guba, 1985).

Researcher as Data Gathering Instrument

While traditional, quantitative methods generate data through the use of instruments such as questionnaires, checklists, scales, tests, and other measuring devices, the principal data for qualitative researchers are gathered directly by the researchers themselves. These data usually include field notes from participant observation, notes from or transcriptions of interviews with informants, and unobtrusive data such as artifacts from the research site or records related to the social phenomena under investigation. Even when mechanical or electronic devices are used to support qualitative work, data take on no significance until they are processed using the human intelligence of the researcher. The logic behind the researcher-as-instrument approach is that the human capacities necessary to participate in social life are the same capacities that enable qualitative researchers to make sense of the actions, intentions, and understandings of those being studied (Bogdan & Biklen, 1992; Hammersley & Atkinson, 1983; Lincoln & Guba, 1985; Spradley, 1979). As Hymes (1982) put it, "Our ability to learn ethnographically is an extension of what every human must do, that is, learn the meanings, norms, patterns of a way of life" (p. 29).

Extended Firsthand Engagement

I began my Ph.D. program with the expectation that I would refine the quasiexperimental study I did for my master's degree and complete the whole study, write-up and all, within six months of finishing my coursework. I discovered alternative ways of thinking about the world and doing research in my doctoral program and became a convert. I remember sitting with my mentor and deciding that I needed to add at least 18 months to my timeline in order to follow my convictions and do a qualitative project. The unofficial standard for qualitative dissertations when I was in graduate school was at least one year in the field and an equal amount of time for analysis and writing. While I often negotiate back from that standard when working with most of my own students, extended engagement continues to be one of the hallmarks of high-quality qualitative work.

If researchers are to understand participant perspectives in natural contexts, it makes immanent sense that they must spend enough time with those participants in those contexts to feel confident that they are capturing what they claim (Erickson, 1986; Spindler, 1982; Walsh, Tobin, & Graue, 1993; Wolcott, 1992). The fieldwork tradition remains strong, and critics of the rising popularity of qualitative approaches worry that some researchers select data collection strategies from the ethnographic tradition but spend far too little time in research settings, a phenomenon Rist (1980) labeled "Blitzkrieg Ethnography." My own experiences as an editor and editorial board member lead me to believe that spending insufficient time in the field continues to be a serious flaw in the qualitative work I see. I understand the practicalities of doing research, especially doctoral dissertation research, but overall, qualitative researchers are not spending enough time being intensely engaged in the settings they are studying.

Centrality of Meaning

The philosophical roots of qualitative research can be traced to the German intellectual tradition expressed in the social sciences in the "interpretive sociology" of Max Weber (Giddens, 1971, p. 143). In contrast to the nineteenth-century French positivist sociologists (e.g., Comte and Durkheim), Weber and his followers stressed the importance of *verstehen* (understanding) in their social analyses. They were interested in describing the meanings individuals used to understand social circumstances rather than trying to identify the "social facts" that comprise a positivist social theory (Hatch, 1985, p. 143). Blumer (1969) contributed symbolic interactionist theory as a conceptual tool for systematically exploring understandings. Three premises of symbolic interactionism signal the central importance of meaning: (a) human beings act toward things on the basis of the meaning that the things have for them; (b) the meaning of such things is derived from, or arises out of, the social interaction that one has with one's fellows; and (c) these meanings are handled in, and sometimes modified through, an interpretive process used by individuals in dealing with the things they encounter (Blumer, 1969). Not all qualitative research is done within the symbolic interactionist framework, but all qualitative research is about understanding the meanings individuals construct in order to participate in their social lives (Bogdan & Biklen, 1992; Erickson, 1986; Lincoln & Guba, 1985; Schwartz & Jacobs, 1979).

Wholeness and Complexity

Qualitative work starts with the assumption that social settings are unique, dynamic, and complex. Qualitative methods provide means whereby social contexts can be systematically examined as a whole, without breaking them down into isolated, incomplete, and disconnected variables. Qualitative data are objects, pictures, or detailed descriptions that cannot be reduced to numbers without distorting the essence of the social meanings they represent. Qualitative reports are usually complex, detailed narratives that include the voices of the participants being studied. They build the case for the researcher's interpretations by including enough detail and actual data to take the reader inside the social situation under examination (Bogdan & Biklen, 1992; Erickson, 1986; Hammersley & Atkinson, 1983; Peshkin, 1988).

Subjectivity

Qualitative research is as interested in inner states as outer expressions of human activity. Because these inner states are not directly observable, qualitative researchers must rely on subjective judgments to bring them to light. Wolcott (1994) draws distinctions among qualitative studies that emphasize description, analysis, and interpretation. Subjective judgment is necessary in all three but more is required as researchers move from description toward interpretation. Most qualitative researchers would deny the possibility of pure objectivity in any scientific endeavor. Most would argue that all their findings, including interpretations, are grounded in empirical evidence captured in their data. Instead of pretending to be objective, the stance of qualitative researchers is to concentrate on reflexively applying their own subjectivities in ways that make it possible to understand the tacit motives and assumptions of their participants (Hamilton, 1994; Jacob, 1987; Lincoln & Guba, 1985).

Emergent Design

It is characteristic of qualitative research that studies change as they are being implemented. Because the goal is to get inside a social phenomenon in a special social setting, it is impossible to construct a design *a priori* that takes into account what the researcher finds out upon actually entering the social setting to be studied (Lincoln & Guba, 1985). This often becomes a sore spot between doctoral candidates and their committees. Many committees expect a research proposal that represents a contract specifying exactly what students will do, when and for how long they will do it, and what questions will be answered in the doing. Some students prepare proposals that specify very little or nothing, claiming that the design will emerge once they are in the setting. Although they differ on the extent to which research designs should be left to emerge (cf., Wolcott, 1992), most qualitative researchers would agree that research questions, methods, and other elements of design are altered as studies unfold (Jacob, 1988).

Inductive Data Analysis

Qualitative researchers do not begin with a null hypothesis to retain or reject. They collect as many detailed specifics from the research setting as possible, then set about the process of looking for patterns of relationship among the specifics. In Bogdan and Biklen's (1992) words, "You are not putting together a puzzle, whose picture you already know. You are constructing a picture that takes shape as you collect and examine the parts" (p. 29). Findings generated from this process are said to be grounded in the data—generated from the ground up. Qualitative data analysis involves a deductive dimension. As patterns or relationships are discovered in the data, hypothetical categories are formed, and the data are then read deductively to determine if these categories are supported by the overall data set (see Erickson, 1986). Still, the overall pattern of data analysis in qualitative work is decidedly inductive, moving from specifics to analytic generalizations (Lincoln & Guba, 1985).

Reflexivity

In qualitative work, it is understood that the act of studying a social phenomenon influences the enactment of that phenomenon. Researchers are a part of the world they study; the knower and the known are taken to be inseparable. For Hammersley and Atkinson (1983), "this is not a matter of methodological commitment, it is an existential fact. There is no way to escape the social world in order to study it; nor, fortunately, is that necessary" (p. 15). Being reflexive places qualitative researchers in a distinctly different position than that of the "objective scientist" usually prescribed in more traditional research activities. The capacities to be reflexive, to keep track of one's influence on a setting, to bracket one's biases, and to monitor one's emotional responses are the same capacities that allow researchers to get close enough to human action to understand what is going on (Lincoln & Guba, 1985; Walsh, Tobin, & Graue, 1993). Reflexivity, "the process of personally and academically reflecting on lived experiences in ways that reveal deep connections between the writer and his or her subject" (Goodall, 2000, p. 137), is essential to the integrity of qualitative research.

The foregoing discussion is meant to portray characteristics of qualitative research in broad strokes. As will be evident later in this chapter (and throughout the book), not all qualitative approaches feel bound by these characteristics. Across the spectrum of qualitative research possibilities, some approaches will include attention to all these characteristics, some will pick and choose from among these, and some will include alternative characteristics that seem to be in opposition to those listed here. Still, understanding the characteristics listed provides a starting place for understanding qualitative research in relation to more traditional forms of scholarship.

5 RESEARCH PARADIGMS

Paradigm is one of those words that is overused to the point that its meaning has been lost. Writers of popular books about everything from business to gardening use the notion of a paradigm shift to sell the importance of their products or ideas. I've heard television preachers use the term, seen it on the backs of trucks going down the highway, and read a brochure that touts a new paradigm in termite control.

In the social sciences, the notion of scientific paradigm was brought to the fore by Thomas Kuhn (1970) in his landmark book, *The Structure of Scientific Revolutions*. Kuhn argued that the history of science is a history of revolutions wherein scientific paradigms have emerged, suffered crises, and been replaced by competing paradigms. In order for a school of scientific thought to ascend to the status of "normal science," it must meet the criteria for paradigms. That is, it must have generated firm answers to the following questions: What are the fundamental entities of which the universe is composed? How do these interact with each other and with the senses? What questions can legitimately be asked about such entities and what techniques employed in seeking solutions? Answers to these questions reveal sets of assumptions that distinguish fundamentally different belief systems concerning how the world is ordered, what we may know about it, and how we may know it. It is in this sense that *paradigm* will be used here.

Based on Kuhn's notion, I have organized the following discussion around five research paradigms: positivist, postpositivist, constructivist, critical/feminist, and poststructuralist. For each paradigm, I present an abbreviated answer to the ontological question (What is the nature of reality?), the epistemological question(s) (What can be known, and what is the relationship of the knower to what is to be known?), and the methodological question (How is knowledge gained?). In addition, I outline what forms knowledge takes when produced within the assumptions of each paradigm.

The objective is to give novice qualitative researchers a framework for exploring their own assumptions about what research is and how it works. Having tried to help scores of advanced graduate students, I have learned that unpacking assumptions is no simple matter. The very nature of assumptions is that they are unexamined, so it gets intellectually tricky right away. Plus, graduate students who are at the stage of thinking about dissertation research often want to start with research questions. They have been told or have assumed that you begin with a question then shop around for the kind of research approach that best allows you to answer that question. Many professors and some institutions encourage this research-question-first approach. For example, Metz (2001, p. 13) begins her description of a "common anatomy for social scientific research" by identifying the research question as "the starting point and most important issue in developing research." As will be seen throughout this book, I agree that research questions are central to the inquiry process; but they ought not be the starting point. Starting with a research question begins in the middle and ignores the fundamental necessity of taking a deep look at the belief systems that undergird our thinking. For me, struggling with paradigm issues, exploring assumptions, and coming to grips with differences in worldviews and what they mean for doing research are essential first steps. Too few doctoral-level students actively confront these issues at any point (see Pallas, 2001), but when such considerations don't come early in the process, researchers risk producing work that lacks logical consistency at the least or flies in the face of theoretical integrity at the worst.

As the paradigms are discussed, I recommend that the reader consider his or her own answers to each set of questions. This can be a good starting place for digging inside what we all take for granted. Figure 1.1 offers a schematic representation of the basic ideas in the sections that follow. Although my labels and organization are different, and I have added "products" to the analysis, the discussion travels the same path as chapters by Denzin and Lincoln (1994) and Guba and Lincoln (1994). The reader will find it useful to explore these frameworks as well.

Positivist Paradigm

Ontology. What is the nature of reality? Positivists are realists who believe in an objective universe that has order independent of human perceptions. Reality exists and is driven by universal, natural laws. Positivism treats reality as being componential, that is, consisting of components that can be taken apart for study, separately verified, then put back together again.

Figure 1.1:

Research Paradigms

	Ontology (Nature of reality)	Epistemology (What can be known; Relationship of knower & known)	Methodology (How knowledge is gained)	Products (Forms of knowledge produced)
Positivist	Reality is out there to be studied, captured, and understood	How the world is really ordered; Knower is distinct from known	Experiments, quasi-experiments, surveys, correlational studies	Facts, theories, laws, predictions
Postpositivist	Reality exists but is never fully apprehended, only approximated	Approximations of reality; Researcher is data collection instrument	Rigorously defined qualitative methods, frequency counts, low-level statistics	Generalizations, descriptions, patterns, grounded theory
Constructivist	Multiple realities are constructed	Knowledge as a human construction; Researcher and participant co-construct understandings	Naturalistic qualitative methods	Case studies, narratives, interpretations, reconstructions
Critical/Feminist	The apprehended world makes a material difference in terms of race, gender, and class	Knowledge as subjective and political; Researchers' values frame inquiry	Transformative inquiry	Value mediated critiques that challenge existing power structures and promote resistance
Poststructuralist	Order is created within individual minds to ascribe meaning to a meaningless universe.	There is no "Truth" to be known; Researchers examine the world through textual representations of it.	Deconstruction; Genealogy; Data-based, multivoiced studies	Deconstructions; Genealogies; Reflexive, polyvocal texts

POSITIVIST PARADIGM (cont'd)

Epistemology What can be known, and what is the relationship of the knower to the known? The world has order, and it is possible to discover that order. The world is, in effect, giving off signals regarding its true nature, and it is the job of science to capture that immutable truth. Positivists claim to be objective in their search for the truth. Researchers and the objects of their study are assumed to be mutually independent, so researchers do not influence and are not influenced by the phenomena they study.

Methodology How can knowledge be gained? Methods of choice within the positivist paradigm are those that allow for careful measurement, manipulation, and control. A deductive model built on empirically verifying propositional hypotheses dominates, and experiments, quasiexperiments, correlational studies, and surveys are widely used. Sophisticated sampling and statistical techniques are in place to ensure reliability, validity, and generalizability.

Products What forms of knowledge are produced? For positivists, knowledge equals accumulated "facts" that have been scientifically verified and generalizations, theories, and laws based on those facts. Most reports have a cause-and-effect dimension, and prediction is the ultimate product. If conditions are controlled, positivist science can predict what will happen when certain changes are introduced.

Postpositivist Paradigm

Ontology Postpositivists agree with positivists that reality exists, but they operate from the assumption that, because of the limitations of human inquiry, the inherent order of the universe can never be known completely. Reality can be approximated but never fully apprehended. Postpositivists are critical realists who subject truth claims to close critical scrutiny in order to maximize chances of apprehending reality as closely as possible—but never perfectly (Cook & Campbell, 1979; Guba & Lincoln, 1994).

Epistemology Postpositivist researchers work to capture close approximations of reality. They seek to maintain an objective position in relation to the phenomena they are studying. Researchers in this paradigm see themselves as data collection instruments, and they use disciplined research techniques such as "constant comparison" (Glaser & Strauss, 1967) or "analytic induction" (Robinson, 1951) to ensure that empirical data, and not their impressions, drive their findings.

Methodology Qualitative methods that prescribe rigorous techniques to improve validity and reliability are used by postpositivists. Low inference, systematic procedures dominate data analysis processes (e.g., Glaser & Strauss,

1967; Kirk & Miller, 1986; Miles & Huberman, 1994), and frequency counts and low-level statistics are sometimes used. Postpositivists are interested in capturing participant perspectives but in rigorously disciplined ways.

|Products.|Knowledge forms produced in this paradigm include analytic generalizations, descriptions, patterns, and grounded theory. Data collection and analysis processes lead to descriptions of patterned behavior that participants use to make sense of their social surroundings. Generalizations are induced from systematic analyses of data that take the form of|searches for patterns.| When potential patterns are discovered, deductive processes are used to verify the strength of those patterns in the overall data set. Grounded theory (Glaser & Strauss, 1967) is the archtypical product of this type of inquiry.

|Constructivist Paradigm|

|Ontology| Constructivists assume a world in which universal, absolute realities are unknowable, and the objects of inquiry are individual perspectives or constructions of reality. While acknowledging that elements are often shared across social groups, constructivist science argues that multiple realities exist that are inherently unique because they are constructed by individuals who experience the world from their own vantage points. Realities are apprehendable in the form of abstract mental constructions that are experientially based, local, and specific (Guba & Lincoln, 1994).

|Epistemology| It follows that individual constructions of reality compose the knowledge of interest to constructivist researchers. They assert that "knowledge is symbolically constructed and not objective; that understandings of the world are based on conventions; that truth is, in fact, what we agree it is" (Hatch, 1985, p. 161)/Researchers and the participants|in their studies are joined together in the process of coconstruction. From this perspective, it is impossible and undesirable for researchers to be distant and objective. It is through mutual engagement that researchers and respondents construct the subjective reality that is under investigation (see Mishler, 1986).

| Methodology.|Naturalistic qualitative research methods are the data collection and analytic tools of the constructivist (Lincoln & Guba, 1985). Researchers spend extended periods of time interviewing participants and observing them in their natural settings in an effort to reconstruct the constructions participants use to make sense of their worlds. Hermeneutic principles are used to guide researchers' interpretive coconstructions of participant perspectives (Guba & Lincoln, 1994).

| Products.|Knowledge produced within the constructivist paradigm is often presented in the form of case studies or rich narratives that describe the

interpretations constructed as part of the research process. Accounts include enough contextual detail and sufficient representation of the voices of the participants that readers can place themselves in the shoes of the participants at some level and judge the quality of the findings based on criteria other than those used in positivist and postpositivist paradigms. As Denzin & Lincoln (1994) explain, "Terms such as credibility, transferability, dependability, and confirmability replace the usual positivist criteria of internal and external validity, reliability, and objectivity" (p. 14).

Critical/Feminist Paradigm

In earlier drafts, I divided critical and feminist approaches into their own paradigms. As I have thought them through, studied others' conceptualizations (e.g., Lather, 1991a), and taught students about them, I have concluded that it is useful to think of them as being in the same research paradigm, but having different emphases. I place them in the same paradigm because they share the metaphysical elements that make up a paradigm. Even as I do this, I hesitate because I know that there are critical and feminist scholars who operate within each of the other paradigms identified (see Reinharz, 1992). Still, the worldview represented by the metaphysical assumptions below qualifies as a research paradigm (Carr, 1995), and sufficient work has been done based on this worldview to qualify for inclusion in a book about qualitative methods in educational research. As these elements are addressed, I will acknowledge the emphases that distinguish critical from feminist perspectives.

Ontology. For critical theorists and feminists, the material world is made up of historically situated structures that have a real impact on the life chances of individuals. These structures are perceived to be real (i.e., natural and immutable), and social action resulting from their perceived realness leads to differential treatment of individuals based on race, gender, and social class. According to Guba and Lincoln (1994), "these structures are, in the absence of insight, as limiting and confining as if they were real" (p. 111). Feminist scholars are most interested in exposing material differences gender makes in women's life chances, and critical scholars focus on issues related to race and social class.

Epistemology. Knowledge within this set of assumptions is subjective and inherently political. Knowledge is always "value mediated" in the sense that "the investigator and the investigated object are assumed to be interactively linked, with the values of the investigator inevitably influencing the inquiry" (Guba & Lincoln, 1994, p. 110). This is in sharp contrast to the objective stance taken in positivist and postpositivist work. In critical/feminist work, philosophies and values are seen as "integral rather than antithetical" to the research process (Carr, 1995, p. 97). In this worldview, it is assumed that knowledge is always mediated through the political positionings of the researcher.

|Methodology.| One of the purposes of this kind of inquiry is to raise the consciousness of those being oppressed because of historically situated structures tied to race, gender, and class. With raising consciousness comes providing understandings that lead to social change. Such methods have been called ("transformative") (Carr, 1995; Giroux, 1988), in that they require dialogue between researchers and participants that can lead to social change that transforms the lives of the participants in positive ways. Data collection takes many of the same forms as constructivist research, but the emphasis for critical researchers is to improve life chances for individuals at the bottom of the social hierarchy, while feminists' primary focus is on making conditions better for women.

|Products.| Critical and feminist scholars produce critiques of the perceived material world in an effort to expose the structures that ensure the maintenance of control by those in power (e.g., capitalist economics for critical theorists and male hegemony for feminists). The object is to reveal for others the kinds and extent of oppression that are being experienced by those studied. With the exposure of oppression comes the call for awareness, resistance, solidarity, and revolutionary transformation.

Poststructuralist Paradigm

It is not easy to capture the complexity of poststructuralist approaches to inquiry in an analysis such as this. In some ways, poststructuralism is an antiparadigm because its tenets can be used to deconstruct all of the paradigms above. In a broader sense, it offers a fundamental challenge to all "modernist versions of social science" (Graham, Doherty, & Malek, 1992, p. 11). Further complicating matters, many contemporary critical and feminist scholars have moved in the direction of poststructuralist thinking in their work. I have some reservations about the logical consistency of being a "critical poststructuralist" or "feminist poststructuralist" because poststructural theory deconstructs grand narratives, including critical theory and feminism (see Hatch, 1999). Poststructuralism also rejects the ideal of emancipation as it rejects the notions of progress and perfectibility and therefore problematizes the critical and feminist project at a fundamental level (see Graham, Doherty, & Malek, 1992). Some critical theorists acknowledge the incompatibility of the two perspectives, reject the claims of poststructuralists, and favor returning to a more purely Marxist form of critical theory (see McLaren and Farahmandpur, 2000). Some feminist scholars argue that a strategically refigured poststructural feminist "hybrid" is developing that goes well beyond a simple synthesis of feminist and poststructuralist thought (St. Pierre, 2000, p. 477). The issues are complex, but the reader should know that many post-structuralist scholars in the social sciences identify themselves as critical theorists or feminists. In order to provide a beginning sense of how poststructuralist thought relates to other worldviews, I will identify paradigmatic elements using the same format as above. As will be evident, distinctions between ontological and epistemological assumptions are blurred in poststructuralist thinking (see Guba & Lincoln, 1994).

Ontology. Sartre (1964) wrote: "Nothing really happens when you live. The scenery changes, people come in and go out, that's all. There are no beginnings. Days are tacked on to days without rhyme or reason, an interminable monotonous addition" (p. 39). These powerful sentences capture poststructuralists' view of the nature of reality. They believe that order is created in the minds of individuals in an attempt to give meaning to events that have no "intrinsic or immanent relations" (Freeman, 1993, p. 95). Thus, there are multiple realities, each with its own claims to coherence, and none can be privileged over another (Graham, Doherty, & Malek, 1992). Those claims take form in the discourses that we construct to make sense of our lives. Those discourses are, in effect, texts that represent our lives, and we can only know the world through textual representations of it.

Epistemology. What *cannot* be known is Truth with a capital T. Poststructuralists start by deconstructing the notion of universal Truth. Their analyses reveal how grand narratives are constructed in particular social-historical circumstances to serve the purposes of those in power. For poststructuralists, multiple truths exist, and these are always local, subjective, and in flux. Researchers do not have direct access to the truths experienced by their subjects; they can never know or represent the lived experiences of those they study—hence, the crisis of representation discussed above. For some, this means that research is impossible (see Clough, 1998). Others are working at the fringes between poststructuralist and other paradigms to produce alternative forms of inquiry that include queer theory (Warner, 1993), performance theory (Phelan, 1993), postcolonial theory (Moore-Gilbert, 1997), critical race theory (Parker, Deyhle, Villenas, & Nebeker, 1998), and cultural studies (Peters, 1999),

Methodology. I divide poststructuralist researchers into three camps: (a) deconstructivists who, following Derrida (1981), use deconstruction as a methodological tool to examine textual representations of the world, searching for aporia, inconsistencies, or gaps where the internal logic of the text unravels (see Sarap, 1993; Tobin, 1995); (b) genealogists who, using historical methods developed by Foucault (1977), problematize particular practices by revealing "the ways in which the practice was historically justified, the discourses that were used for that justification, and the assumptions underlying forms of representation that are part of the practices" (Cannella & Bailey, 1999, pp. 23–24; see also Meadmore, Hatcher, & McWilliam, 2000); and (c) poststructuralists doing data-based research. I agree with Graham, Doherty, and Malek (1992) that the latter are searching for new ways to do social science but that those new ways are still poorly worked out. As a result, they are using many of the methods of other qualitative paradigms. What makes poststructuralists distinct is their focus on understanding data as texts that represent one of many stories that could be told. They acknowledge distinctions among lives as lived, lives as experienced, and lives as told (Bruner, 1984). They accept that they create lives as they hear lives told, process them through their own perspectives, and put them to text as lives as written (see Hatch & Wisniewski, 1995).

Products. Deconstructivists produce analyses that reveal the internal incongruities of discourses and expose the consequences of actions taken based on the assumed Truthfulness of those discourses. Poststructuralists doing genealogical work produce critiques that reveal historical ruptures that challenge the foundations of modern structures, institutions, and discourses. Other poststructuralist researchers generate research reports that attempt to include multiple voices, that acknowledge the specific, local, situational, partial, and temporary nature of the stories being told (see Van Maanen, 1988), and that are framed within a reflexive mode that acknowledges the researchers' prominent place in the research and writing process.

As Kuhn (1970) made clear, when you are standing within the circle of logic created by the assumptions of your paradigm, the positions taken by those working in other paradigms simply do not make sense. Paradigms are indeed completing ways of thinking about how the world is or is not ordered, what counts as knowledge, and how and if knowledge can be gained. It's logical, for example, that critical/feminists will not count the apolitical subjective stance taken by positivist researchers as legitimate (e.g., Lather, 1991a), or that poststructuralists will not buy into constructivist notions of mutually constituted realities (e.g., Garrick, 1999). I have tried to identify key elements that define the conflicted territories dividing the paradigms outlined. The goal is to give beginning researchers a starting place for exploring their metaphysical beliefs. Of course, each paradigm has its own defenders and detractors, and students are encouraged to explore paradigms much more deeply based on the beginning structure provided here.

Should I do a qualitative study? What if my answers to the ontological and epistemological questions indicate that I'm a positivist. Can I still do a qualitative study? What if I'm not sure? I have spent many hours talking with students about these and related questions. Most students, like most individuals socialized into Western belief systems, hold a taken-for-granted metaphysical view that fits best within the positivist paradigm. When they start to think about what that means about them and about research, it is often a troubling experience. For some, such contemplations include a religious dimension—they are intellectually attracted to belief systems that challenge the notions of absolute Truth while at the same time holding that certain truths are unquestionable. Some just don't buy into the notion that a researcher's methodological choices ought to be bound by his or her assumptions about how the world is ordered and how it can be known. This is especially common among students who want to mix quantitative and qualitative methods.

I don't stand in the way of students who are unable to find a natural fit within one of the paradigms associated with qualitative research. I sometimes decline invitations to serve on doctoral committees, and occasionally I do so because students do not seem able to articulate their metaphysical assumptions. But when students generate their own answers to these tough questions and, where necessary, acknowledge the potential conflicts in mixing paradigms and/or methods, I do my best to help them chart a reasonable path.

KINDS OF QUALITATIVE RESEARCH

It could be said that there are as many kinds of qualitative research as there are qualitative researchers. Each qualitative study has its own unique character that develops and often changes as studies are implemented. Still, students new to the field want to know what are the kinds of qualitative research from which to chose. I include this section because it is useful to think about some specific kinds of qualitative research that will give potential researchers an idea of what has been done and what it is possible to do. Again, this is territory that is hard to describe because of its complexity and dynamic nature. The attempt is not to be comprehensive, but to offer examples of the array of possibilities. I give brief descriptions of each type of qualitative study and provide citations that will make it possible for readers to find examples and more detailed discussions. I also note the relationship of each kind of research identified to the paradigms discussed above. As will be seen, most kinds of qualitative research fit within multiple paradigms, excluding the positivist.

Ethnographies

Ethnography is not synonymous with qualitative research. It is a particular kind of qualitative research that seeks to describe culture or parts of culture from the point of view of cultural insiders (Jacob, 1987; Malinowski, 1922; Spradley, 1979; Wolcott, 1982). Ethnography is the classic form of qualitative research that was developed by anthropologists who spent extended periods of time doing fieldwork within cultural groups. Fieldwork usually involves participant observation, informant interviewing, and artifact collection in an effort to come to understand the cultural knowledge that group members use to make sense of their everyday experiences. Contemporary ethnographers often study subcultures, communities, or even classrooms, but their goals remain consistent with classic fieldworkers, that is, "to account for the behavior of people by describing what it is that they know that enables them to behave appropriately given the dictates of common sense in their community" (McDermott, 1976, p. 159).

Classic anthropological ethnographies were mostly framed within the postpositivist paradigm. Some of the best examples of contemporary ethnographies done in education are those of Peshkin (e.g., 1986; 1991; 1997). Some scholars call their work "critical ethnography" (e.g., Britzman, 1991), "feminist ethnography" (see Behar & Gordon, 1995), or "poststructuralist ethnography" (see Clifford & Marcus, 1986). When such labels are applied, the adjectives signal the paradigm, while *ethnography* usually refers to the writers' intent to represent cultural knowledge in some form.

Microethnographies

Jacob (1987) makes a distinction between macro- and microethnographies, Macroethnographies fit the description of ethnographies above, but microethnographies are not just "small ethnographies." They are a particular kind of qualitative research usually undertaken by sociolinguists or others interested in verbal and nonverbal communication (Collins, 1979; Jacob, 1987; Wilkinson, 1982). Scholars doing microethnographic work make fine-grained analyses of face-to-face interactions within specific social contexts. They use participant observation, often supported with videotape, as their basic data collection method in order to discover the linguistic rules that participants in certain settings use to construct meaning together.

Most microethnographies are undertaken based on the assumptions of the postpositivist paradigm. The best examples of such studies that have direct implications for classroom teaching were done by Erickson and his students (e.g., Bremme & Erickson, 1977; Erickson & Mohatt, 1982; Shultz & Florio, 1979; Shultz, Florio, & Erickson, 1982).

Ethnomethodology

The term *ethnomethodology* is a reference not to research methods but to the subject matter of ethnomethodological studies, that is, the methods that people use to navigate their everyday lives (Bogdan & Biklen, 1992; Morris, 1977). Ethnomethodologists use observation and interview techniques to capture commonsense understandings that their subjects apply to accomplish the taken-for-granted tasks of daily living. They are interested in assessing an individual's stock of knowledge (e.g., rules of thumb, recipes for doing things, maxims, definitions). They do so by examining everyday talk that takes place in real contexts to study how people do their jobs, watch television, cook, eat, and accomplish the other practical realities of ordinary life (Morris, 1977; Potter, 1996).

Ethnomethodologists operate within the postpositivist paradigm. They apply rigorous discourse analysis procedures in their work and produce generalizations and theories to explain contextualized human behavior. An example of ethnomethodology applied to the study of everyday discourse in schools is McBeth's (1994) study of how order is restored after problems or distractions disrupt high school classrooms.

Participant Observation Studies

Qualitative studies that place researchers in social settings but do not have the broad purpose of capturing the cultural knowledge that insiders use to make sense of those settings I classify as participant observation studies. Fieldwork methods that include interviewing, artifact collection, and especially direct observation recorded in field notes are the data collection tools in this type of study. Such studies are not ethnographies because they are much narrower in scope and usually involve less time in the field. Researchers often enter the field with specific interests (e.g., what is the nature of principal-teacher relationships?) and/or specific questions (e.g., how do these students understand reading instruction?) that concentrate their studies in ways that ethnographers do not. Even though considerable time in the field is required to do participant observation studies well (see the discussion of extended firsthand engagement above), the tighter focus allows graduate students to do fieldwork on interesting and important topics without spending the time required to do and write full-blown ethnographies.

Participant observation fieldwork involves a set of data collection strategies that can be utilized within any of the qualitative research paradigms. An example of a participant observation study in education settings from each paradigm follows:

- Postpositivist: *Life in Classrooms* is Jackson's (1968) classic analysis of the hidden curriculum of everyday life in elementary schools.

- Constructivist: Graue's (1993) study of the social construction of school readiness across multiple communities is reported in *Ready for What? Constructing Meanings of Readiness for Kindergarten.*

- Critical/Feminist: Fine's (1991) *Framing Dropouts* is a critical account of the policies and practices of an urban public high school with a high dropout rate.

- Poststructuralist: In their chapter "Carnival in the Classroom: Elementary Students Making Videos," Grace and Tobin (1997) describe a study of children's filmmaking in a Hawaiian elementary school.

Interview Studies

Informant interviewing can be the basis for another kind of qualitative study. While it is often a part of participant observation research and other approaches, interviewing can be the primary data collection strategy in a qualitative project. Qualitative researchers utilize special interview strategies that are different in nature from interviews done in quantitative studies. Most quantitative interviews are closed-ended questionnaires with yes/no questions, forced choices, and Likert-scale categories. These are administered face-to-face or over the phone, then analyzed using statistical procedures. Qualitative interviewers create a special kind of speech event during which they ask open-ended questions, encourage informants to explain their unique perspectives on the issues at hand, and listen intently for special language and other clues that reveal meaning structures informants use to understand their worlds (Mishler, 1986; Seidman, 1998; Spradley, 1979). Interviewers enter interview settings with questions in mind but generate questions during the interview in response to informants' responses, the social contexts being discussed, and the degree of rapport established.

Again, qualitative interview studies can be undertaken from within any of the paradigms outlined, except the positivist. The nature of the interviews and findings will change based on the paradigm being applied. Postpositivists will see themselves as data collection instruments and report generalizations based on rigorous analysis of the interview data—for example, Smith's (1989) study of teachers' beliefs about retention. Constructivist interviewers will work with informants to coconstruct understandings that are reported as interpretations or narratives as in Ladson-Billings' (1994) study of successful African American teachers. Critical/feminist interviewers are involved with their informants in bringing about social and political change, and their products include calls for action—for example, Ceglowski's (1994) examination of Head Start salaries and teachers' views on their value as workers in a gender-segregated field. Poststructuralist interviewers are in an interesting position in relation to their informants because they acknowledge that they can never really know the lived experience of those individuals. They seek to explore "truths" that are local, temporal, and in flux. I was not able to locate an educational research project that I would classify as a poststructuralist interview study, but Bloom and Munro's (1995) poststructuralist narrative study of female administrators used interviewing as its primary data source.

Focus Group Studies

Using focus groups is a qualitative interview strategy that has its roots in sociology (e.g., Merton & Kendall, 1946) but has been utilized most widely in marketing research (Berg, 1998). Focus groups are sets of individuals with similar characteristics or having shared experiences (e.g., beginning teachers) who sit down with a moderator to discuss a topic. The focus is on the topic, and fundamental data are transcripts of group discussions around the topic. Group discussion provides a different kind of information than can be generated from individual interviews and/or observations (Krueger, 1994). In Morgan's (1997) words, "the hallmark of focus groups is their explicit use of the group interaction to produce data and insights that would be less accessible without the interaction found in a group" (p. 2).

Focus group interviews are often used to supplement other qualitative data, but they can be the basic data collection strategy of a qualitative study. Like individual interviews, researchers from any of the qualitative research paradigms in this chapter can utilize focus groups. Examples include the following:

- Postpositivist: Eisenberg, Wagenaar, and Neumark-Sztainer (1997) conducted focus groups with high school students to capture their views on sexuality education.
- Constructivist: Parent and professional perspectives on inclusion and early intervention were examined by Wesley, Buysse, and Tyndall (1997).
- Critical/Feminist: Lather and Smithies (1997) applied focus group methods to study support group meetings for women with AIDS/HIV.
- Poststructuralist: Tobin's (1997) cross-national study involved Irish and American preschool teachers in discussions of their attitudes towards children's sex play.

Artifact Analysis

The collection of unobtrusive artifact data is a part of many qualitative research projects, but it is unusual for artifacts to be used as the primary data source, except when they are text-based materials in archival, policy-based, or historical studies (see below). Hodder (1994) argues that artifacts, "the intended and unintended residues of human activity, give alternative insights into the ways in which people perceive and fashion their lives" (p. 304). Artifact collection is the gathering of "indicators" or "non-reactive measures" of group or individual life (Schwartz & Jacobs, 1979). For school-based research, these might include school records, official documents, children's work, teachers' lesson plans, parent newsletters, or any materials used in the settings being studied. The main advantage of this type of data collection is that it does not influence the social setting being examined. The major disadvantage is that interpreting the meaning and significance of objects is difficult because connecting them to relevant contexts is highly inferential.

Again, studies having artifact analysis as the primary methodology are unusual, and examples from education are hard to find. I did a study with a colleague in which we analyzed report cards from kindergartens across the state of Ohio. While this was part of a larger study with other data, we were able to complete and write up an artifact analysis on the report cards collected (Freeman & Hatch, 1989). Because of the static nature of the data and a reliance on the researcher as data collection instrument, artifact analyses fit most neatly within the postpositivist paradigm. Our study was undertaken from a postpositivist perspective; we reported patterns and made generalizations based on frequency counts and percentages.

Historical Studies and Historiography

Historical studies or historiographies involve the collection and analysis of data for the purpose of reconstructing events or combinations of events that happened in the past (Berg, 1998; Denzin, 1978). Those data are classified by historiographers as deriving from primary or secondary sources. Primary sources include oral or written testimony, original documents, photographs, diaries, journals, drawings, mementos, or other original artifacts. Secondary sources are elements created by others that relate to the event or events in question, such as textbooks, journal articles, newspaper accounts, public records, and other information about individuals or groups (Berg, 1998; Salkind, 1991). It is the job of the historiographer to examine potential sources of data for authenticity and accuracy, to make interpretations based on multiple data sources, and to weave these into a "meaningful set of explanations" (Berg, 1998, p. 202).

Qualitative educational historians operate within several research paradigms. Some collect and interpret data using postpositivist assumptions, generating careful descriptions of events or characters from the past, for example, Holmes and Weiss's (1995) collection of histories of women public school teachers from the 1830s. Others produce histories from feminist or critical perspectives, for example, Weiler's (1992) study of California teachers who taught from the 1920s through the 1950s. And some systematically deconstruct history, applying approaches developed within the poststructuralist perspective (e.g., Derrida, 1981; Foucault, 1972), as in Cannella's (1997) analysis of the genealogies of child psychology and early childhood education.

Grounded Theory Studies

Glaser and Strauss (1967) created a model that has had a powerful influence on the development of qualitative research. Their landmark book, *The Discovery of Grounded Theory*, provides a guide for collecting and analyzing qualitative data in rigorous, systematic, and disciplined ways. The original book and elaborations that have followed (e.g., Schatzman & Strauss, 1973; Strauss, 1987; Strauss & Corbin, 1998) detail procedures for generating theories that are inductively derived from careful examination of the data (i.e., *grounded* in the data). Vital to these procedures is the notion of constant comparison, through which researchers engage in detailed analytic processes that require repeated confirmations of potential explanatory patterns discovered in the data. Doing constant comparison requires incessant immersion and microscopic familiarity with the data. My experience is that many novice qualitative researchers call their work (or at least the products of their work) "grounded theory" but that few have actually followed the well-defined methods described by Glaser, Strauss, Corbin, and others. My reaction is that you can claim your findings are grounded in the data (if they are), but if you call it a grounded theory study, you must actually *do* grounded theory.

Grounded theory is clearly a postpositivist method. It works from the assumption that rigorous methods can be used to discover approximations of social reality that are empirically represented in carefully collected data. Constant comparison engages the researcher in a give and take between inductive and deductive thinking. Potential categories of meaning are said to emerge from the data, then data are carefully read to determine if those categories are valid. In some ways, grounded theory is the quintessential postpositivist research approach. An example of the application of grounded theory in education settings is Henry's (1992) study of rituals in Waldorf and college prep schools.

Naturalistic Inquiries

Naturalistic methods is a general term that is roughly synonymous with qualitative research. The term makes direct reference to the goal of capturing naturally occurring activity in natural settings. *Naturalistic inquiry* is a specific kind of research within the domain of naturalistic methods and is described best in the work of Lincoln and Guba (1985). In contrast to conventional positivist research, Lincoln and Guba offer design elements that include the following: (a) determining a focus for the inquiry; (b) determining the fit of paradigm to focus; (c) determining the fit of the inquiry paradigm to the sub-stantive theory selected to guide the inquiry; (d) determining where and from whom data will be collected; (e) determining successive phases of the inquiry; (f) determining instrumentation; (g) planning data collection and recording modes; (h) planning data analysis procedures; (i) planning the logistics; and (j) planning for trustworthiness (pp. 226–47). While it is not as prescriptive as other methodological approaches (e.g., grounded theory), I do insist that students who call their approach "naturalistic inquiry" pay close attention to the procedures and methods found in Lincoln and Guba's work.

Naturalistic inquiry is the archetype for constructivist qualitative research. Assumptions that define the constructivist paradigm are clearly articulated by Lincoln and Guba (1985). For example: "There are multiple constructed realities that can be studied only holistically"; "The inquirer and the 'object' of inquiry interact to influence one another"; "Knower and known are inseparable"; and "All entities are in a state of mutual simultaneous shaping" (pp. 37–38). An example of a naturalistic inquiry done in a higher education setting is Manning's (1995) study of the cultural rituals of a small liberal arts college for women.

Symbolic Interactionist Studies

The full title of Blumer's (1969) foundational text is *Symbolic Interactionism: Perspective and Method*. Symbolic interactionism as perspective has had a profound impact on qualitative research in general, providing the theoretical groundwork that allowed a clean break from positivism. Symbolic interactionism *as method* is often forgotten. So, lots of qualitative studies are undertaken from a symbolic interactionist theoretical perspective, but few identify symbolic interactionism as their methodology. The major premises of this perspective are fundamental to all postpositivist work: (a) "Human beings act toward things on the basis of the meanings that the things have for them"; (b) "The meaning of such things is derived from, or arises out of, the social interaction that one has with one's fellows"; and (c) "These meanings are handled in, and modified through, an interpretive process used by the person in dealing with the things he encounters" (Blumer, 1969, p. 2). Symbolic interactionist methods, according to Blumer's original account, are comprised of "exploration" (i.e., collecting observations, interviews, life histories, letters, diaries, public records, and group discussions) and "inspection" (discriminating analytic elements and isolating relations between elements) (pp. 40–47).

Blumer described symbolic interactionism using postpositivist ontological and epistemological assumptions. His science was decidedly empirical. He was convinced that the real world exists but that it can only be known through studying the perspectives of those experiencing that world. In Charon's (1998) words, "The central principle of symbolic interactionism is that we can understand what is going on only if we understand what the actors themselves believe about their world" (p. 210). Curry's (1993) description of a student athlete's experience of pain and injury throughout an amateur wrestling career is an example of a study applying symbolic interactionist principles.

Narrative Studies

Qualitative research that is focused on gathering and interpreting the stories that people use to describe their lives is called by various names that fit under this heading. Different types of narrative studies include life histories, life story research, biography, personal experience methods, oral history, and narrative inquiry (see Hatch & Wisniewski, 1995; Yow, 1994). All are based on the notion that humans make sense of their lives through story. Bruner (1986) distinguished between paradigmatic and narrative ways of knowing. Paradigmatic knowledge is characterized by the logical-scientific mode. Narrative knowledge is storied knowledge, and Bruner argued that it is not inherently inferior to paradigmatic knowledge, even though it is less highly valued in Western culture. Narrative studies seek to capture storied knowledge. Clandinin and Connelly (1994) identify the following methods for generating the data of narrative studies: oral history; annals and chronicles; family stories; photographs, memory boxes, and other personal/family artifacts; research interviews; journals; autobiographical writing; letters; conversations; and field notes and other stories from the field.

Narrative work fits most comfortably within the paradigmatic boundaries of constructivist and critical/feminist thinking, although it is possible to apply postpositivist analytic techniques to narrative data (see Polkinghorne, 1995). The emphasis in this kind of work is on the meanings individuals generate through stories, and constructivist researchers and their participants coconstruct the stories that are told as part of the research. Critical/feminist narratives involve the researcher and participants in telling stories that raise awareness and promote resistance. Cohen's (1991) *Lifetime of Teaching: Portraits of Five Veteran High School Teachers* and Casey's (1993) *I Answer with My Life: Life Histories of Women Teachers Working for Social Change* are good respective examples of constructivist and critical/feminist work. Poststructuralists are concerned about the possibilities of representing the complexity of individual lives in text. Some are calling for "different ways of representing the other and ourselves as researcher-author . . . [such as] creating impressionist tales, dramas, fictions, and poetic representations of lives" (Sparkes in Hatch & Wisniewski, 1995, p. 121). An example of such a poststructuralist approach to narrative is Tierney's (1993a) "Self and Identity in a Postmodern World: A Life Story."

Educational Criticism

Eisner (1991) presents an approach to examining educational contexts that he calls "educational connoisseurship" or "educational criticism." Educational criticism as a form of qualitative research relies on the abilities of the researcher to study school life in much the same ways an art critic studies a painting or symphonic work. Researchers must be both "connoisseurs" and "critics" of school life. For Eisner, connoisseurs know works of art because of well-developed abilities to see the special qualities that make art great, and critics are skilled at helping others see the qualities that works of art possess. Educational researchers doing this kind of qualitative work are connoisseurs and critics of educational events and practices. They observe, interview, and collect artifacts and documents like other qualitative researchers. From these data, educational critics construct stories or portraits of what they experienced and understood in the settings explored. Their findings look more like the essays of art critics than the "objective" reports found in positivist journals.

educ research

 Eisner and his students have made an impact on qualitative research, working mostly within the assumptions of the constructivist paradigm. It is constructivist because educational criticism assumes that multiple realities exist, the researcher is portraying only one, and researcher interpretation is at the center of analysis procedures. Barone's (1983) study of a high school art program is an example of one of Eisner's students' work. It is important to note that *criticism* here refers to art criticism rather than the neo-Marxist orientation of many critical theorists. It is also important to recognize that contemporary art and literary criticism has been influenced by feminist and deconstructivist perspectives; however, I could find no examples that I would classify as critical/feminist or poststructuralist educational criticism.

Phenomenological Studies

While principles of phenomenology are at the roots of most qualitative work (e.g., the belief that phenomena should be studied without preconceived notions), particular kinds of qualitative inquiry can be identified as phenomenological studies. The approach most widely used in education Van Manen (1990) called "hermeneutic phenomenological research." This approach combines both interpretive/hermeneutic methods and descriptive/phenomenological methods for the purpose of examining the lived experiences or lifeworlds of people being studied. In Van Manen's (1990) words, "Phenomenology describes how one orients to lived experience, hermeneutics describes how one interprets the 'texts' of life" (p. 4). Phenomenological researchers seek to reveal the essence of human experience by asking, "What is the nature of this phenomenon?" In an effort to "bracket" their biases and preconceptions, they usually begin their investigations by exploring their own experiences with and understandings of the phenomena they study (Marshall & Rossman, 1995; Patton, 1990). The methods they use to gather experiential descriptions from others include: (a) protocol writing (asking individuals to write their experiences down); (b) interviewing (gathering experiential narrative material through conversation); (c) observing (collecting anecdotes of experience through close observation); (d) studying experiential descriptions in literature and art (examining poetry, novels, stories, plays, biographies, works of art, and the phenomenological literature for insight into the nature of the phenomena under investigation); and examining diaries, journals, and logs (searching for meaning in writings individuals have done for themselves) (adapted from Van Manen, 1990, pp. 62–76).

Hermeneutic phenomenology is a constructivist approach. It assumes that multiple, socially constructed realities exist and that the meanings individuals give to their experiences ought to be the objects of study (Bogdan & Biklen, 1992; Eichelberger, 1989). Further, phenomenological researchers often view participants as coconstructors of the descriptions and interpretations of their studies (Van Manen, 1990). An example of a phenomenological research project is Howard's (1994) study of adult learners' first experiences with computers.

Case Studies

Researchers from many disciplines and many paradigms (qualitative and quantitative) call their work "case studies." It is not perfectly clear that qualitative case study research is distinct from ethnography or participant observation studies. When students decide to use the term *case studies*, I insist that they be able to make such distinctions. The best sources for doing so are Yin's (1994) general text on case study research and Merriam's (1988) book on case studies in education. Both argue that case studies are a special kind of qualitative work that investigates a contextualized contemporary (as opposed to historical) phenomenon within specified boundaries. Merriam (1988) offers examples of such bounded phenomena in education: "a program, an event, a person, a process, an institution, or a social group" (p. 13). Defining the boundaries, or specifying the *unit of analysis* is the key decision point in case study design. According to Patton (1980), identifying the unit of analysis means deciding "what it is you want to be able to say something about at the end of the study" (p. 100). Data collection and analysis procedures parallel those of other qualitative approaches. It is their focus on "bounded systems" (Smith, 1979) that makes qualitative case studies different.

Case study is a term that has become a catchall for identifying qualitative studies of various types. I mentioned above that students should be able to rationalize their decisions to use case study methods. Both Merriam (1988) and Yin (1994) advocate postpositivist approaches to case study research, but this does not mean that case studies do not fit in other qualitative paradigms. There is nothing inherent in a bounded system approach that precludes the application of constructivist, critical/feminist, or poststructuralist principles. A highly regarded example of qualitative case studies is Lightfoot's (1983) descriptive portrait of six high schools, and Smulyan's (2000a) study of women principals is a good recent addition.

Action Research Projects

Action research has a rich tradition in education. As its name implies, action research is concerned with activity and change. It is undertaken for the sake of investigating practice, usually in concert with those working on the front lines, and improving that practice based on what is discovered. Action research is usually organized in a cycle of identifying a problem through careful observation, reflecting on the dimensions of the problem, designing a change that addresses the problem, implementing the change, and assessing its effectiveness through careful observation (Hitchcock & Hughes, 1995). Its major concern is not with generating theory or generalizations that can be applied in other settings. Action research may provide a basis for theorizing and knowledge production, but its "primary purpose is as a practical tool for solving problems experienced by people in their professional, community, or personal lives" (Stringer, 1999, p. 11). Action research can include the collection of quantitative data and can be done by teachers working without the support of university researchers.

The assumptions of action research fit most neatly within the critical/feminist paradigm. There is recognition that the values of the researcher have a prominent place in the inquiry, and change is the desired endpoint. Critical action research has a strong presence in Western scholarship (e.g., Carr & Kemmis, 1986; Kincheloe, 1991; Shor & Friere, (1987). Still, some action research in education is undertaken without an explicitly critical or feminist orientation, in the tradition of Lewin (1952) and Stenhouse (1975). Because of their focus on immediate change in particular settings, action research projects are seldom published. A notable exception is Cochran-Smith and Lytle's (1993) collection of projects by Philadelphia teachers, *Inside/Outside: Teacher Research and Knowledge*.

Collaborative Studies

It is possible to do research in collaboration with practitioners but not with the specific intent of changing the practices of research participants. *Collaborative research* here refers to work that is distinguished from action research because its principal aims are the generation of knowledge and understanding. It is assumed in collaborative qualitative research that it is valuable to bring both insider and outsider perspectives to the analysis of phenomena under investigation. It is also considered desirable to include research participants as full partners in the research process, thus addressing concerns that researchers sometimes "use" the individuals they are studying, taking more than they are giving in the research bargain (see Hatch, 1995b; Mishler, 1986; Reinharz, 1992).

Because raising participant consciousness or bringing about social or political action is not the primary goal and because researchers and participants coconstruct knowledge based on data, collaborative studies are most often undertaken within the constructivist paradigm. The classic collaborative study in education is Smith and Geoffrey's (1968) investigation of an urban elementary school classroom. Collaborative studies (or action research projects) that include extensive involvement by school personnel are legitimate forms of scholarly inquiry, but graduate students who elect to do these kinds of research projects will have to be sure their committees and graduate schools count such studies as doctoral-level inquiry.

Conclusion: What Do I Call It?

These are not all the kinds of qualitative studies, but they do represent broad categories that give those considering qualitative work a starting place for exploring what's possible. As has been mentioned several times in this chapter, I believe unpacking individually held metaphysical assumptions is a key step in deciding if one should do a qualitative study. Without this step, it is possible to start down a road that leads to a dead end. I know it happens that researchers operating on positivist assumptions try to do qualitative research. As an editor and editorial board member, I have seen manuscripts that purport to be reports of qualitative research but appear to be based on positivist assumptions. I have also had students in my qualitative research classes who are die-hard positivists who take the class because of program requirements or an interest in "knowing the enemy." They have a great deal of trouble with the assignments of the course, and class activities (and sometimes lectures) often turn into debates. They don't get it, and they shouldn't get it. The point is that individuals who are uncomfortable outside the assumptions of traditional science should not do qualitative research.

Once a new researcher has come to grips with his or her ontological and epistemological beliefs and finds a place among the qualitative paradigms, the field of methodological choices is narrowed, but the decision about what kind of methods to use is not made. As my examples demonstrate, several kinds of qualitative research are available within each of the four qualitative paradigms identified. Methods decisions will be made based on what the researcher wants to find out. These decisions will be addressed head on in the next chapter, but a brief discussion of naming qualitative work fits here.

Advanced graduate students and other novice qualitative researchers often struggle with deciding what to call their work. Some researchers, for example, know that their assumptions about how the world is ordered and what can be learned place them firmly within the critical/feminist paradigm. They may want to do "feminist research." My response is that they should learn as much as possible about feminist approaches to research, look at the kinds of research that fit comfortably within the critical/feminist paradigm, think carefully about what questions they want to ask, and design a project accordingly. Their studies will be feminist research, but their methods will be feminist ethnography, feminist historiography, feminist action research, or whatever. Calling the work "feminist" or "critical" or "constructivist" or "poststructuralist" identifies the paradigmatic framework but not the research methodology.

I give students a hard time about the issue of what to call their work. As I mentioned above, if they want to call it "grounded theory" or "naturalistic inquiry," I insist that they be true to the methods that the field understands to be those specific kinds of research. I also expect students to be consistent in their terminology, and this is difficult because qualitative researchers as a group are not known for such consistency. For example, some researchers call their work "ethnography" and "case study" (or "action research" and "phenomenological research," etc.) in the same paragraph. This can be just sloppy writing, but sometimes it reveals a lack of basic understanding about information summarized in this chapter. More subtle problems are revealed when qualitative researchers identify themselves within one paradigm but select arguments and methods that don't fit. For example, when they call their work "constructivist," but build cases and select methods designed to capture an assumed reality using rigorously defined data collection and analytic tools that fit best in the postpositivist camp. Worst of all are researchers who use a "shotgun" approach to describing their work. They select terms and methods indiscriminately and blast them onto the page without rhyme or reason.

Often, students don't know what to call their work until they are well into the design process, and that's fine, so long as they are aware of the need to tie it all together in an internally logical package. In the next chapter, I will go through the process of designing qualitative studies step by step. The basis for design will be a solid understanding of research paradigms and associated methods.

The goal of this chapter has been to introduce the foundations of qualitative research and help novice researchers make initial decisions about doing this kind of scholarship. If the chapter worked, it gave readers a starting place for making decisions and for finding out more about particular perspectives and methods. Successful researchers at any level find out what others with like interests and perspectives have done and are doing. Once students identify with certain research paradigms and become interested in particular kinds of research, I encourage them to find and read everything they can—both work about their interests and work that exemplifies the kinds of studies they might do. That kind of background gives readers the grounding they need to create their own unique approaches to doing qualitative work.

CRITERIA FOR DECIDING TO DO A QUALITATIVE STUDY

One of my objectives in this book is to provide researchers with criteria for making assessments about the quality of qualitative work. While it is easier to talk about such criteria in relation research design, data collection, or data analysis, I want to provide some guidance for decisions about choosing to do a qualitative study in the first place. While the questions are framed for doctoral students trying to decide if qualitative research is the way for them to go, other novice researchers will find the questions useful in examining their fit for qualitative work. Honestly addressing the issues embedded in the following questions will lead some away from an unhappy experience with qualitative research and help others to establish a solid foundation on which to build successful qualitative research projects.

1. Has the researcher investigated the foundations of qualitative inquiry?
   A. Does the researcher have a basic understanding of the historical roots of qualitative research?
   B. Can the researcher articulate characteristics that distinguish qualitative from quantitative work?
   C. Has the researcher written a description that defines what qualitative research means to him or her?

2. Has the researcher unpacked his or her metaphysical assumptions?
   A. Can the researcher articulate his or her ontological and epistemological beliefs?
   B. Can the researcher locate himself or herself in relation to particular qualitative paradigms?
   C. Can the researcher identify appropriate qualitative research approaches, given his or her metaphysical assumptions and paradigm choices?

3. Is the researcher prepared to do qualitative research?
    A. Has the researcher had the equivalent of two formal courses in qualitative methods?
    B. Has the researcher had experience collecting and analyzing qualitative data?
    C. Has the researcher studied examples of qualitative work done in areas related to his or her substantive interest?

CHAPTER TWO

Designing Qualitative Studies

How do I design a qualitative study? What should be included in a qualitative research proposal? Once students have decided that their worldviews place them in the qualitative research camp, they are faced with the task of conceptualizing and designing a research project and, at most universities, putting their plans into a dissertation prospectus or proposal. Experienced researchers working in university settings are required to present their research designs to institutional review boards for human subjects approval, and researchers who seek financial support submit research proposals to funding agencies. This chapter is about designing qualitative research studies. It is not organized as a guide for writing research proposals (cf., Marshall & Rossman, 1995), but I will make suggestions throughout that address concerns related to proposal writing.

One of the issues that must be addressed early in the design process is the tension between flexibility and structure. Part of the lore of qualitative work is that researchers enter their research contexts without specific questions, plans, or foci. This probably dates to early anthropologists who were sent into the field without formal training and expected to learn field methods on the job (see Hamilton, 1994). I have sat on committees where students came to proposal meetings with very sketchy plans, claiming that their designs would emerge as their studies progressed. They were sometimes armed with quotes from respectable sources, for example, Lincoln and Guba's (1985) statement that "the design of a naturalistic inquiry . . . cannot be given in advance; it must emerge, develop, unfold" (p. 225) or Bogdan and Biklen's (1992) injunction that "[i]nvestigators may enter the research with some idea about

37

what they will do, but a detailed set of procedures is not formed prior to data collection" (p. 58). While it is characteristic that qualitative projects do have an emergent quality (see chapter 1), my stance is that novice researchers need to begin their work with a solid plan that includes attention to all of the design elements discussed in this chapter.

While it sounds oxymoronic, I encourage students to design qualitative studies with a *flexible structure.* It is understood that studies will develop and change as they are implemented, but it is better if projects develop within a framework and change when real circumstances dictate than to go into a research setting without a fundamental plan of action. Further, at my university, a signed dissertation prospectus is a contract between the student and his or her committee. Both the student and the committee are protected when proposals have enough specific information about the project so that is clear when the contract is or is not completed. When changes are made in the research process, it is important to keep the committee informed so that the "contract" can be amended. Experienced researchers who expect human subjects approval or funding know that institutional review boards and funding agencies need specific plans in order to evaluate research proposals.

The basic elements that need to be addressed in a qualitative research design are the place of theory, research questions, contexts, participants, data collection strategies, data analysis procedures, and the nature of anticipated findings. The body of this chapter details what needs to be included under each element. Institutional review (i.e., human subjects) concerns and ethics are then addressed, and the chapter concludes with criteria for assessing design adequacy.

DESIGN ELEMENTS

Methodological and Substantive Theory

What is the place of theory in qualitative research? Should I start with theory, or will that bias my data collection and analysis? Will I have to do a literature review before I begin my study? These are questions that come up as students consider how to start putting together a research proposal. Answers will depend in part on expectations of doctoral committee members, university traditions, and the nature of particular studies. I will offer my answer to these questions, not *the* answer for every circumstance.

As qualitative studies are designed, attention should be given to two types of theory: methodological and substantive. An exposition of methodological theory places the proposed study in a research paradigm and identifies what kind of study is being planned. It is the formal expression of the researcher's answers to the ontological and epistemological questions that framed the discussion of paradigms in chapter 1. Writing a paradigm declaration forces researchers to look closely at their assumptions about how the world is or is not ordered and how we can come to know about it. It encourages them to establish a foundation on which to build their design.

The next logical step is to identify what kind of qualitative research is to be done within the paradigm described. Telling the committee (and later, dissertation readers) that theirs is an interview study done within the constructivist paradigm, a feminist narrative study, or a grounded theory study based on postpositivist principles sets the stage for understanding what is to follow. This early step is not the place to present and defend the nuts and bolts of the study; it is the place to articulate the researcher's metaphysical assumptions and to explain his or her rationale for selecting the methods identified. The extent and depth of methodological rationale will differ by situation, but I hope it is no longer necessary to justify the integrity of qualitative research as a general approach to scholarly inquiry. I wrote such an elaborate justification in the early 1980s, and, even then, my Ph.D. committee told me it was "overkill." It is necessary to explain how the particular qualitative methods selected fit with the researcher's paradigmatic assumptions and why those methods are appropriate means for studying the topic being proposed.

Theory that is used to describe and explain the phenomena to be investigated—the substance of the study—is substantive theory. In order to place their work within a theoretical framework that is recognized and understood by the scholarly community, it is necessary for researchers of any ilk to provide a conceptual frame of reference that includes an exposition of substantive theory (see Marshall & Rossman, 1995). This exposition may include reference to a single, overarching theory or several related theories (Berg, 1998), but it is essential to locate the study in relation to theory that has already been generated in the appropriate area.

The place of substantive theory has been the subject of disagreement among qualitative researchers. Some recommend extensive literature reviews and thorough understanding of relevant theory prior to entering the field (e.g., Yin, 1994). Others see the generation of theory as the outcome of research and prefer to delay reference to extant theoretical literature until late in the research process (e.g., Glaser & Strauss, 1967). I like Wolcott's (1995) statement: "Theory is supposed to help researchers of any persuasion clarify what they are up to and to help them to explain to others what they are up to" (p. 189). It reminds me that substantive theory is important up front, to help researchers "clarify what they are up to" and important at the writing stage to "help explain to others what they are up to."

The theoretical development of one of my studies serves as an example of how substantive theory can be important at different stages of research design and implementation. It was a participant observation study of children's social interactions undertaken within the assumptions of the constructivist paradigm. At the outset, and in my funding proposal, I declared my interest in studying peer interaction from a sociological theoretical perspective articulated by Goffman (1959; 1969) as "self-presentation." As the study progressed, I became interested in the social relations of a particular child who appeared to be treated as "less than normal" by his peers (Hatch, 1988). I focused more attention on social interactions involving this child in my data collection and made a study of this particular child's social behavior in relation to his peers a major part of the overall project. Trying to understand this emergent area of investigation led me to search the theoretical literature related to the "sociology of deviance" (e.g., Becker, 1963; Goffman, 1963; Pfuhl, 1980), so my findings were framed within a perspective that was not a part of my initial substantive theory base. The point of the example is that substantive theoretical grounding is necessary during the design phase, but that does not preclude the importance of continuing to explore alternative theoretical explanations as the study progresses and reports are written.

New researchers are also concerned that too much front-loaded theory will make their qualitative studies more like deductive, quantitative work than they would like. They reason that familiarity with established theory will lead them to see social phenomena in ways that they would not if they were not conversant with the theory, thereby leading them to processes that feel like confirming or disconfirming hypotheses. They sometimes resist doing full-blown literature reviews for the same kinds of reasons. The concern is that knowing what others have found will bias the ways they look and the ways they interpret what they see. They are also concerned about efficiency, asking, "Why should I spend the time doing a thorough exploration of theory and/or a comprehensive literature review when I may end up using different theories and placing my work within different literature bases?"

These are good questions, and the concerns they reflect are important. It is true that having strong theoretical predispositions can influence the design and implementation of a study in negative ways. As will be discussed in the next chapter, these and other sources of bias need to be monitored and bracketed. But entering a potential study without theory is dangerous in other ways. Instead of seeing what he or she expects, the researcher may end up seeing nothing or become overwhelmed at seeing everything. In addition, as with the tension between structure and flexibility in design, it is much easier to alter or reject theoretical orientations than to create them. As always, the balance will be different for different kinds of qualitative research. Someone doing grounded theory work will require less substantive theory on the front end than someone doing critical historiography.

Not knowing anything about the literature allows the researcher to start from scratch, but that can be a disadvantage too. Part of the logic of doing research of any kind is to add to the body of knowledge, and part of the rationale for many projects is that they fill a gap in the literature (see Marshall & Rossman, 1995). Knowing something about studies already done gives the researcher a sense of what the field takes to be known, what is possible, and what needs further exploration. It may seem inefficient to do a complete literature review on the front end, but that is much preferred to doing a study only to find that many versions of the same work have already been completed. A solid grounding in the substantive and theoretical literature related to the study places it in a frame of reference for the researcher and the reader. Without such grounding, the researcher may generate inquiry that wanders aimlessly, and readers may disregard findings because they do not connect to anything they recognize.

One of the first discussions of the place of theory that I remember reading was Denzin's (1978) argument that unfortunate consequences result when theory, methodology, and substantive interests are fragmented. In his words,

> Research methods are of little use until they are seen in the light of theoretical perspectives. Substantive specialty is of little use or interest until it is firmly embedded within a theoretical framework and grounded upon sound research strategies. (Pp. 3–4)

Solid research designs and compelling research proposals are founded on internal logical consistency. When there is a bad fit between methodological and substantive theory, between substantive theory and methods, or between methodological theory and methods, the logic of the design falls apart. That is why I encourage new researchers to spend time clarifying their methodological and substantive theoretical bases as a first step in research design.

Research Questions

Identifying research questions is a critical step in research design because questions give direction to the study, limit the scope of the investigation, and provide a device for evaluating progress and satisfactory completion. They are critical to research design because they are the only component that ties directly to all of the other elements of design (Maxwell, 1996). A solid set of research questions gives direction to a study by carving out a piece of territory for exploration. Traditional ethnographers were interested in capturing as much insider knowledge as possible, and their questions reflected that broad focus (Chiseri-Strater & Sunstein, 1997). They asked big, open-ended questions such as "What do the members of this group know that allows them to operate within their culture?" Most other qualitative researchers have a narrower purpose, and the questions that guide them establish boundaries that focus the work. Their questions remain open-ended, but take in less territory—for example, "What are high school teachers' perspectives on zero tolerance policies?" or "What is the nature of interactions between children with and without disabilities in this preschool?"

When I meet with students at various stages of the research process, I always remind them to refer back to their research questions. New researchers almost always feel overwhelmed when they first enter the field. There is so much going on that they can barely take it all in, let alone make a record of it. Referring back to research questions puts a frame on what to look for. Even more debilitating for most students are initial attempts at data analysis. Qualitative data are usually voluminous, and research questions give initial structure to an inherently messy process. Later, students don't know when to stop their analysis, and this is a genuine problem because qualitative researchers can always do more. Asking if research questions have been answered provides a way to judge if enough has been done. If the research proposal represents a contract, then answering the research questions becomes the starting place for deciding if the contract has been fulfilled. Research questions are often refined and sometimes changed during the course of qualitative studies, but without them, studies can lack direction, focus, or the means to evaluate their effectiveness.

Formulating research questions is not easy work. It will help a great deal for the student to have gone through the process of identifying methodological and substantive theory bases and to have done a literature review. New researchers who skip these steps and try to begin with research questions run the considerable risk of adopting questions that do not fit with their basic assumptions, are not answerable given the kind of research they want to do, and/or have already been answered in similar settings. The questions selected will build logically from the researcher's theoretical orientation and substantive interests. Individuals who see themselves as post-positivists and want to use interview methods to study administrator perspectives on race relations in a school district will have a different frame of reference and different research questions than critical researchers who want to use focus groups to study the experience of black students in a majority white high school.

Students who have not explored their metaphysical assumptions sometimes pose questions that are simply unanswerable using qualitative approaches. These are often individuals who assume research is supposed to generate facts, laws, predictions, and cause-and-effect relationships (see Bogdan & Biklen, 1992), and their questions reveal their positivist orientation. Qualitative research questions will look different depending on the paradigm, but none will based on assessing the effects of factors, variables, causes, or determinants (Hatch 1995c).

Even within the qualitative paradigms, answerability is an important issue. I make students work hard to generate a few broad, answerable questions. I like the idea that researchers should be able to describe the intent of their projects in one or two sentences (Bogdan & Biklen, 1992). I also like the model of one overarching research question followed with subquestions that remain general in nature but offer more specific direction. An overarching question ought to reflect the general intent of the study but be specific enough to delimit its breadth. In graduate school, I did a study of summer school reading programs with a colleague. We wanted to find out what happened to primary children who were forced to attend summer programs because of the threat of retention (Hatch & Bondy, 1984). Our overarching question was "What is the nature of reading instruction in a remedial summer program?" The question signaled the basic intent of the study, established some boundaries on its breadth, and was answerable given our constructivist participant observation design.

Our subquestions were "What do teachers do to help children who have been identified as having difficulties learning to read?" and "What kinds of activities and experiences do teachers provide for these children?" (Hatch & Bondy, 1984, p. 29). We could have studied any number of phenomena in the programs we looked at, but our research questions kept us focused on what teachers did and had students doing during reading time. Our questions were open-ended, few in number, and stated in straightforward language. I recommend all these qualities to new researchers. Closed-ended questions are better suited for quantitative studies, too many questions can lead to a fragmented approach to data collection and analysis, and complex language or jargon increases the possibility of confusion and misinterpretation. Again, it would be unusual if research questions did not change during a qualitative project, but having them in place at the outset is essential to the design and implementation process.

Notice too that our questions were specific to the summer schools we were studying. We did not frame our questions as if we were claiming to describe all remedial or all summer programs. Questions such as "What is the nature of remedial reading instruction?" or "What is summer reading instruction like?" are pretentious and misleading. Part of the power of qualitative work is that it provides careful description and analysis of social phenomena *in particular contexts*. Identifying such contexts is the next step in the research design process.

Contexts

In what contexts can my research questions best be answered? To what contexts do I have access? Will I be able to gain entry into contexts that I want to study? Deciding where to do a study is a key decision, and making a plan for how to negotiate access and entry is an important element in qualitative research design. In qualitative work, a context always includes the physical setting in which social action occurs, a set of participants and their relationships to one another, and the activities in which participants are involved (Bondy, 1983). In addition, as Graue and Walsh (1995) point out, "A context is a culturally and historically situated place and time" (p. 141). Contexts are not, as is assumed in most quantitative studies, static entities that can be controlled or manipulated. They are complex, dynamic, and nested within larger cultural, political, and historical frameworks that must be considered as studies are planned.

Decisions about contexts are driven by many factors. The primary consideration ought to be the concern that the settings of the study will provide data that make it possible to answer research questions. Other concerns such as accessibility, feasibility, and familiarity are important, but it makes no sense to go into a school to study teacher relations with teaching assistants when monies for teaching assistants have been cut or to plan a study of teacher induction in a system that hires only experienced teachers. While it is true that interesting findings may be generated in a wide variety of settings, some contexts are better than others for answering particular research questions. In the study of summer school mentioned above, we were interested in the nature of remedial reading programs, and it was essential to locate contexts in which reading instruction was a discrete and observable part of the curriculum for children who had "failed" reading during the regular year. An activity-based program open to any child would not have been a good context for our study.

The kind of research planned is an important consideration as well. Not only does the kind of research selected frame the generation of questions, but also it influences context selection decisions. For example, microethnographies and ethnomethodological studies depend on the careful recording and analysis of face-to-face interactions, so contexts where such interactions take place (and are observable) are required. In contrast, artifact analyses and many historical studies rely on data that can be gathered unobtrusively in a variety of contexts. Identifying contexts for all studies requires selecting settings appropriate to the kind of research proposed and finding environments in which research questions can be answered.

Just because the social action of interest is happening in a particular setting does not mean that that context is available for study. Issues of access and entry also need to be addressed in the design of qualitative studies. Every setting will be different and require different approaches. Most education projects will take place in institutional contexts, meaning that designing access and entry will require a careful analysis of the formal and informal structures of the organizations in which the research contexts are imbedded. Of particular importance is the identification of gatekeepers who formally or informally control access to the settings of interest. Research designs ought to include step-by-step plans for finding out the rules and regulations of the institutions involved (e.g., schools, school districts, state agencies); identifying the names and/or positions of key gatekeepers; specifying who will be contacted, when, and how; detailing what gatekeepers will be told about the study; and articulating how formal permission will be acquired.

Careful planning is important because the research will not be possible without access to the contexts of interest and because initial contacts with research participants or gatekeepers set the tone for the rest of the study (see Johnson, 1975). When researchers have not done their homework about entry requirements or have not taken the time to find out who controls access, they risk sabotaging their own projects. Virtually all school institutions have written policies about research approval. Large school districts will likely have an office that is responsible for granting formal permission, and these offices usually make their permission contingent on the approval of a school-level administrator if a study is to be done at a school. Formal information is usually available via a phone call, and application materials will often be mailed. Still, it may be a good idea to make a face-to-face visit to district offices to make a personal contact and to begin to get a handle on the informal structures that inevitably influence access and entry. Professors, other researchers, and contacts inside the system may also be valuable sources of information about how "things really work."

If a study involves spending time in classrooms, interviewing teachers, videotaping children, or having contacts with parents, researchers need plans for when and how to explain the study to the gatekeepers and participants involved. Even though school district permission will be required, it may be a good idea to make contact informally with building principals, teachers, and parents to assess the likelihood that they will agree to participate or allow access. As a researcher, you are trying to find out if you will be able to get into the setting, if you will be welcome there once you get in, and if you are going to have access to the data you will need to complete your study. I am not recommending an "end run" around district requirements. I am saying that starting at the top may lead to a situation in which you have district permission to do a study but nowhere to do it. Or you may end up with a place to do the study but have no willing participants. Your informal talks with teachers, principals, and parents might be framed as, "If the district research office (and your principal) agrees, do you think I could do the study here?" This is also a good time to seek school-level advice about how the system really works, to find out who would be best to talk to, and to ask for help in deciding how best to package the formal application.

I did my dissertation study in the school district in which I was employed. Using my contacts within the system, I found a school principal who would allow me to do a participant observation study in her school and identified a kindergarten teacher at the school who was interested in participating. I collected the necessary application materials and made arrangements to meet with a representative of the district research office, who turned out to be a friend of mine. Because I had known her for several years, and because I knew she had recently completed a Ph.D., I did not prepare well for our meeting. She asked good questions: "What is the purpose of your study? What will you actually be doing? Why do you want to do the study in our district? What will you do with your findings? How will the district benefit from your study?" I generated answers that were barely satisfactory, but I was embarrassed. I learned to anticipate such questions and have gone to subsequent meetings of the same type much better prepared (see Bogdan & Biklen, 1992).

I recommend that researchers outline the elements of a research bargain that they are able to explain to potential gatekeepers and participants. The bargain should specify the roles and responsibilities of the researcher and each participant. It should explain what the researcher will be doing, when, and for how long. It should tell what will happen to the data of the study and indicate if and when the participants will have access to the data and/or the results of the study. An informed consent document will have to be signed as part of human subjects requirements, and this is a formal contract that is signed when formal permission is granted. The research bargain will have elements in common with informed consent forms but is less formal and more flexible. I recommend that qualitative researchers use both and that the research bargain be introduced during initial contacts with potential participants and revisited regularly throughout the research process (see Hatch & Bondy, 1986).

My view is that researchers should come clean with gatekeepers and participants about their research interests and intentions. It is possible to do covert research in education settings, either hiding the very fact that research is being done or misleading participants and gatekeepers about real research objectives. I am against such approaches on principle. It is wrong to lie to people about what you are doing. I recommend general statements of purpose (e.g., "I am here to study what it's like to be a freshman student") that allow a degree of latitude as the study unfolds, but I believe it is an ethical necessity to signal everyone involved that you are a researcher studying something with identifiable boundaries. If those boundaries change during the course of the study, participants have the right to know. Methods for dealing with such contingencies should be built into the research bargain.

Negotiating entry and access to research contexts is a continuous process. Having a solid plan as part of research design is essential, but being prepared to make adjustments as the plan unfolds is also important. In ways, access is renegotiated every time the researcher reenters the context. Educational settings are complex professional, social, and political contexts. Part of the power of qualitative work is that complexity becomes more comprehensible as data are gathered and analysis is begun. As researchers learn more about the settings they study, their awareness of what goes on where and who controls what will increase. Using this kind of insight to improve the quality of studies requires ongoing attention to entry and access issues.

Feasibility is an important element in decisions about research contexts (see Kvale, 1996). Most graduate students do not have the time or resources to complete studies in distant places that require long stays away from campus. Most are living on patchwork budgets of savings, loans, and assistantships, so they are looking for research projects that are manageable in terms of time and seeking contexts that are available and convenient. Many doctoral candidates are teachers, administrators, or former educators with direct connections to local school systems. For them, doing a study in their home system, school, even in their own classroom seems like a good solution to the feasibility problem.

While I sometimes capitulate, my general stance is to discourage students from studying their own contexts. This applies especially to teachers studying their own classrooms or principals or supervisors studying their own schools. It is just too difficult to balance the sometimes-conflicting roles of researcher and educator when the enactment of both roles is required in the same setting. It is just too difficult for educators to pull back from their insider perspectives and see things with the eyes of a researcher. It is just too difficult for participants in the study to respond to the researcher as researcher not teacher, colleague, or boss. While it may improve chances for access and ease the sometimes-cumbersome task of building rapport, studying settings with which you are familiar is generally a bad idea.

This is also true for graduate students who want to study the college students for whom they have teaching or supervisory responsibility. Again, it is tempting to study what you are close to and know a lot about, but students you have taught or are supervising will respond to you and frame their actions around you in particular ways because of your role as university instructor. Further, it will be difficult to bracket your preconceptions about these students and what they have learned under you, so all your data will be muddied in ways that jeopardize the believability of your findings. One of the most memorable quotes from my own graduate education is "It may be true that familiarity breeds contempt; more relevantly for the interpreting social scientist, familiarity breeds inattention" (Berger and Kellner, 1981, p. 34). The phrase *familiarity breeds inattention* summarizes my biggest concern for anyone proposing a "backyard" study. Capturing what insiders take for granted is one of the objectives of qualitative work. If the researcher is also an insider, that which is taken for granted may never come to the surface.

Identifying research contexts is an important decision point in qualitative design. Contexts must provide opportunities for research questions to be answered, and issues of accessibility and feasibility must be addressed as part of research design. The more time spent on the front end considering these issues, the more likely that entry into an appropriate context will be successful.

Participants

Selecting contexts and identifying participants are closely connected. Indeed, participants make up a large measure of context according to the definition above. Decisions about context necessarily include decisions about participants. Still, including plans for selecting and establishing working relationships with participants is an important part of research design. The terms used signal very real differences between the ways qualitative and quantitative researchers think about those they study. Qualitative researchers try to understand the perspectives of their participants or informants; quantitative types are interested in samples and subjects. In general, samples for quantitative studies are better when the number of subjects (n's) is high; samples are thought to represent some larger population; and samples are often homogeneous in an effort to control for extraneous variables. Qualitative researchers argue that no direct relationship exists between the number of participants and the quality of a study; questions of number are answered in reference to research questions and levels of analysis; contexts are carefully described so that readers can make their own judgments about applicability to their own contexts; and there are no extraneous variables—any element that is perceived to be important by participants is important to the study (see Hatch, 1995c).

The criteria for participant selection grow out of different assumptions depending on the research paradigm and the kind of study. In postpositivist studies, the researcher is interested in discovering the patterns of understanding that participants use to make sense of their worlds. They require participants who are willing to allow researchers to watch them acting in their natural environments and/or talk with them about their actions and intentions. Postpositivists see themselves as data-gathering instruments, so they need close relationships with informants in order to have access to the data they require. They often enlist the assistance of key informants or guides with whom they have a special relationship that gives them insight into the settings they are studying and access to people and events they could not obtain on their own (Berg, 1998; Spradley, 1980). Analysis is usually accomplished by the researcher alone, using rigorous methods that ensure that findings are empirically supported by the data.

Constructivists think of their participants as coconstructors of the knowledge generated by their studies. They are likely to enlist their informants in much more collaborative relationships that postpositivists. While their level of involvement will vary across studies, participants in constructivist projects often help decide how research questions might be modified, what other participants might be involved, how richer data might be collected, and how analyses might be framed. It is usual in these studies for participants to have a say in how the final product will look. If they are not involved in the analysis process directly, they are almost always given an opportunity to see and give feedback on findings before they are finalized (see Lincoln & Guba, 1985).

Researchers in the critical/feminist paradigm are interested in raising the consciousness and transforming the lives of those they study. Researchers and participants work together to expose injustices in society. Critical and feminist research purposes include helping participants recognize and challenge the oppressive conditions under which they operate. While this stance is often critiqued by positivists as not scientific because it is not objective, transformative inquiry makes perfect sense within its own paradigmatic assumptions. Still, selecting participants who understand the transformative intent of critical or feminist work is obviously important. It would be unfair and unethical not to describe exactly what expectations are for participants in any study, but it is especially important when the study is designed to raise awareness, evoke resistance, and encourage political action.

No particular relationship with participants is logically specified from poststructuralist assumptions. Tentativeness about the ability to know the lived experience of participants and reluctance to try to represent lives in text make relations with participants ambiguous. The specifics of particular studies will dictate more about participant-researcher relations than the fact that a poststructuralist perspective is taken.

The kind of research approach selected will affect participant selection criteria within all paradigms. Graduate students are rightly concerned about how many participants are needed to make their studies sufficiently robust to count as a dissertation. I am ever ready to give my best professorial answer: "It depends." It depends on the purpose of the study, what kind of study is planned, and, again, what questions the study is trying to answer.

As designs are proposed, students and I often negotiate a balance between breadth and depth. It's a simple formula, but in most studies I can imagine, the fewer the participants involved, the more time must be spent with each one. By way of illustration, if the research is a qualitative interview study of high school guidance counselors' perspectives on their jobs, 30 counselors from around the country could be interviewed once, 10 counselors from one district could be interviewed three times, or three counselors from the

data source

fewer + deeper
more important multiple

same school could be interviewed multiple times. This approach to deciding the number of participants to interview fits within the spirit of Kvale's answer to his students: "Interview as many subjects as necessary to find out what you need to know" (1996, p. 101). It would be possible to study a single guidance counselor, but interviewing alone would not provide sufficient data to generate the depth necessary to justify such a study. In fact, the fewer the number of participants, the more important it is to include multiple data sources. Similar negotiations of balance are common in all kinds of studies. When a grounded theory, narrative, phenomenological, or any other kind of study is proposed, issues of "how many?" have to be balanced with concerns about "how deep?" Finding that balance is not easy, but specifying the projected number of participants and estimating the amount of time to be spent with them is a key element in qualitative research design.

Deciding exactly who the participants will be is determined in part by the context and unit of analysis selected for study. If it is a case study of a college sorority chapter or an ethnography of a third grade classroom, the participants will likely be all of the actors in those settings. If the project is a focus group study of private school teachers' perspectives on merit pay, decisions about who to include will be framed by concerns around how many schools to involve, what kinds of private schools to include, how many focus groups to have, and what kinds of teachers (by experience, discipline, grade level, etc.) to invite.

While the perspective is decidedly postpositivist and heavily influenced by evaluation research, Patton (1990, pp. 169–86) offers a variety of "purposeful sampling" strategies that are useful for thinking about selecting participants in any kind of qualitative study. For example, Patton includes homogeneous samples, maximum variation samples, and intensity sampling among his 16 strategies. Homogeneous samples are made up of participants who share common characteristics, and these selection strategies are useful for studying small subgroups in depth. Maximum variation samples are the opposite of homogeneous samples because participants are selected based on differences in characteristics. This kind of sampling is used in studies that seek to find central themes that are shared by a variety of participants. Intensity sampling seeks to identify participants who manifest intense forms of the phenomena of interest, and this kind of sampling is useful in studies that seek to understand the development and expression of such phenomena.

Many students and some experienced researchers are drawn to projects because a readymade sample is convenient and available for study. I agree with Patton (1990) on both counts when he says that "convenience sampling . . . is probably the most common sampling strategy—and the least desirable" (p. 180). For students who see their doctoral programs as nothing more than a series of hoops to jump through, a "quick and dirty" dissertation study that starts with identifying a readily accessible group of willing participants may seem like the perfect setup. It is tempting to go with what you know, and feasibility is a real concern in any study; but if a study is to have integrity and make a solid contribution, starting with convenience sampling strategies is not the way to go.

Thinking through and describing the anticipated relationships between researcher and participants is a vital part of designing a qualitative project. It should be expected that developing relationships with participants will take time and energy. It is likely that, as in any relationship, things will not always go smoothly. While the particulars cannot be anticipated, making general plans for building and maintaining rapport is important.

Participants are the ultimate gatekeepers. They determine whether and to what extent the researcher will have access to the information desired. In their discussion of field relations between researchers and informants, McCall and Simmons (1969) point out that the reason such relations are often problematic is that participants "do not know how to be studied" (p. 28). Building good working relationships is the responsibility of the researcher, and it is the researcher who must make and implement a plan for helping participants "learn how to be studied."

In the context section, I mentioned that researchers should have the outline of a research bargain in hand before approaching potential research participants and that these bargains should include descriptions of the roles and responsibilities of researcher and participants. Before such roles and responsibilities can be drafted, the researcher should think carefully about what kind of researcher-participant relationship is desirable given the paradigm in which the study is framed, the kind of study to be done, and the research questions to be asked. Different paradigms and different research approaches require different kinds of relationships. Researchers who want to join with teachers in a critical action research project will approach relationship building differently than those planning an interview study of state school board officers. Collaborative studies, by definition, require close working relationships, but historiographies may or may not be facilitated by building rapport with potential informants. Thinking through relationship issues ahead of time will save time in the long run.

Once the level of desired relationship is identified, plans can be made for building and maintaining that level of relationship. Depending on the study, researchers may decide that initial interview, focus group, observation, or artifact collection sessions will be devoted heavily to relationship building. They may decide to implement data collection strategies incrementally to allow participants to become familiar and comfortable with the process and their presence. In any case, researchers should take time to go over what the study will involve and what will be expected of participants before the study actually begins. They should be able to tell participants what the purpose of the study is in words that are easily understood. Researchers should be prepared to explain what they will be doing, when, and for how long. Participants need to know what they are supposed to do to prepare for the researcher, what to do when he or she is with them, and what they can tell others about the project. Participants need a systematic way to let the researcher know when they have questions about the research process or are uncomfortable in the research setting. I recommend that the research bargain specify periodic checkpoints at which time the researcher and participant actively discuss how the participant perceives the research process. If this is built into the plan, such questions as "How are you feeling about the way things are going?" will be more than polite conversation (Hatch & Bondy, 1986).

Every study will be different, but when researchers ask others to participate in their studies at any level, they owe them respect, concern, and consideration. Identifying participants and inviting their involvement are important steps in designing an effective research project. Selecting the right participants and building working relationships with them can make or break a qualitative study. Careful planning will not guarantee success, but failure to plan leaves far too much to chance.

Data Collection Strategies

Even though these sections are written in serial fashion, I hope it is clear that qualitative research design is not strictly linear. Questions of data collection will be part of the thinking all along the design process. As researchers come to grips with their assumptions about substance and method and identify research questions, they are thinking within a conceptual framework that opens certain kinds of options (and closes others) when decisions about data collection strategies are made. When all this comes together, the logic of the study will be tight and easy to explain. When the study is put together from the middle out, starting with research questions, a convenient context, or the desire to use a particular kind of data collection strategy, logical justifications will probably be difficult.

The next chapter of this book is devoted to an extensive discussion of data collection strategies, and the details of how to collect data via various methods will be left for that chapter. In the design phase of a qualitative project, it is necessary for researchers to specify what data will be collected, how and when the data will be collected, and why the data will be collected. The answer to the "why" question should flow logically from the issues addressed throughout this chapter and the last. If a researcher operates within the post-positivist paradigm and wants to do an ethnomethodological study of turn taking during advanced math instruction in a magnet high school, participant observation records of classroom interactions are the logical data. If a critical historiography of desegregated schools in a Southern city in the 1950s is the goal, then archival data will logically include public records, newspaper accounts, and private diaries, but the collection of interview data from individuals involved in the schools may also be justified. The rationale for data collection strategies should flow directly and smoothly from considerations of paradigm, research questions, contexts, and participants.

The design of qualitative projects must include a description of what the data of the study will be and how they will be collected. With a colleague, I did a yearlong study of the social adjustments of four highly creative children in a preschool classroom (Johnson & Hatch, 1990). The qualitative data for the study were videotapes of classroom activity, participation observation field notes, notes from informal interviews, transcripts of formal taped interviews, and unobtrusive data such as school records, reports, program descriptions, material from children's cumulative folders, photographs, and teacher- and student-made artifacts. We were interested in watching how social relations developed among four target children who had been identified as highly creative and the rest of their preschool classmates. The data gathering strategies selected fit our purposes and our assumptions that social relationships are constructed among children through their interactions with peers.

We wanted to be in the classroom the first week of school and continue to gather data throughout one school year. Our data collection design was built on being in the classroom at least one full morning per week throughout the year. We tried to balance visits across days of the week, and we always let the teacher know which day we would be coming week to week. We collected field notes during each visit, sometimes following a particular child, sometimes going where the social action was happening in the room, and sometimes recording observations where video taping was being done. Informal interview notes were recorded in field-note records as they occurred throughout the day. Field notes were filled in and converted to typed research protocols as soon after observation visits as possible. We hired a technician to videotape social interactions in three activity centers in the room. Twenty minutes in each center were recorded on tape during each weekly visit. Formal interviews with the teacher and her assistant were conducted at the beginning, middle, and end of the data collection phase of the study, and parents of the target students were interviewed near the end. Unobtrusive data were collected throughout the study.

The foregoing is offered as an example of the kinds of data and data collection strategies that might be specified in a qualitative design. Doctoral committees, funding agencies, institutional review boards, and/or potential gatekeepers and participants will need to know what kind of data the researcher is after and how he or she plans to get it. I ask students to be as specific as possible about these issues. Again, it is understood that data collection strategies will evolve in the process of doing the study, but starting with a solid plan is essential.

If it's a study using participant observation, initial plans should include projections concerning how many observational visits will be made and how long each visit will last. If interviews or focus groups are planned, the estimated number and duration should be specified. Artifact collection should be articulated in some detail. This is another place for negotiation between students and committees. Data collection strategies are important elements of the design contract, and I often argue for language that stipulates "at least" so many hours of observation, so many interviews, or so much artifact data. My experience reviewing proposals for qualitative studies and manuscripts reporting qualitative work is that too many are based on too little data. Extended engagement and rich data that lead to thick descriptions help distinguish qualitative research from more traditional inquiry. Qualitative designs should establish clear plans that make a strong case that the researcher will spend sufficient time and collect appropriate data. It makes no sense to put energy into a project that will be dismissed out of hand because the data set is thin or ill matched to the purposes of the study. These and related issues will be taken up in more detail in the next chapter.

Data Analysis Procedures

Analysis is the most mysterious and most difficult part of qualitative research. It is fair to say that the only way to understand the data analysis process is to do it. That is why effective qualitative research courses build some kind of data analysis experience into course requirements. For novice qualitative researchers, describing data analysis strategies as part of their research designs is difficult because most have never done a full-scale analysis. I devote a long chapter describing several approaches to qualitative data analysis that I hope will provide guidance in forming, describing, and implementing data analysis plans. That chapter should be studied before analysis designs are formulated, but now, I want to give an overview of what needs to be included at the design stage in terms of data analysis strategies.

Readers of design proposals want to have confidence that researchers know what they are doing. Funding agencies don't want to risk their money, human subjects committees don't want to risk their institutional reputations, and doctoral committees don't want to risk wasting their students' time (or their own). Knowing what they're doing includes having a firm idea of how data will be analyzed. Just saying that data will be analyzed qualitatively or inductively will not be enough for most critical readers. More details about when and how analysis will be accomplished are needed to build confidence in the research design.

Of course, data analysis choices will build on previous design decisions. With some kinds of research, especially those within the postpositivist paradigm, specific kinds of data analysis are prescribed when the research approach is identified. Grounded theory (Glaser & Strauss, 1967) is a good example. If the researcher is doing grounded theory, then readers know that systematic, rigorous data collection and analysis procedures are well defined. The researcher will be formulating potential explanations and searching for potential patterns through close reading and rereading of data throughout the analysis process, and constant comparison will be used to determine if these potential "theories" are grounded in the data. In positivist studies, naming an analytic approach such as analysis of covariance or multiple regression tells the reader a great deal about how analysis will be accomplished. Identifying grounded theory as an analytic strategy is as close to such an approach as will be found in qualitative work. But, as I mentioned in chapter 1, if the study is called "grounded theory," it must really be grounded theory, or the conceptual shorthand falls apart.

Other postpositivist research models have been developed to a level of specificity that identifying them gives the reader a good idea of how analysis will be done. Spradley's (1979, 1980) developmental research sequence (DRS) is an example, as are techniques described by Miles and Huberman (1994). In addition, analysis strategies, such as "analytic induction" (Denzin, 1978; Lindesmith, 1952; Robinson, 1951), have been articulated, and naming these strategies signals readers who know qualitative work that certain systematic rigor will be built into the analysis.

Most qualitative studies will not fit neatly into a specific model, so describing data analysis procedures will be more complicated than saying, "I will analyze my data using Miles and Huberman's approach." It is much more likely that researchers will say things like, "I will adapt Spradley's DRS" or "I will apply principles of analytic induction" then proceed to explain the adaptations or articulate how the principles will be applied. Studies based on other than postpositivist assumptions will have far fewer "models" to adopt or adapt because the metaphysics of the other paradigms don't easily lend themselves to the development of prescribed procedures. Naturalistic inquiry as described by Lincoln and Guba (1985) is close to a constructivist exception, but my read is that analytic procedures in *Naturalistic Inquiry* are not intended to be prescriptive to the point that researchers can say, "I will analyze my data using Lincoln and Guba's approach."

Since prescribed models are unusual in most qualitative paradigms, analysis procedures need to be spelled out in straightforward terms. Proposal readers need to know what researchers expect to do and when. The when part will likely be that the analysis will begin after all the data for the study are collected, that analysis will be recursive and begin with the first data collected, or that analysis will occur at set stages during the study. All are legitimate approaches depending on the kind of study being done. I have used all three in various studies. In an interview study, I have collected data from all my informants before beginning analysis. In classroom participant observation studies, I have begun analysis with the first observational data and shaped future observations based on that analysis. And in a study with multiple data sets, I have collected one set of data, analyzed that, and moved through the next data collection phase before analyzing its data.

Deciding if data will be analyzed in an ongoing fashion, at certain points, or only at the end will depend on the study. While none is inherently better than the others, there is some risk for researchers who wait until they are removed from the research context to do any analysis. These researchers may not know if they have sufficient data to support their findings. They may get into their data and find that something really interesting is going on, but have insufficient depth in the data for making the case in a final report. Or they may find conflicting evidence in their analyses and have no way to gather more information to resolve the conflict. A rule of thumb is that the more open the research questions, the more important to have analysis built into the data collection process. If researchers start with more specific questions, they will be looking for data that answer those questions and the risks of waiting to do analysis go down. If they are asking, "What's going on in this setting?" kinds of questions (see Goffman, 1974), then a recursive cycle of data collection and analysis is called for.

Telling proposal readers *how* analysis will be accomplished is more difficult. Again, the chapter on data analysis will provide several possible approaches. All will be based on organizing data analysis in ways that answer research questions and follow the logic of qualitative design described in the first two chapters of this book. All will require careful reading and rereading of the data. All will identify certain procedures to be followed, and all will specify some method for dealing with counterevidence or discrepant cases. These elements will look different depending on the paradigm, kind of study, and research questions; but addressing them in the research design is important for explaining the research and for framing the study in the researcher's mind. For example, in chapter 4, I detail typological analysis procedures I have developed for working with interview data around research questions that address fairly specific topics. These can be adapted to fit most approaches that use interviewing as a data collection strategy. Listing the steps here will give a sense of what kind of information should be included in the data analysis section of a research design: (a) identify topic areas to be analyzed; (b) read the data, marking entries related to topics; (c) read entries by topic, recording main ideas in entries on a summary sheet; (d) look for patterns, categories, relationships within topic areas; (e) read data, coding entries according to patterns identified (keep a record of what entries go with what elements in your patterns); (f) search for nonexamples of your patterns—decide if your patterns are supported by the data; (g) look for relationships among the patterns identified; (h) write your patterns as one-sentence generalizations; and (i) select data excerpts to support your generalizations.

A trap that novice qualitative researchers sometimes fall into is to assume that merely identifying a computer program designed to support qualitative data analysis is a sufficient description of their data analysis procedures. They sometimes write declarations such as, "Data analysis will be accomplished using NUD.IST software" and leave it at that. As will be discussed later, there are some computer programs that can be helpful in accomplishing the mechanics of data analysis (see Tesch, 1990; Weitzman & Miles, 1995), but no program can be developed to do the "mindwork"(Wolcott, 1995, p. 155) necessary to interpret and analyze qualitative data. Identifying a specific program that will be used to organize data as part of the analysis process is fine; saying that the program will do the analysis is not.

Many new researchers collect their data then hit the wall because they have no idea how to make sense of it through data analysis. While this is understandable at some level because analysis is always a complex task, having a plan for data analysis as part of research design will force researchers to think through what they anticipate doing before they are faced with a mountain of data and nowhere to start climbing. My view is that most qualitative methods texts do not give enough data analysis guidance to new researchers, and I try to do better in this book. Reading this and other sources will help researchers project data analysis strategies, but spending time with real data through course projects or pilot studies is the best way to come to terms with data analysis issues. Developing data analysis procedures as part of research design will always be a challenge, but it will get easier with knowledge and experience.

Nature of Anticipated Findings

As they are designing studies, qualitative researchers will not be able to describe their anticipated findings. They do not begin with a null hypothesis to retain or reject. But, they can anticipate the form that their findings will take; they can describe the nature of anticipated findings. Again, this is an important conceptual step for the researcher and those evaluating his or her research proposal. Having a basic idea of what findings will look like gives researchers a frame of reference for thinking about what they are doing at

each step of the research process. Being able to describe the nature of anticipated findings to committee members gives them confidence that the product of a great deal of effort will be worth the trouble.

For some studies, the form will flow directly from the kind of research
approach that is applied. The products of ethnographic fieldwork are ethnographies. Historiographies may be organized in different ways, but they are
historic accounts by nature. Narrative studies of the type that Polkinghorne
(1995, p. 15) calls "narrative analysis" are reported as stories that unite and
give meaning to the data. Critiques are the natural product of studies done
using the principles of educational criticism.

Most kinds of qualitative research, however, will produce insights that
can be presented in a number of ways. Wolcott (1994) provides a useful tool
for thinking about the form findings will take. He describes three options for
organizing and presenting qualitative data: description, analysis, and interpretation. Wolcott argues that all three are present to some degree in all qualitative studies but that deciding what gets emphasized in the balance deter-
mines the nature of the findings. In descriptive findings, the data are said to
speak for themselves. The goal is to provide accounts that represent as far a
possible what is going on in particular contexts. Wolcott recognizes that pure
description is impossible because researchers are observing through their own
interpretive lenses and making choices about what to describe, but, on balance, description emphasizes data presentation as the source for understanding the contexts under examination.

Analysis, for Wolcott, means transforming data by way of searching for
relationships and key factors that can be supported by evidence in the data.
It requires careful, systematic methods that lead to careful documentation
that is grounded in the data. The products of analysis are generalizations that
represent essential features or relationships, and the case for the accuracy of
these generalizations is made using excerpts from the data. Again, analysis
cannot be completely divorced from description or interpretation, but an
emphasis on analysis leads to findings that look substantially different from
descriptive or interpretive accounts.

Interpretation involves mental processes through which the researcher
goes beyond "factual data and cautious analysis and begins to probe what is
to be made of them (Wolcott, 1994, p. 36). Understanding and explanation
are the goals of interpretation, and it is here that the researcher inserts his or
her own thinking into the data transformation process. Interpretive work is
not undertaken without regard for the data; indeed, the plausibility of interpretations comes from the researcher's ability to use the data to make the case
for his or her interpretations.

Astute readers will see connections between qualitative paradigms and
Wolcott's three-pronged data transformation construct. Postpositivist

research may include some description, but the obvious emphasis will be on analysis. Constructivists will be comfortable emphasizing description, doing analysis, or coconstructing interpretations in concert with their participants. Critical/feminists may include some description and analysis, but their orientation assumes interpretation from particular sociopolitical perspectives. For poststructuralists, everything, including "reality" itself, is an interpretation.

By following the sequence in this chapter, researchers will put limits on what is logical when it comes to deciding on the form their findings will take. Whether Wolcott's construct is used or not, the kind of research and paradigm selected will point toward certain kinds of findings. For example, someone doing a focus group study of first-grade teachers' perspectives on whole language approaches to reading instruction will have research questions and select data analysis procedures framed by the assumptions of a particular paradigm. The questions for a constructivist will likely be open-ended, and participants and contexts will be selected based on whether the researcher wants to include a homogeneous or heterogeneous group in terms of whole language experience, commitment, training, and so on. The constructivist researcher will seek to coconstruct with his or her focus group participants the meanings that they bring to the concept of whole language. The analysis will be set up to describe the meaning structures participants use to understand whole language, and the findings will logically take the form of descriptions that rely heavily on the voices of the teachers in the study.

A postpositivist may approach the study as a way to identify the components of whole language teaching from the perspectives of first-grade teachers. This researcher may form focus groups of teachers doing whole language and ask questions that get participants talking about what it looks like in their classrooms. The data would be systematically analyzed for patterns of shared meaning across the group, and findings would be presented in the form of analytic generalizations that are supported with excerpts from the transcripts of the focus group interviews.

A researcher from the critical/feminist paradigm may develop research questions designed to confront teachers with social, economic, and political implications of using whole-language approaches with children from backgrounds that are said to place them "at risk" of school failure. He or she may select teachers based on their willingness to think critically about such issues, and analysis may lead to interpretive findings that read like an exposé of the hidden consequences of implementing whole-language approaches with certain groups of children. In addition, the teachers and researcher may develop action plans for revealing these consequences to others and resisting them in their own workplaces. The point of the example is not to argue that whole language is bad for poor kids (phonics programs or any other approach could be critically examined), but to show that the nature of findings in most studies will flow logically from their design.

Describing the nature of anticipated findings is not the same as anticipating the findings themselves. In *The Art of Fieldwork*, Wolcott (1995, p. 204) admonishes researchers to "work 'start to finish' but think 'finish to start.'" Thinking carefully about what the products of the research will look like gives the researcher a reference point for making decisions at each step along the way (see Kvale, 1996). Anticipating the nature of projected findings gives the researcher (and readers of his or her proposal) confidence that the journey proposed will lead to some productive place.

In sum, building a research design that has a flexible structure is a kind of balancing act. Having had experience with research designs that need to be modified as their studies unfold, seasoned qualitative researchers will be more comfortable with the flexible side of the equation. Those new to qualitative work will want to emphasize the structure side of the balance, expecting that studies will evolve and change but starting with a solid plan that gives them and their committees confidence that the work will lead to a positive conclusion. In the chapters to follow, more detail will be provided that will help guide researchers as they plan and do data collection, data analysis, and write-up.

INSTITUTIONAL REVIEW

When research is done under the banner of an institution such as a university, researchers are usually required to submit their research designs to human subjects committees or institutional review boards (IRBs). These committees review research projects to be sure they are designed in ways that protect research participants—the human subjects—from harm. Different institutions have different requirements, but doctoral students can be virtually certain that their dissertation preparations will include getting clearance from their university's IRB. In this section, I outline the elements that need to be included in an institutional review application and discuss research ethics that go beyond basic human subjects concerns.

Institutional review boards are usually made up of experienced researchers who are charged with insuring that any project with their institution's name on it "does no harm" to individuals who agree to participate as research subjects. Universities where large numbers of studies are being done often construct their boards so that expertise in a variety of disciplines and research approaches is represented. Representatives with knowledge of the legal risks associated with research either sit on or act as council to such boards. Institutional review committees publish guidelines to help researchers in preparing materials, and they meet regularly to approve, reject, or ask for modification of applications. Some institutions have different levels of review depending on the risks associated with individual studies. Some have "short forms" and/or "expedited review procedures" for projects that appear to offer little or no risk. These contrast with standard procedures requiring a complete application and "full review" by the entire board. Most universities build in procedures at the department and/or college level so that colleagues from the same discipline review materials before being forwarded to university IRBs. The elements presented here are drawn from my experience serving on the institutional review board at my present university (University of Tennessee IRB, 1999). They represent elements of a full review, but of course, researchers must refer to the guidelines of their own institutions as they prepare human subjects materials.

Identification of Project

Information in this section tells the reviewers who will be doing the project, who will be advising the researcher (if it is a thesis or dissertation), the type of project proposed, the title of the project, its starting and estimated completion date, and if any external agencies are involved in funding the project. Much of this detail is completed by filling in blanks on a form. If it is a thesis or dissertation, a faculty member approved to direct such work must be identified either as advisor, principal investigator (PI), or co-principal investigator (Co-PI), depending on the institution. Students will be listed as PIs or Co-PIs.

Project Objectives

This is a narrative describing the rationale, goals and objectives, and anticipated significance of the research. This will be a short version of similar sections of the research proposal. Before I served on my IRB, I had my students submit their full proposals as attachments to their IRB applications, and some universities require this. Since serving, my advice is to just give institutional review committees what they ask for and to give it to them in clear, understandable language. Institutional review boards are in the business of making decisions about risks. They need information that helps them make good decisions about potential risks. They don't necessarily need all the detail included in a full proposal to determine the degree of risk. Portions can be lifted intact from the proposal, but care should be taken to use language in the IRB application that is easily understood by individuals from other disciplines.

Description of Research Participants

In this section, reviewers want to see a clear description of who the participants will be and how many, how access to these individuals will be gained, and the criteria for selection and exclusion of potential participants. If groups whose ability to give voluntary and informed consent may be questioned are to be used (e.g., children, prisoners, or individuals with cognitive impairments), researchers must provide a rationale. Sources for participants and methods for recruiting them must be identified. If those sources are institutions such as schools, hospitals, or government agencies, researchers must provide letters of permission from these institutions that authorize researchers to contact potential participants, use the facilities, and/or access records. If incentives are to be offered to potential subjects, a rationale must be provided. Any relationships between investigators and participants must be disclosed and safeguards described so that no individuals will be coerced into participating. Methods of obtaining informed consent from these individuals are taken up in a later section.

Methods and Procedures

This section should spell out exactly what will be done in terms of data collection and analysis. Again, the language should be accessible to reviewers not conversant with the specialized language of particular disciplines and research approaches. Data collection techniques (e.g., interviews, observations, video or audio taping) need to be described, as do plans for how data will be analyzed and interpreted. This information will be an abstracted version of the research proposal with an emphasis on exactly how participants will be affected by such procedures and anticipating any potential risks. It is not the job of IRBs to evaluate the adequacy of data collection and analysis procedures except when inadequacies lead to risks for participants. The reason for requiring a clear description of research procedures is to make an informed decision about the value of a research project in relation to the risks associated with its implementation.

Specific Risks and Protection Measures

In this section, researchers should spell out the nature and amount of potential risk. Precautions to be used to reduce risks should be described and the effectiveness of the precautions assessed. Means of assuring confidentiality must be described, including the storage and disposal of data (e.g., tapes, photographs) through which identification of participants is possible. Who will have access to data should be specified and rationalized. In qualitative studies, it will be unusual for participants to be exposed to risks associated with treatments or procedures, but their anonymity will need to be protected unless they give direct permission to the contrary.

Benefits

It is not expected that all research will be risk free; but whatever risks are evident must be justified in terms of some benefit. In this section, benefits to participants and/or society should be described. It is understood that most projects contribute to knowledge in the field of research, and this is a benefit, but care should be taken not to inflate the incidental benefits to individuals who agree to participate. Payments are considered incentives, not benefits. Participants in qualitative studies often give a great deal of time and reveal sensitive information that may make them vulnerable. This is sometimes justified by claiming that participants benefit from having someone observe and talk to them, as if it will be automatically therapeutic to have someone studying your every move or asking you about your motives. While it sometimes happens that researchers become close to participants and that both benefit personally and professionally from those close relationships, to make such claims on the front end is presumptuous (see Measor & Sikes, 1992). It is essential that qualitative researchers think carefully about protecting informants and that they portray potential benefits honestly. This kind of information should be clearly spelled out in IRB applications and research bargains.

Methods of Obtaining Informed Consent

Informed consent is a key feature of a human subjects review. The elements covered in the complete application need to be part of the information that participants receive prior to giving their official consent. The exact methods for obtaining informed consent must be specified in this section, and copies of the actual forms to be used must be included. Methods must give the potential participants the opportunity to consider whether or not to consent and minimize the possibility of coercion or undue influence. Capable adults give "consent," children and others who may be incapable of making informed decisions give "assent," and legally authorized representatives give "permission" for their charges to participate. Different forms and procedures are required in each case. Forms must be in language that is understandable to participants, and means must be specified for explaining procedures to those who may not be able to read or understand consent documents. The basic elements of informed consent are summarized below (abstracted from University of Tennessee IRB, 1999, pp. 20–21):

- State that the study involves research
- Explain the purpose of the research and the expected duration of the participant's involvement
- Describe the procedures that directly involve human participants
- Describe any foreseeable risks or discomforts
- Describe any benefits to participants or others
- Describe the extent to which confidentiality will be maintained, how records will be stored, and who will have access to data
- For research involving more than minimal risk, explain whether any compensation is available if injury occurs
- Identify persons participants can contact with questions about the research or their rights
- State that participation is voluntary and that participants can withdraw at any time without penalty or loss of benefits to which they are otherwise entitled.

These elements are required for studies of all types, and additional elements may be required depending on the study. Some elements fit better with qualitative methods than others. IRBs at most universities will include members who know qualitative research and understand the special concerns of qualitative researchers for their participants. Some of these concerns will be addressed in the ethics section below.

Qualifications of the Investigator(s)

When human subjects are involved, IRBs need assurances that researchers know what they are doing. This is partly why dissertation advisors are usually carried as principal or co-principal investigators. The more vulnerable the participant group, the more important that researchers have the appropriate experience and expertise.

Facilities and Equipment

This section will include a description of the facilities and equipment to be used as part of the research and an evaluation of their adequacy for the intended project. If facilities other than those of the university are to be used, then letters of permission from the organization supplying the facilities must be included. This is especially important in education studies that involve work in school buildings. As mentioned above, written permission from appropriate school representatives will need to be acquired before submitting institutional review applications.

Responsibility of the Principal/Co-Principal Investigator

At the University of Tennessee, all IRB applications must include the following verbatim statement that includes acknowledging ethical responsibilities as prescribed in the Belmont Report (National Commission, 1979):

> By compliance with the policies established by the Institutional Review Board of the University of Tennessee, Knoxville, the principal investigator(s) subscribe to the principles stated in "The Belmont Report" and standards of professional ethics in all research, development, and related activities involving human participants under the auspices of the University of Tennessee, Knoxville. The principal investigator(s) further agree that:
>
> A. Approval will be obtained from the Institutional Review Board prior to instituting any change in the research project.
>
> B. Development of any unexpected risks will be immediately reported to the compliance section.
>
> C. An annual review and progress report will be completed and submitted when requested by the Institutional Review Board.
>
> D. Signed informed consent documents will be kept for the duration of the project and for at least three years thereafter at a location approved by the Institutional Review Board.

Preparing IRB applications is an important part of learning how to do qualitative research. Application forms and procedures will be different in different places, but the basic concern for protecting participants will be the same. My view is that ethical responsibility goes beyond "first do no harm." Some of the special ethical concerns of qualitative research in education are taken up below.

ETHICS

Qualitative researchers are interested in exploring the world from the perspective of cultural insiders. Their methods are designed to allow them to get close to the action and close to their informants. Most qualitative studies require some level of active involvement by research participants. Many only work when that involvement is extensive, and some studies require involvement at the level of collaboration. We ask a lot when we ask individuals to participate in our qualitative studies. We usually ask for a considerable amount of time, but more important, we ask participants to reveal what goes on behind the scenes in their everyday lives. We ask them to trust us to the point that they are comfortable sharing the intimate details of their lifeworlds. We make some sort of record of these, then we leave. We ask a lot, take a lot, and, if we're not careful, give very little.

Reciprocity is an ethical issue in any research effort, but it is especially important when participants invest themselves in close relationships with researchers and trust them with sensitive information. It is fair to ask who benefits from these relationships and who benefits most? It's easy to see how researchers benefit, but what are the rewards for participants? When research bargains are struck, it is important to build in reciprocal arrangements that specify what the researcher will be contributing to the bargain. These can be labor-related contributions such as driving parents to Head Start meetings or monitoring students during study hall, or they might be expertise-related activities such as helping to organize presentations for a school board meeting or providing inservice for teachers. It gets tricky for researchers in some classroom studies because volunteering to work as a coteacher or assistant or agreeing to consult with the teacher on his or her teaching practices may put researchers in roles that conflict with their researcher role and change the nature of the study. Others will design studies with the expectation that collaborations in labor, like coteaching, are a positive element that allows for benefits to participants to become part of the study and its findings (see Zigo, 2001). No matter what the anticipated relationships with participants, giving back something of substance needs to be considered as qualitative projects are planned.

Plans also need to made for leaving the scene once the research process is complete. This is an especially sensitive issue when participants and researchers have formed close personal bonds. The conventional model has been for researchers to take what they want from the research site then abruptly pull out (see Reinharz, 1979), but this is ethically unacceptable when participants have made themselves vulnerable through close personal contact with researchers. Standard research bargains will specify if and how research findings will be shared with participants, but they typically do not discuss how exiting the project will be accomplished. I am not suggesting that bargains say things like, "The researcher will remain friends with the participant." I do think that ceremonial events such as a final debriefing or wrap-up celebration are important if the researcher is planning not to have future contact with participants. When the expectation is that the relationship will continue, building in a session to plan future activities might be appropriate. The point is to signal both sides what will be expected of the relationship at the end of the study. This will be more important in some studies than in others, but protecting the feelings of those who have given themselves to any project is an ethical imperative.

Qualitative researchers doing research in education contexts have special ethical responsibilities when the participants in their studies are students and teachers. Students are especially vulnerable to exploitation because of their youth and their positioning as a kind of captive audience in the school. While informed consent procedures will require parents to agree to their children's participation, it is often questionable if children, especially young children, understand what is going on or agree to participate themselves. Even procedures for acquiring "assent" from children through verbal explanations that seek their agreement to participate do not guarantee that children really understand or that they do not feel coerced into going along with an agreement that their parents and teachers have already made. This is difficult territory, but using children to accomplish research purposes in ways that we would not use adults is wrong. The fact that they are children should make us more, not less, sensitive to ethical concerns. A genuine effort should be made to help children comprehend exactly what their participation will mean, and a thoughtful attempt to assess their degree of agreement should be a part of research design.

Teachers, as an occupational group, have relatively little power or status (Clifford, 1989; Gitlin & Margonis, 1995) and often perceive themselves to be in a subordinate position in relation to educational researchers (Hatch, 1995b; Tripp, 1994). They too can be subtly coerced into participating in studies about which they have reservations. When district officials and principals have already agreed, it may be difficult for teachers to decline an invitation to participate. In addition, some teachers may be reluctant to say no to individuals from universities whom they see as "experts" in the field, or they may think that refusal to participate sends the message that they have something to hide. Here again, full disclosure of research intentions and the clear message that participation is voluntary are essential elements of genuine informed consent. To take advantage of teachers by not giving them the full right to refuse participation is wrong. Being sensitive to their potential vulnerability is essential.

Qualitative researchers in any setting may face ethical decisions about what to do if they observe illegal activity, behavior that is unsafe, or practices that place individuals at risk (see Berg, 1998; Marshall & Rossman, 1995). Because children are involved, such decisions may be even more important for educational researchers. The law in my state requires that suspicions of child abuse be reported no matter what the circumstances, so that information must be stated directly in informed consent documents. The reporting of other illegal activity such as drug use, theft, or truancy is not as clear-cut. It is possible that studies of the "underworld" of schooling will require that researchers agree to keep confidential the identities of individuals who commit illegal acts. If the goal is to understand the thinking of children who join gangs, for example, access to that understanding is not going to be possible if researchers report gang activities to police or school authorities. However, if researchers have reason to believe that the safety of the school is threatened by gang plans, they have a moral obligation to intervene.

In other circumstances, educational researchers may see practices or observe children behaving in ways that they believe put others at risk. School policies or teacher practices that discriminate against children with disabilities or the social ostracism of a minority child by his or her peers might be examples. In cases like these, it's easy to rationalize that you are there to record what actually happens, to argue that it would be happening if you were not there, and to ask how such phenomena can be studied in their natural context if you blow the whistle or intervene on behalf of individuals. My own take on issues like this is that decisions should not be reduced to the either/or level. It is sometimes possible to make an effort to help reduce risks for participants without abandoning the research project. The nature of the study may change, but that may be preferable to completing a study and then regretting that you did not try to help (see Ceglowski, 2000; Hatch, 1995b).

These are difficult issues, and simple formulas for resolving them do not exist. Familiarity with guidelines for ethical research practices such as the Belmont Report (Commission) is essential, and carefully planned informed consent procedures and research bargains are important, but every study will generate its own special ethical concerns. I have designed a list of questions that help get at some of the special ethical issues related to qualitative research in education settings. Answering these questions will set the stage for thinking about ethical issues particular to individual research contexts. The questions are:

Why am I doing this study?

Why am I doing it at this site?

What is my relationship to the participants?

What are the participants' roles in the design, data collection, analysis, and authorship of this study?

Who owns the study?

Who benefits from the study?

How do I benefit?

How do the participants benefit?

Who benefits most?

Who may be at risk in the contexts I am studying?

Should I intervene on behalf of those at risk? (Hatch, 1995b, p. 221)

Paying honest attention to such questions may be helpful, but ethics finally come down to individual researchers making the best judgments they can to insure that the individuals they study are treated with fairness and dignity.

CRITERIA FOR ASSESSING DESIGN ADEQUACY

The following are questions that provide a framework for making judgments about the adequacy of qualitative research designs. They are built on the structure of this chapter, and readers should refer to this and other chapters in this book for explanation and clarification. Every study will be different and every design unique in some respects. Answers will vary by paradigm and research type, but my view is that researchers should be able to point to their proposals and generate answers to each question prior to implementing their projects.

1. Has the researcher described his or her methodological and substantive theory bases?
    A. Is it clear which qualitative paradigm will frame the research?
    B. Are the researcher's metaphysical assumptions explicated?
    C. Is the kind of qualitative research identified and justified?
    D. Has a theory (or theories) that grounds the substance of the study in some established body of knowledge been identified and justified?

2. Has the researcher articulated a set of research questions?
    A. Do the research questions make sense given the researcher's methodological and substantive theories?
    B. Are the questions answerable given the kind of qualitative research proposed?
    C. Are the questions open-ended, clearly stated, and few in number?

3. Has the researcher identified a research context and explained how access and entry will be negotiated?
    A. Is it clear where the study will be undertaken and why that context was selected?
    B. Is the study doable, and are the research questions answerable in the context identified?
    C. Are procedures for obtaining formal permission described?
    D. Has a research bargain been developed?
    E. Are procedures for gaining entry and acquiring informed consent described?

4. Has the researcher described procedures for selecting participants and establishing working relationships with them?
   A. Are criteria for selecting participants spelled out?
   B. Are procedures for contacting and inviting participants described?
   C. Are the projected number of participants and anticipated amount of time to be spent with them specified?
   D. Has the anticipated level of involvement by participants been described and justified?
   E. Are plans in place for building and maintaining the desired researcher-participant relationships?

5. Has the researcher identified and justified data collection procedures to be used in the study?
   A. Are the anticipated data of the study described?
   B. Is it clear how and when the data will be collected?
   C. Do data collection plans make sense given the paradigmatic assumptions and methodological orientation of the study?
   D. Are the research questions answerable given the data identified?

6. Has the researcher described data analysis procedures to be used in the study?
   A. Are anticipated data analysis procedures articulated?
   B. Is it clear how and when data will be analyzed?
   C. Are procedures for dealing with discrepant cases or counterevidence spelled out?
   D. If utilized, is the role of computer programs designed to support data analysis described?
   E. Does the data analysis plan make sense given the research paradigm, the kind of research to be done, the data to be collected, and the research questions to be answered?

7. Has the researcher described the nature of his or her anticipated findings?
   A. Has the anticipated form that research findings will take been described?
   B. Does the nature of anticipated findings build logically from the preceding elements of research design?
   C. Will anticipated findings be in a form that will answer research questions?

CHAPTER THREE

Collecting Qualitative Data

How do I start collecting data? How do I take field notes? What do I write down when there is so much going on? What kinds of questions should I take to an open-ended interview? What artifact data are needed for my study? When will I start analyzing the data? How will I know when I have enough data? This chapter is about how to collect qualitative data, and it is designed to answer these and other questions that novice researchers have about the data collection process. I devote separate sections to the primary data gathering strategies of qualitative research (observation, interviewing, and unobtrusive data collection), then address other strategies (video recording, focus-group interviewing, and participant journaling). I try throughout to connect the generic descriptions of data collection strategies to specific kinds of qualitative research within specific qualitative paradigms. The chapter concludes with the presentation of criteria for assessing data adequacy.

While the researcher's stance in relation to his or her data may be different across qualitative paradigms, the basics of doing observation, interviewing, and unobtrusive data collection are similar. So, for example, even though a postpositivist sees interview data as an empirical representation of a situated reality from which a set of generalizations can be drawn, and a critical/feminist sees similar data as evidence of political, economic, or sexual oppression, both might use parallel techniques to generate the interview data in the first place. Similarly, constructivist researchers will do observation in ways that look the same as poststructuralists, even though the former sees the data to be obtained as coconstructed with participants and the later as nonunitary text from which any number of stories might be told. The goal of the sections to follow is to present a clear description of data collection strategies that can be adapted to a variety of research approaches within the qualitative paradigms that frame this book.

OBSERVING

In chapter 1, I described *participant observation* as a special kind of qualitative study that involves all of the field methods of ethnography (observation, interviewing, and artifact collection) but has a narrower focus than a full ethnography. Here I am using the term *observation* to describe a specific data collection strategy that can be applied across many kinds of qualitative studies. The kind of observation used in most qualitative work is usually called "participant observation" because the researcher acts as a participant at some level in the settings he or she is studying. Distinctions between participant observation as a kind of qualitative study and as a data collection strategy are blurred throughout the literature. I will not be able to solve that problem in this book, but the reader should be aware that my discussion of observation parallels others' descriptions of participant observation as a data collection strategy.

The goal of observation is to understand the culture, setting, or social phenomenon being studied from the perspectives of the participants. Observers attempt to see the world through the eyes of those they are studying. They observe carefully in an effort to acquire "members' knowledge and consequently understand from the participants' point of view what motivated the participants to do what the researcher has observed them doing and what these acts meant at the time" (Schwartz & Jacobs, 1979, p. 8).

Patton (1990, pp. 202–05) identified several strengths of observational data for qualitative program evaluation. I have adapted these strengths for general qualitative research as follows:

- Direct observation of social phenomena permits better understanding of the contexts in which such phenomena occur.

- Firsthand experience allows the researcher to be open to discovering inductively how the participants are understanding the setting.

- The researcher has the opportunity to see things that are taken for granted by participants and would be less likely to come to the surface using interviewing or other data collection techniques.

- The researcher may learn sensitive information from being in the setting that informants may be reluctant to discuss in interviews.

- Getting close to social phenomena allows the researcher to add his or her own experience in the setting to the analysis of what is happening.

The idea is to be there in the social setting, to make a careful record of what people say and do, and to make sense of how the participants make sense within that setting. Systematic tools for making analytic sense of observational data will be described in the next chapter, but the basic process of making sense is a very human activity. Whenever people enter social situations with which they are not familiar, they are anxious to find out the rules for appropriate behavior in those situations. They watch others operate and gradually build up a storehouse of knowledge about the norms and expectations of the setting. They take action themselves and get feedback about the appropriateness of those actions from the reactions of those around them. While the roles of ordinary participant and research observer are very different (see Spradley, 1980), researchers using observation as a data collection strategy are applying the basic cognitive processes they use to negotiate new social situations and to understand the social behavior of others.

Level of Involvement

The level of participation that an observer takes in the research setting is a key issue in doing qualitative observations. Classic ethnographers assumed that observation meant "conscious and systematic sharing, insofar as circumstances permit, in the life-activities . . . of a group of persons" (Kluckhohn, 1940, p. 331), and Chicago-style sociologists operated from the belief that the "observer participates in the daily life of the people under study" (Becker & Geer, 1957, p. 28). Other qualitative researchers have described continua with extremes from "complete observer" to "complete participant" (Reinharz, 1979, p. 156),"limited observer" to "active participant" (Wolcott, 1988, p. 194), and "nonparticipation" to "complete participation" (Spradley, 1980, pp. 59–62). Whatever the framework, observers need to think carefully about their level of involvement in the settings they study.

Several factors should influence decisions about researchers' levels of participation in the activities of their participants. One is the issue of intrusiveness. If the goal is to capture naturally occurring activity, then a complete participant will have a more obvious impact on a social setting than a complete observer. While it is true that the very presence of a researcher makes any natural context unnatural to some degree (Labov, 1972), researchers who take on the role of teacher, teacher assistant, or student in school-based studies will influence the way that life plays out in those settings more than the observer who acts as a fly on the wall. The level of involvement does not have to be *either* nonparticipation *or* complete participation. Spradley (1980), for example, identifies passive, moderate, and active levels of participation between the extremes, but part of deciding about level of involvement means considering how the researcher's participation in the context influences the natural flow of events in that context.

A second and related factor is the researcher's ability to act as a true participant. In anthropological field studies, researchers spend long periods of time living in the cultures they are trying to describe. Their goal is to understand the rules of behavior that define cultural insiders' perspectives, and they work hard over time to learn to think and act like their informants. Educational researchers who are not ethnographers usually have different research objectives and do not have the time to develop insider perspectives through complete participation.

Full participation is especially problematic when adult researchers attempt to participate as students or young children. Examples of successful attempts to participate as children in studies of peer culture (Corsaro, 1985) and children's perceptions of race and ethnicity (Holmes, 1995) are available, but the limitations of an adult being accepted as a peer by students are obvious. Less evident are problems that educational researchers face when attempting to participate as teachers or administrators. I made it clear in chapter 2 that I believe clandestine research agendas in which those under examination are unaware that they are being studied are unethical in education settings. Participants should know that the researcher is acting as a researcher even if he or she is also taking on the role of teacher or administrator. This knowledge will influence the behavior of those being studied and influence the researcher's ability to be effective in both roles. A good example is Hargreaves's (1967) study of social relations in a British secondary school. Teachers accepted and confided in him as a teacher/colleague until he started doing formal observations, at which time they began treating him like an inspector. It's reasonable for participants to ask, "Why should I take you seriously as a teacher/administrator when I know you are here to study us?" or "How do you want me to act so I won't mess up your study?"

Again, participation need not be an all or nothing proposition. I have had graduate students who enter classrooms as "helpers" for teachers, then gradually shift to a more passive observer role. I have also supervised those who chose to politely avoid interaction with students at the beginning, then move to more active participation as their studies move forward. In each of these cases, decisions about taking and shifting roles were deliberate and strategic. The former emphasized building rapport with teachers and children early on, and the latter wanted to start with descriptive information about classroom routines without her influence. Finding a balancing place on the continuum is important, but changing the balance as studies progress is sometimes a good strategy.

A third issue has to do with what data might be missed while the researcher is participating instead of taking field notes. If the researcher is acting as teacher, student, or administrator, stopping to make a record of what is happening may be impossible, and trying to remember without some kind of field note record will be very difficult. In the case above where the student acted as a classroom helper in the early stages of the research, her data record from those early stages was thin. She worked all day in the classroom, then wrote her recollections that evening. The data were little more than a set of general impressions of the time she spent in the setting. As she shifted the balance to less active participation and more formal observation, she was able to capture more verbatim classroom conversations and more explicit descriptions of classroom interactions. These richer data allowed her to do the constructivist analysis she planned for her study. While it is true that building rapport early might be a strategy that leads to higher quality data down the line (see Dean, Eichhorn, & Dean, 1969), it should be recognized that tradeoffs exist between the degree of involvement and the ability to concentrate on making a rich data record.

Proximity to the action is the fourth issue that needs to be considered as decisions about degree of involvement are made. Field anthropologists act as full participants because they want to experience firsthand what their informants experience in their home cultures. As much as possible, they want to know what it's like to live as a member of the cultural groups they are studying. The principle is the same for other qualitative studies that seek to get at insider perspectives: the more involved the observer is as a participant in the setting, the closer he or she is to the action. Not only does acting as a participant allow access to the places where the action happens, but it places the researcher in a position to experience feelings similar to those they are studying. So in school-based studies, participating as a cafeteria worker, for example, would give the researcher a richer perspective on what life is like for such a worker than would observing from the sidelines. The benefits of such involvement would have to be weighed against the other factors discussed in this section.

A final consideration has to do with issues of "going native" in the participant observer role. Those who act as full participants have some small chance of going native in the classic sense (i.e., joining the cultural group that is under investigation), but there is a larger chance that researchers will overidentify with those they are studying and lose their perspective as researchers (see Hammersley & Atkinson, 1983). It seems like a long shot that researchers would decide to become cafeteria workers as a result of studying them, but it could be possible to build a kind of "overrapport" that influences researchers to fail to see certain evidence that might cast the workers being studied in a negative light. It is not unusual for qualitative researchers to identify with those they are studying (see Reinharz, 1979), and it is not necessarily a bad thing. But it can be problematic if participant observers give up important parts of their observer role to their participant role. If seeing the world through the lenses of their participants creates a kind of myopic vision that leaves out other important perspectives, then overidentification can lead to distorted findings. No matter what the level of involvement, the influences of potential overrapport need to be monitored; the higher the level of participation, the more careful the monitoring needs to be.

The level of involvement researchers take in relation to their participants depends on balancing all of the factors discussed above and on the kind of research planned. Researcher-participant relationships within different paradigms were discussed in chapter 2, and that discussion will not be repeated. Here, I present a set of generalizations about levels of researcher participation within different paradigms using different kinds of qualitative research to summarize my views. I have framed these using Spradley's (1980) continuum that runs from nonparticipation, through passive participation, moderate participation, and active participation, to complete participation. These generalizations are not hard and fast rules, but they are intended to be guidelines for making decisions about levels of participation within each paradigm:

- Nothing about *postpositivist* research assumptions limits the level of researcher participation in studies involving observation. Individuals doing traditional ethnography will, by definition, be heavily involved as participants, but other postpositivists doing grounded theory, ethnomethodology, case study, participant observation, or symbolic interactionist research can justify operating within the full range from nonparticipation to complete participation.

- *Constructivist* assumptions lead logically in the direction of more participation when observation is chosen as a data collection strategy. If participants are to be involved in coconstructing the findings of the study, then constructivist researchers doing naturalistic inquiry, case studies, participant observation, educational criticism, phenomenological studies, collaborative studies, or action research are likely to be at least moderately involved as participants in their observational work.

- The assumptions of *critical/feminist* research also indicate the need for active involvement on the part of researchers. When observation is used for data collection in critical or feminist ethnographies, case studies, participant observation studies, or action research projects, researchers will most often be engaged in at least moderate participation in order to work with participants in the effort to raise consciousness and bring about social change.

- *Poststructuralist* researchers will find no insight into what constitutes appropriate participation from their paradigmatic assumptions. If they design ethnographic, participant observation, or case studies that include observation as a data collection strategy, their reluctance to assign anything but transitory meaning to their observations does not translate into a preference for involvement at either end of the continuum.

Field Note Processes

The principal data generated through observation take the form of field notes. Observers need to make a record of what they observe in the settings they are studying, and these records usually take the form of raw field notes that are written on the spot while the researcher is in the setting. Raw field notes are usually descriptions of contexts, actions, and conversations written in as much detail as possible given the constraints of watching and writing in a rapidly changing social environment. Raw field notes are converted into research protocols through a process of "filling in" the original notes. Filling in means going through the raw data as soon as possible after leaving the field and making a more complete description based on the raw notes and what is remembered from the setting. Research protocols are filled-in field notes organized in a consistent format (most often in a word processing program) in preparation for analysis. As field notes are taken and research protocols produced, researchers also keep track of impressions and preliminary interpretations that go beyond the descriptions reserved for the field-note record. This is usually done by bracketing certain sections within field notes and/or by keeping a separate research journal. After a discussion of what to attend to when entering a research setting, a variety of approaches to each of these processes will be addressed in detail (appendix B is an excerpt from a protocol done as part of a study of creative and social behavior in a preschool, and it includes examples of many of the elements described below).

Figuring Out What to Attend To. I remember my first attempt to take field notes. As part of an introductory qualitative research course, we were assigned to find a public place and make as accurate a record as possible of what happened there over an hour's time. I chose to sit in the gallery and take notes on a session of traffic court. I thought I had made a good choice because the physical setting is fairly static, movement around the courtroom is limited, and people generally talk one at a time. I was trained to start by making a map of the setting, so I started with that task, but as soon as the action started, I felt I had to get down what was being said, so I put the map aside. I quickly learned that I could not write fast enough to keep up with the conversations in the courtroom. As my head was down to write, I would lose track of who was talking and get behind on what the last person had said. The defendants were at a table with their backs to me, and I had a hard time hearing what they had to say. Panic set in! Since I was not getting everything, I had the feeling I was getting nothing. The action was moving so fast, and I was processing so slowly that I was sure I could never learn to do observational research.

I was right about the courtroom. It is a much easier place in which to take field notes than other, more dynamic settings (like classrooms), but the problem of knowing what to attend to and what to write down got my attention right away. The feeling of being overwhelmed and of knowing that you are not recording all of the action going on around you does not go away even as you become more experienced at doing field observations. At some level, observers always experience what Woods (1986, p. 46) calls the "elsewhere syndrome"—the nagging feeling that the really important action is happening elsewhere. But, with practice and with a general plan, it is possible to feel more comfortable in the setting and more confident that you are capturing important data that fairly represent the contexts you are observing.

Some tips that will help novice researchers develop a general plan for beginning field-note data collection are offered below. These are drawn from my own experiences and from qualitative researchers who have written about their experiences collecting observational data.

The first tip is *don't expect to be perfect*. All researchers are limited in what they can see and hear, what they can pay attention to, what they can write down, and what they can remember. When I became frustrated with all I was missing when taking field notes in a busy kindergarten class, I tried to ease my anxiety by considering all I was getting that I would be missing if I were not there at all or if I were there recording tallies on some kind of standardized observational checklist. Wolcott's (1995, p. 97) advice in this regard is well taken: "Don't worry about all that you are *not* getting; focus on what you *are* getting" (emphasis in original). No researcher is able to capture the complete picture of all that is happening in any social situation. As Patton (1990, p. 216) has noted, "It is not possible to observe everything. The human observer is not a movie camera, and even a movie camera has to be pointed in the right direction to capture what is happening." Ways to focus the researcher's lens and point him or her in the right direction follow, but these have little utility unless it is understood that all pictures are incomplete.

Since it is impossible to attend to everything, it is important to *make a careful record of what you attend to*. Data that are useful for generating descriptions, analyses, and interpretations are detailed, verbatim accounts of events and conversations. I have seen data from students and scholars trained in other approaches that were little more than general descriptions of events and paraphrased accounts of what participants said. I believe that no matter what qualitative paradigm is framing the study, observational data should be as careful a representation as possible of the action observed in the research setting. If data are only researchers' impressions of what happened, then it turns out to be a study of researcher impressions of the social action observed, not a study of the action itself. I realize full well that all observation is interpretation at some level (see LeCompte & Schensul, 1999). Our own perspectives color what we see when we look. We decide what settings to study, what to pay attention to, and what to write down—all interpretive acts. But if our claim is to be doing data-based research, then data should be, insofar as possible, an accurate descriptive account of what the participants did and said while we were watching. Wolcott (1995, p. 98) calls such accounts "reportable data," that is, data "recorded in sufficient detail that you can report it verbatim." So the suggestion is to not worry about recording everything that's going on, but to record what you do pay attention to in the form of reportable data.

But what should researchers pay attention to, especially at the beginnings of their observational work? It is usually a good idea to *start by describing the contexts that frame the study*. One of the strengths of qualitative work of any type is that it is contextualized—that the behaviors of participants can be understood only within an understanding of their particular circumstances. Giving readers a solid sense of the contextual world of the participants is part of any good qualitative report, and developing an understanding of contexts during the study will help frame the researcher's approach to what to look for and where. I mentioned that I was trained to make a map of the social settings in which I was observing. This is a good way to start any observation. It forces you to pay attention to the physical features of the context and supplies you with points of reference that you can go back to as data collection and analysis continue. Spradley (1980, p. 78) identifies contextual dimensions that define any social situation. I have adapted these dimensions and framed questions that might be used to guide early observations:

- What are the places where social activity occurs?
- Who are the people involved in the social action?
- What individual activities are people engaged in?
- What group activities are people engaged in?
- What are the objects people use?
- What is the sequence of activity that takes place over time?
- What things are people trying to accomplish?
- What emotions are expressed?

Taking these or similar questions to the field will give new researchers something to look for and help build a database on which a rich contextual description can be grounded.

A related general strategy is to *start with a broad focus and narrow as you go*. Ethnographers (e.g., Agar, 1980; Ely et al., 1991; Spradley, 1980) often recommend starting fieldwork with a broad, general focus that gradually narrows as researchers spend time in the setting and begin their analyses. This approach seems essential if researchers start their work, as ethnographers do, with broad questions about cultural groups, but it is also a good strategy for other researchers doing qualitative observational research. Spradley (1980) describes first forays into the field as "grand tour observations" (p. 77). During these initial observations, researchers pay attention to the major features of the social context rather than the particulars. If the study is designed with general research questions, the grand tour observations will be useful for early analyses that will lead to more focused observations. If the study is framed by more specific research questions, the grand tour approach serves to ground the specifics on a firm contextual base. Even though I have done observational studies that focused on particular classroom phenomena (e.g., child-to-child interaction, remedial reading instruction, social adjustments of creative children), I have always begun the data collection cycle with grand tour observations that set the stage for exploring the social action of interest.

That leads to the next tip: *bring questions to each observation*. I take field notes on legal pads attached to a clipboard. When I do classroom observations, I write one or two questions at the top of the pad before entering the setting. Early in the study, the questions will likely be broad, contextual questions like those above (e.g., What are the activities that children engage in away from the supervision of the teacher?). Later, questions become more focused and are often related to gaps that I am finding in the data as I begin analysis (e.g., What are peer relations like for children who spend most of their day working and playing alone?). Near the end, questions are usually more specific and often framed to get more information on tentative patterns (e.g., What do children do when other children put them down?). Questions evolve and usually become more focused as the study progresses (see Ely et al., 1991). The idea is not to find a definitive answer to your questions on a particular visit, but to give you a point of reference from which to decide where you will place yourself in the research scene and what you will look for as you go about your observation. Sometimes events in the setting will be so compelling that your questions will not be addressed that day, but having a question or two in mind gives you a place from which to start.

Another strategy is to *use sensitizing concepts to focus early observations* (Denzin, 1978; Patton, 1990). When researchers from different disciplines or different paradigms enter the field, they bring with them different ways of organizing and conceptualizing knowledge. So a feminist anthropologist may enter a magnet school for the arts with an interest in issues of social justice and gender equity, while a constructivist doing educational criticism may enter the same setting looking for evidence of aesthetic quality and artistic integrity, and a postpositivist social psychologist may be tuned into student socialization and leadership processes. Every field of inquiry has particular sensitizing concepts that distinguish the interests of that field from others, and those sensitizing concepts are further circumscribed by the research paradigm being applied. This is one of the important reasons why new researchers need to spend time becoming grounded in their disciplines and coming to grips with their paradigmatic assumptions. In the field, knowing the important frames of reference within disciplines and paradigms will make it easier to identify sensitizing concepts that can be used to focus observations. For example, poststructuralist scholars are particularly interested in issues of knowledge and power (see Flax, 1990; Sarap, 1993), so knowledge/power relationships often become sensitizing concepts for poststructuralist researchers entering a research setting to do observation. Sensitizing concepts can tie to the last suggestion about bringing questions to the field, so the poststructuralist may enter the magnet school of the arts with questions such as "What are situations in which knowledge/power relationships are evident?" Whatever the field of inquiry or paradigm, using sensitizing concepts to focus observations is a useful strategy.

As data collection proceeds, researchers should *refer back to research questions* to keep their observations on track. Wolcott (1995) makes this recommendation:

> Try to assess what you are doing (that is, your participation), what you are observing, and what you are recording, in terms of the kind of information you will *need to report* rather than the kind of information you feel you *ought to gather*." (P. 78–79, emphasis in original)

My own experience and my knowledge of others learning how to do observations is that this is good advice that is hard to follow. New researchers are afraid that they are missing the really good stuff or not being faithful to their methodology if they confine their attention to what they will need to report. I encourage students to be sure they are getting data that will answer their research questions. They will likely have much more data than are needed at the end of the study, but they must have adequate data to justify the reporting of findings related to their original purposes. Research questions often change as a result of experiences in the research setting, and other analyses are often completed in addition to those originally proposed. But, Wolcott's advice is on target for managing what can become unmanageable in observational work. By continually referring back to research questions, researchers have an additional framework for organizing observations so that they get at what they will need to report.

A final suggestion is to *focus on what matters to participants*. On my office bulletin board I have a yellowed note that I wrote to myself while I was doing my dissertation research. It says, "What matters is what matters." While others find it more confusing than profound, if I have a gravestone, this is what I want on it. In the qualitative research context, what matters to the actors in a social setting is what ought to matter to the researcher. The power of observation done well is that it allows access to participants' experiences of their worlds. No matter what the paradigm or research question, the reason for selecting observation as a data collection tool is to try to see the phenomena under investigation from the viewpoint of those being observed. A big part of that is learning to notice what is important to them (LeCompte & Schensul, 1999). Figuring out what matters to participants and paying attention to expressions of what matters is an important goal that can serve to guide observations during a qualitative study.

Writing Raw Field Notes. Once the researcher has a general strategy for deciding what to attend to, how are field notes actually produced? The first basic issue is deciding how notes will be physically recorded. I take a clipboard into the field because I like to have a hard surface on which to write as I move around classrooms. Some observers use small spiral notebooks because they are less obtrusive and less cumbersome. Others use laptop computers because they believe the computers facilitate the accurate recording of details. I think laptops can be intrusive, and I want to write more detail in my field notes than can easily be recorded on small notebook pages, but each researcher will have to find his or her own preferred data recording medium.

It is impossible for researchers to remember all that is done and said in any social setting, and it is impossible for the researcher to make a complete record on the spot of the rapidly changing events in that setting. Qualitative researchers make "field jottings" (Bernard, 1994, p. 181), "scratch notes" (Sanjek, 1990, p. 96), "condensed accounts" (Spradley, 1980, p. 69) or what I call "raw field notes" that are accurate, but incomplete, written descriptions of what was observed in the field. Raw field notes will be converted into research protocols, so it is important that they include enough detail to make an accurate representation possible. Contextual details should include a record of where the observer is in the research setting, what general activity the participants are engaged in, and what time observations start and stop. I like to keep a record of the time down the side of my legal pad so that I can put events in temporal perspective as I am filling in and interpreting my notes. In a preschool study, a raw field note entry might begin with "8:30—I am sitting at the edge of the rug as teacher and students begin circle time."

Since the goal is to produce an accurate account, raw field notes need to include "key words, names, apt phrases to prompt the memory later" (Woods, 1986, p. 44). Conversations should be recorded as close to verbatim as possible, and since it will be impossible to record everything that is said, important sentences, phrases, and words should be written down as they are spoken. Paraphrasing what was said is not a good strategy. Try to get the flavor of the interchange by writing the participants' actual words, and these will facilitate reconstructing conversations as protocols are written. Early in the research process or later as new participants enter the research scene, it is vital to include descriptions of the actors you are studying (Berg, 1998). Taking time to get this information in your field notes will save lots of time and energy later on.

I have yet to meet a qualitative researcher who was not frustrated by his or her first attempts at taking notes in the field. It takes time to develop the skills and confidence necessary to take good notes. As mentioned above, I recommend practicing in public settings. Taking along a notepad when you go to the library, airport, or fast-food restaurant can provide you with an opportunity to learn what it feels like to try to record social activity in different settings. I also agree with others (e.g., Berg, 1998; Bogdan & Biklen, 1992) who recommend that early observations be kept relatively brief in order to give the researcher a chance to become acclimated to the research scene and facilitate developing note-taking skills. Some of these specialized skills include using abbreviations and developing a personal shorthand (see Woods, 1986), learning to pick out key words and phrases, learning to write and listen at the same time, leaning to concentrate when things seem to be happening too fast to keep up with, and developing the ability to continue to write when your fingers go numb. Making good raw field-note records is a special skill that will improve with lots of practice. Understanding that virtually everyone gets frustrated and that everyone who takes it seriously improves will make it easier for novice researchers to persevere in the face of this daunting task.

Working on the development of some other, more general, skills before going into the field will facilitate success in doing observational research. Bernard (1994, pp. 147–53) identified several skills that participant observers need in order to do anthropological fieldwork. I have adapted Bernard's suggestions and added some examples of my own. The list that follows identifies a skill area that is important to qualitative observation, suggests an approach to working on the development of that skill, and provides an example of a specific activity:

- Building explicit awareness—practice paying close attention to the details of ordinary events (e.g., write detailed descriptions of the most mundane things you can think of).

- Building memory—work on developing short- and long-term memory (e.g., walk past a storefront, then try to recall everything you saw, going back to check on your accuracy, or try making a complete record of a church service after it is over).

- Maintaining naivete—learn to suspend judgment, especially when you think you already understand participant motives and actions (e.g., learn a new skill such as archery or pottery that requires you to interact with experts and keep a journal of the experience of being a novice).

- Building writing skills—develop your abilities to write (e.g., form a writing workshop with others who are interested, set regular writing tasks, and critique each others' work).

- Understanding biases—learn to watch yourself watching in order to become more aware of your opinions, experiences, and values and their potential impact on observations (e.g., write a self-disclosure statement that details your biases about what you are studying).

Several of these skills are addressed at various points throughout this book. They are included here to give novice researchers information about some of the skills required to become an effective observer and some strategies for developing those skills. Janesick (1998, pp. 14–24) also offers "stretching exercises" that may be useful for individuals learning to be observers.

Filling in Research Protocols. As soon after leaving the field as possible, researchers should convert their raw field notes into research protocols, that is, expanded accounts of what was observed on that particular visit. This is the time to fill in the details that the researcher did not have time to record during the observation. The idea is to rewrite the raw notes using a format that the researcher selects for use throughout the data collection process. The filling in process takes at least as much time as was spent in the field, and often longer, and it is vital that this activity be undertaken before memories begin to fade or other observations are made.

A well-written research protocol should provide a sense of being in the research scene. The raw field notes should be expanded in enough detail that readers can visualize what the observer saw (Berg, 1998; Clifford, 1990). They should be as accurate a record as possible of everything that happened during the observation period. I recommend filling raw field notes in by typing protocols into word processing programs. Early on, I typed protocols on a typewriter, and I have filled in notes by talking into a tape recorder, then having a transcriptionist type protocols. Some researchers still prefer to write their expanded accounts by hand, but the advantages of using computer technology are obvious—errors can be corrected on the spot, revisions and additions are easy to make, files can be produced and organized with ease, and later analytic work and writing are greatly facilitated.

Whatever the process, it is important that raw field notes be filled in before they "go cold." Even though researchers become better able to remember details with practice, making protocols as soon as possible after leaving the field improves the chances that the abbreviated descriptions in the raw notes will be turned into accurate representations of what was observed. My rule of thumb is to fill in notes *as soon as possible*. I like to go directly from the research context to my desktop, so I try to block my "research time" so that it includes time for both observation and filling in. Of course, this is often impossible, but even when I cannot get to protocol writing immediately, I never sleep on raw field notes, I never do another observation before making an expanded account of what I have already observed, and I try to avoid talking about an observation before writing it up (see Bernard, 1994; Woods, 1986).

New researchers often find that filling in raw field notes is an arduous task that requires time, energy, and concentration. As they start writing up their field jottings, researchers will get better at taking field notes because they learn what kind of raw notes lead to solid protocols. As they practice filling in notes, researchers will become better at recalling the details of events and conversations in the research context. Woods (1986) describes qualitative researchers' memory development as parallel to how actors learn their lines, musicians memorize their scores, and writers develop an ear for dialogue. While it may never become second nature, filling in raw field notes will become easier.

As with recording raw field notes, care should be taken to keep protocols as descriptive as possible. Spradley (1980, p. 80) describes three principles to keep in mind as raw field notes are expanded: the language identification principle, the verbatim principle, and the concrete principle. Spradley points out that different groups use different words and language patterns to communicate and that researchers often create a kind of amalgamated language that loses the flavor of the participants' original language. In school studies, students, teachers, and parents are likely to have different ways of talking. Applying the language identification principle means making an accurate record of these differences by keeping track of who says what to whom. The verbatim principle has been discussed above; it stresses the importance of recording exactly what was said as opposed to summarizing or paraphrasing. The concrete principle means recording the details of events using concrete language rather than making generalizations. Attending to these principles will help researchers keep their protocols descriptive, not interpretive.

In the rewriting process, raw notes will be "partly cooked—at least to the extent that all the blanks are filled in" (LeCompte & Schensul, 1999, p. 33). It is natural that impressions, interpretations, and hypothetical categories will come to mind as data are being recorded, but care should be taken to keep interpretations separate from the descriptive data. As with notes taken in the field, when possible interpretations or impressions come to mind during the filling in process, these should be bracketed in the protocol and/or recorded in a separate format such as a research journal (see below).

The form that protocols take will be idiosyncratic with each researcher. It will serve the novice well to develop some kind of standard organization for protocols, then to be consistent in using it throughout. I was trained to double-space my protocols and to leave wide margins to facilitate later analysis. I have seen protocols typed on only the left side of a page to leave room for bracketed information on the other half. Some word processing programs have a feature for numbering lines, and some researchers use this feature because it makes analysis (especially computer-assisted analysis) easier later on. I like to start each protocol with the date and a note describing where the observation took place. So if I am doing a classroom study in several schools, I can identify protocols related to that school easily. If I am looking at contexts within particular settings or paying attention to particular social events or individuals, I note that at the top. For example, I pulled a protocol from an early study that reads across the top: "December 5, 1983. Edgewood Kindergarten. Today I will follow Kara and keep track of her interactions with peers." As I mentioned above, I always keep a record of the time in my notes, and I always number my pages. Having the date and page numbers allows me to keep track of data in the analysis phase; I can find data excerpts on page four of the protocol above by coding them as 12–5–4, leaving out the 83 since the study did not last for more than a year. I keep separate files for each observation, as opposed to a giant file with ongoing observations, and I back up files with hard and disc copies. Again, each researcher will develop his or her own style when it comes to creating research protocols, but finding a consistent format will save headaches down the road.

Bracketing. Bracketing has been mentioned several times above. Bracketing is a general concept from phenomenology that dates to Husserl (1913). In its conceptual form, it means holding a phenomenon up for inspection while suspending presuppositions and avoiding interpretations (Ashworth, 1999; Denzin, 1989b; Giorgi, 1985). It is a state of mind from which qualitative researchers approach their experiences. Ely and her colleagues describe this general mindset: "Bracketing requires that we work to become aware of our own assumptions, feelings, and preconceptions, and then, that we strive to put them aside—to bracket them—in order to be open and receptive to what we are attempting to understand" (Ely et. al., 1991, p. 50). Individuals doing phenomenological studies as described in chapter 1 are especially sensitive to the concept of bracketing; researchers taking feminist, critical, or poststructuralist approaches want to be aware of their biases and preconceptions, but they see no need to set them aside.

In addition to the general concept of bracketing, the term is also used to describe a specific strategy for separating impressions, feelings, and early interpretations from descriptions during qualitative data collection. As field notes are taken and protocols are written up, researchers will have reactions to and reflections on what they are observing. These reactions and reflections should be recorded in the raw notes and protocols, but they should be kept separate so that it is clear exactly what they are. I literally use brackets [like this] to separate notes to myself in the data records (see examples in appendix B). Others underline bracketed notations, write them in the margins, or divide their field note pages so that bracketed information is recorded on one side of the page. Bracketed notes can be about many things, from recording hunches about patterns that might be emerging in the data (e.g., [Could asking questions be a way that Tish avoids being put on the spot by teachers?]) to monitoring reactions to powerful events (e.g., [Looks like Lester is being excluded by the other kids]) to writing reminders about what you want to do later (e.g., [Remember to ask his teacher why Rodney was sent back from the computer lab]) to writing notes that make connections to other parts of the data (e.g., [Check other records of lounge talk to see if Colleen and Chester shared information about their students]).

Some bracketed notes will be important as you continue to do observations, some will help with starting or shaping analysis, and some will be ignored. The key is to keep them separate from the descriptive data. Learning to bracket what you see by taking on the mindset of the phenomenologist and writing bracketed notes to make a record of impressions, feelings, and potential interpretations are skills that will develop with practice. I remember the exhilaration of beginning my first observational studies. I had the feeling I was acting out the part of researcher. I had a pretty good idea of what I was supposed to do, but I didn't really believe my own performance. One of my strong memories is of being very self-conscious about managing my own impressions and biases in an effort to keep my data descriptive. Bracketing was a useful tool in these early experiences because it gave me a way to make distinctions that made me feel like I was doing what researchers do. After some time, I started to believe my own performance as a researcher, but being self-conscious about my reactions and preconceptions continues to be important.

Keeping a Research Journal. Anthropologists are trained to maintain diaries or fieldwork journals to keep track of the personal side of their research experiences. Their diaries or journals are records of "experiences, ideas, fears, mistakes, confusions, breakthroughs, and problems that arise during fieldwork" (Spradley, 1980, p. 71). Ethnographers date these entries and refer back to them as analysis is undertaken. The information helps with field note interpretation and provides a means of accounting for personal biases and feelings.

I think all qualitative researchers should keep research journals, especially those doing observational studies. Research journals provide a record of the affective experience of doing a study. They provide a place where researchers can openly reflect on what is happening during the research experience and how they feel about it. Every day that raw data are taken in the field should include time for filling in protocols and writing a journal entry. These entries need not be typed or edited, although high-tech journaling at a desktop will likely be the preferred form for most readers of this book. They should be personal, honest, and reflective accounts of the human experience of studying other people. They are places to "talk to yourself" about how things are going, about your fears, frustrations, and small victories.

If you had a chance to visit my office, you would quickly see that my own style is to keep everything in file folders, including my research journals. I make journal entries on full-size pieces of paper, date them, and stick them in the back of a folder marked "Research Journal." I also create a separate folder called "Research Log." This folder contains a running record of exactly what I have done during the study. Down the left side of the log pages are dates followed by brief descriptions of any data collection done on that day. If I am doing an observation study, it will give the exact time spent in the field and note where the observation took place (e.g., Feb. 2, 1999, 8:15–11:35, Mayfield Elementary Kindergarten). Interviews are recorded the same way, except interviewees, their codes, or pseudonyms are identified. The log gives me a quick look at the overall data set and helps with keeping track of total time spent in the field and/or number of interviews completed. Some researchers keep their logs and journals together, and some combine them, making more systematic journal entries that include the information I would log. The form doesn't matter so much as actually keeping track of both kinds of information and keeping them separate from the descriptive data of the study (see Bernard, 1994). Journaling is an extension of bracketing. It gives the researcher some distance on the research process and provides a way to monitor his or her personal reactions to what is being discovered. Journal entries are useful for self-assessing researcher biases when interpreting data and for constructing the story of the research, which can become a part of the final report. (See appendix C for an example of a research journal entry from the early stages of one of my participant observation studies of children's social relations in kindergarten.)

Knowing When to Stop. Collecting observational data is labor- and time-intensive work. It takes energy and concentration to be in the field taking raw notes, it takes time and effort to fill in protocols, and it takes commitment and discipline to keep up with a research journal. It is hard to imagine that graduate students with assistantships or professors with teaching responsibilities have time to do qualitative research involving observations. It is understandable that new researchers always ask, "How long do I need to be in the field?" While the duration of studies was discussed generally in chapter 2 and the importance of extended firsthand engagement was highlighted in chapter 1, I will address the "how long" question here as it relates directly to observational studies.

It depends. It depends on your research questions. It depends on how much time your participants will give you. It depends on how involved you will become in the research scene and how quickly. It depends on the time of the year, especially in a school-based study. It depends on your own time and resources. It depends on factors that I (and perhaps you) cannot anticipate.

Doctoral students and professors rarely have the luxury of going into the field with the expectation of staying there for as long as it takes to complete the study. They are much more likely to have a year or a semester set aside to complete their observations. Decisions about when to stop will most often be made during the design phase rather than being based on criteria related to sufficiency or completeness. Most data collection phases will end when the researchers' time is up, the term ends, the research bargain is fulfilled, or, if they are lucky enough to have financial support, when funding runs out. That means that researchers must monitor their data collection during the study to be sure they are getting the information they will need to complete their research.

For this and other reasons, I recommend that data collection be paired with data analysis that begins soon after field note data are converted to protocols. It is possible to do observational studies in which all of the data are collected, then researchers retire from the field to analyze that data. This may be the best approach when short-term events are being studied intensely. For example, studying a one-week exchange program for gifted middle school students might require the observer to be present and taking notes for all of the waking hours of a seven-day period, and systematic analysis of the data during that period may be impossible. Still, most studies will involve longer and less intense involvement that will make ongoing analysis possible and advisable. This is not the place to explain how the data analysis will be accomplished; that discussion is saved for Chapter 4. The point here is that by doing analysis as part of the data collection cycle, researchers will have a good idea of what they are getting and make it possible to adjust their observations to be sure they are getting what they need.

For me, getting what they need means, first, having data to answer their research questions (see Patton, 1990). You cannot stop collecting data until you can answer the research questions around which the study is organized. You might change your research questions as the study evolves, but you must be able to answer them before leaving the field. If you are observing how social relations develop in a primary multiage classroom, you cannot go back after summer break and fill in the missing pieces because the social context

how much data?

you have studied no longer exists. Keeping track of research questions and of the information necessary to answer them is vital to making decisions as data are collected. It will be a great help to mix observation and analysis, but thoughtful monitoring of data collection in relation to research questions will be necessary in any observational study.

Another way of thinking about getting what is needed is to be sure that you are seeing a full cycle of the activity you are studying (Wolcott, 1995). In the two studies used as examples above, the full cycle will likely be a week for the gifted program and a school year for the multiage class. The idea behind understanding participant perspectives, which is a prime objective of doing observations in the first place, is to see and record what participants experience. If you are present only for the beginning of the gifted program or only see the middle of a school year, you are missing significant parts of the participants' experience. You have a study of something, but it will be hard to claim that you know participants' experience of the context of interest. As was inferred by the gifted program example, when the cycle is short, more intense engagement will be necessary. When a year's worth of observations are planned, less time per week will be required to capture the full cycle of activity.

Some of my students use the criterion of redundancy to gauge when they have enough data. They want to stop data collection and/or analysis because they are finding nothing new in the data, only repetitions of what they already know. I suspect they are following advice from Lincoln and Guba (1985), who write, "Redundancy is typically eschewed in life, but in this instance it is a most useful criterion: Repeat until redundancy—then just one more time for safety" (p. 219). I am likely to counter with Spradley's (1980) observation that repetition is a means to getting beneath the surface of the context being studied. In his words, "Only through repeated observations and repeated descriptions in fieldnotes does the ethnographer begin to see the complexity of a seemingly simple social situation" (pp. 70–71). When students say they are seeing nothing new, I advise them to keep looking and to look more carefully. Looking "one more time for safety" is better than assuming that you have it covered, but looking with a finer lens may reveal insights that might otherwise be missed.

To summarize this section, observation is a cornerstone of qualitative data collection. No matter what the paradigm, if the researcher is interested in participant perspectives, observing those participants in action provides avenues into their understandings that are unavailable any other way. In order to collect useful observational data, researchers will need to make careful decisions about how involved they will be in the field sites in which they collect their data, what they will attend to at various stages of the research process, how they will take raw field notes, how they will convert those notes to research protocols, how they will bracket their impressions and reactions, and how they will know when observations should stop. While it is sometimes used al[ ] is more common to observe participants in context and to interview them in order to get another take on their perspectives. In some studies, artifact data will be collected as well. The next two sections describe interviewing and unobtrusive data collection as if they were separate from observation and each other, but it is understood that, in practice, researchers design studies that mix and match data collection methods to meet their objectives.

INTERVIEWING

Qualitative interviews are special kinds of conversations or speech events that are used by researchers to explore informants' experiences and interpretations (Mishler, 1986; Spradley, 1979). Qualitative researchers use interviews to uncover the meaning structures that participants use to organize their experiences and make sense of their worlds. These meaning structures are often hidden from direct observation and taken for granted by participants, and qualitative interview techniques offer tools for bringing these meanings to the surface. Spradley (1979) summarizes the stance qualitative researchers take in relation to their informants:

> By word and by action, in subtle ways and in direct statements, [researchers] say, "I want to understand the world from your point of view. I want to know what you know in the way you know it. I want to understand the meaning of your experience, to walk in your shoes, to feel things as you feel them, to explain things as you would explain them. Will you become my teacher and help me understand?" (P. 34)

Learning how to learn from informants is what this part of this book is all about.

In much qualitative work, interviews are used alongside other data collection methods, but they can be the primary or only data source in some qualitative projects. When interviews are used in conjunction with observation, they provide ways to explore more deeply participants' perspectives on actions observed by researchers. They also provide avenues into events and experiences that have not been observed. When used with unobtrusive data collection, interviews can reveal the meanings and significance of artifacts collected in the field. Lincoln and Guba (1985, p. 268) identify five outcomes of interviewing, abstracted as follows:

- *here and now constructions*—participant explanations of events, activities, feelings, motivations, concerns
- *reconstructions*—explanations of past events and experiences,

- *projections*—explanations of anticipated experiences
- *triangulation*—verification or extension of information from other sources
- *member checking*—verification or extension of information developed by the researcher.

Accomplishing these outcomes is the stuff of qualitative interviewing, and discussion of how to accomplish them will be woven through this section. Triangulation and member checking are addressed in other parts of this book as well.

No matter if it is used alone or in parallel with other data collection tools, the central strength of interviewing is that it provides a means for doing what is very difficult or impossible to do any other way—finding out "what is in and on someone else's mind" (Patton, 1990, p. 278). Its limitations are tied to the difficulty of doing just that. Individuals may be reluctant to share what is on their minds, and researchers may lack the sensitivity, time, or interview expertise to help informants do so. This section is intended to guide researchers as they conceptualize interview studies, plan interview strategies, initiate qualitative interviews, and process interview data. It concludes with a presentation of tips for qualitative interviewers.

Kinds of Qualitative Interviews

Types of qualitative interviews are described differently by different scholars (cf., Bernard, 1994; Fontana & Frey, 1994; Rubin & Rubin, 1995). When I talk with students about studies that use interviewing, I break the range of possible interviews down into three basic kinds: informal, formal, and standardized. Some studies will use all three kinds, some one, and some two. Purposes and research questions will lead in the direction of certain kinds of interviewing and away from others. The assumptions of some research paradigms will lead researchers to utilize some kinds of interviews and to see others as inappropriate. As studies that include interviewing as a data collection strategy are planned, understanding the utility of each basic kind will be important.

Informal interviews are unstructured conversations that take place in the research scene. That means that informal interviews will not be the primary data source in a study. They are most often used as a strategic part of observation studies. I say "strategic" because, even though they are informal, that does not mean they are without purpose or are undertaken randomly. Informal interviews provide opportunities to ask participants to explain their perspectives on what the researcher has observed. They take advantage of the immediate context to give informants the chance to reflect on what they have said, done, or seen. I recall going on break with a kindergarten teacher after observing her deal with a child who could not sit through the reading of a storybook. We had a conversation about the incident in the teachers' lounge, and that informal interview provided a completely different picture of what she was doing with that child than I had assumed from my observation.

Informal interviews require researchers to be good listeners and to create pertinent questions on the spot. Because informal interviews are often sidebars to the real action, they are usually not the place for taking out a tape recorder or trying to write verbatim notes. In the teachers' lounge conversation above, I did have my clipboard, and I did take down some key phrases so I could fill in the conversation later. I had an agreement with this teacher that, in essence, "everything is data," so she was not put off or surprised by my note taking. The incident was on both our minds so it was natural to talk about it. The event was related to the purpose of my research (to understand young children's adaptations to the expectations of school), so it was just a matter of engaging the teacher in a reflective conversation about what happened.

Sometimes researchers use informal interview situations to get at particular topics in a more planned way. I mentioned in the section on observation that I write questions on my note pads that remind me what to look for during visits. I have included questions I wanted to ask participants in the same way. So, for the study above, I might have a note like "Ask teacher how she put together her classroom rules" at the top of my pad.

Participants must understand that their informal conversations with you are part of the data collection process. Informal interviews can help build rapport if they are done well because people are generally flattered when someone is interested in what they do, but it would be unfair to mislead informants into believing that friendly conversations are not also data collection events. When sensitive information is shared during informal interviews, I tell my students to be sure that their informants understand that they are "on the record" and to accept and honor their requests when they ask that certain information be kept "off the record."

Informal interview strategies can be adapted to fit within any of the qualitative research paradigms. Postpositivists might be inclined to use informal interview opportunities to verify their hypothetical categories after some extensive observations or to generate data for triangulation (e.g., to confirm information obtained from another informant). Constructivists assumptions fit very well with the idea of informal interviews in that they are places where researchers and participants coconstruct understandings of what is happening in the research context. Critical/feminist researchers may use informal interview settings as opportunities to engage in transformative dialogues that serve to raise the consciousness of participants and plant the seeds of critique and resistance. Poststructuralists may see informal interviews as chances to gather the stories that individuals use to make sense of their lives.

Formal interviews are sometimes called "structured," "semistructured," or "in-depth" interviews. They are structured in the sense that the researcher is "in charge" of leading the interview, there is a set time established for the interview, and they are most often recorded on tape. They are semistructured because, although researchers come to the interview with guiding questions, they are open to following the leads of informants and probing into areas that arise during interview interactions. They are in-depth in that they are designed to go deeply into the understandings of the informants. I call them formal to distinguish them from informal interviews and because they are planned events that take place away from the research scene for the explicit purpose of gathering information from an informant.

Formal interviews are often a planned part of studies that include observations. When research bargains are put together for such studies, they include clear descriptions of how many formal interviews will be conducted, when they will be done, and approximately how long they will last. It is common to try to interview participants before observations start and after they are concluded, with periodic interviews during the data collection phase as dictated by the needs of the study. Formal interviews are also used when interviewing is the only data collection tool of a study. These studies range from a series of interviews with a small number of informants to single interviews with many. While the nature of questions will be different when observation is a part of data collection than when interviews are used by themselves, the general structure of formal interviews is consistent for both types of studies.

In formal interview settings, both researcher and participant know they are there to generate data. Spradley (1979) characterizes formal interviews as a special kind of speech event that can be distinguished from other speech events such as lectures, sales pitches, or friendly conversations. Individuals take different roles and recognize that different rules govern turn taking, asking questions, pausing, and beginning and ending in different speech events. Learning these roles and enacting the rules of formal interviews are part of being a qualitative researcher, and these are explored below.

Researchers enter formal interviews with questions in mind. These vary in their number and specificity based on the kind of research being done. Phenomenologists may bring only one question designed to get informants talking about the nature of a phenomenon, for example, "What does it mean to be a teacher?" (Van Manen, 1990, p. 42). Historians may have an interview schedule with many questions they are asking a number of informants.

In all of the interviews I would classify as formal, researchers have questions about certain topics in mind, but they are open to digressions, they expect the interview to move in the direction that the informant takes it, and they plan to create probes or follow-up questions based on the responses they receive. In keeping with the theme of "flexible structure" introduced in chapter 2, Chiseri-Strater and Sunstein (1997) describe interviewing as an ironic contradiction:

> You must be both structured and flexible at the same time. While it's critical to prepare for an interview with a list of planned questions to guide your talk, it is equally important to follow your informant's lead. Sometimes the best interviews come from a comment, a story, an artifact, or a phrase you couldn't have anticipated. The energy that drives a good interview—for both you and your informant—comes from expecting the unexpected. (P. 233)

Building flexibility into the structured interview is what distinguishes formal interviews from standardized qualitative interviews taken up next. Formal interviews, like their informal counterparts, can be adapted for use within any of the qualitative paradigms. Postpositivists will be most concerned about using interviews as an additional data source from which to triangulate their findings and more likely to use final interviews as a member-checking activity to find out if participants agree with their analyses. These concerns may lead postpositivist researchers to design more structured interviews, while constructivists will be more likely to emphasize flexibility as they seek to create interactive interviews where they share responsibility for questions and answers with informants. Formal interviews with critical/feminist researchers will take on the special transformative relationship that characterizes this paradigm, and poststructuralists may see formal interviews as sources for textual representations of lives.

Standardized interviews are a special type of formal interview that fit most comfortably in the postpositivist camp. Researchers enter the interview setting with predetermined questions that are asked in the same order, using the same words, to all informants. The idea is to gather information from several informants that can be compared systematically. The data generated are comparable to open-ended questionnaires that are used in some qualitative studies, but answers are recorded and transcribed by the researcher rather than written by informants. Such interviews are qualitative in the sense that informants are not limited to forced choices, yes/no answers, or Likert-like scales such as those found in quantitative interviews; but they are standardized in that all interviewees get the same questions, and follow-ups are usually not used. Interviewers sometimes use techniques such as pile sorting (what goes with what?), rank ordering (which comes first?), comparing (what's the same and different?) along with direct questioning (see Bernard, 1994). While some of these might be adapted for use in formal interviews by other than postpositivist qualitative researchers, the assumptions of standardizing any data collection strategy fit most closely with those of the postpositivist paradigm.

Interview Processes

How exactly do I go about doing qualitative interviews? How do I find the right informants? What kinds of questions do I need? How close to my guiding questions do I have to stay? How should I start and end my interviews? What should I do if my informants don't want to talk? These are questions on the mind of any new qualitative researcher who plans to use interviewing as a data collection strategy. My very first interview experience was one of my worst. I didn't have an answer to the "What should I do if my informants don't want to talk?" question. I had spent a semester observing in a classroom as part of a project for my initial qualitative research course and planned to conclude the study by doing a formal interview with the teacher. Relations had been somewhat strained during the observation phase, but I was still surprised when the teacher refused to allow a tape recorder at the concluding interview. I was even more taken aback when my first question in the interview led to the following response:

> RESEARCHER: "My goal for doing this interview is to try to better understand how things work in your classroom by asking you to describe how you see things. What happens in your classroom that's different from what goes on in other classes?" Teacher: "I'd like to know how you saw things. If you'd tell me what you saw that's different, then I could react." (Hatch & Bondy, 1986, pp. 51–52)

The rest of the experience didn't go much better. I tried to stay in role as researcher, and the teacher did her best to resist. In posthoc analyses of this and other researcher-teacher relationships, this situation served as an example of an "antagonistic-defensive" relationship that was larger than just the final interview (see Hatch & Bondy, 1986). The point here is not to paint the teacher as the villain, but to note that I could have done a better job of preparing for and doing the interview. Given the situation, things may not have been much better, but I have knowledge and experience now that would help me do things differently. The goal of this section is to share some of that knowledge in an effort to improve the early experiences of novice researchers.

Preparing for Qualitative Interviews. The first level of preparation is simply deciding what kinds of interviews will be done. If the research is ethnography or a participant observation study, then informal and formal interviewing will likely be part of the design. If the work is a qualitative interview study, then formal interviewing will be the data collection tool. Phenomenological studies rely on phenomenological interviews, and focus group studies, by definition, call for group interviews. However, decisions about other kinds of studies are less clear cut. Some observation-based studies will include no interviewing (an educational criticism might be an example), some will utilize only informal interviews (action research or collaborative studies might be set up this way), and some will use only formal interviews to supplement observations (multisite case studies might use this design). Standardized interviews will likely be used by postpositivist researchers in conjunction with observation and formal interviews (grounded theory studies might take such an approach).

Decisions about kinds of interviews will be based on research aims, research questions, and issues of feasibility. The strength of interviews is that they allow insight into participant perspectives. If capturing those perspectives is a goal, then interviewing at some level seems imperative. Research questions are framed in ways that shape the design of a study (see chapter 2). Questions that are framed to address broad, structural issues may be best answered within more formal interview settings, while questions that are pointed toward narrow, individual issues might best be addressed with informal strategies. Feasibility concerns have to do with the availability of participants for informal interviews and their willingness to do formal or standardized interviews. It will be intrusive to interview participants in some research settings (e.g., talking to children during school lessons), and some informants will be reluctant to sit down with a researcher because of time (e.g., teachers working on advanced degrees in the evenings) or confidentiality concerns (e.g., students suspended for zero tolerance violations). I encourage students to use observation and interviewing and to include both formal and informal interviews whenever it makes sense. Of course, it depends on the study, but gathering information in different forms from different sources almost always improves the quality of qualitative studies.

Once the kinds of interviews are identified, issues of exactly who will be interviewed quickly follow. Identifying participants is discussed at length in chapter 2; special concerns related to interviews are taken up briefly here. If it's an observation study that also utilizes informal, formal, and/or standardized interviews, you will want to talk to participants about their experience in the settings you observe. It's a matter of selecting those individuals you believe will make good informants, be available, and agree to be interviewed.

Good informants have knowledge about everyday life in the settings being studied, and they are willing and able to communicate that knowledge using what Spradley (1979) calls "their native language" (p. 25). School board members and preschoolers learn the native languages of the contexts in which they operate, and effective informants from these and other settings have the ability to describe their contexts in the language of the setting as opposed to translating it into generic or research language.

In studies where formal interviews are the major or only data source, selecting informants will be more complex. As discussed in chapter 2, Patton's (1990) purposeful sampling strategies offer a useful framework for thinking about whom to interview. In an effort to tie his sampling strategies directly to qualitative interviews, I have abstracted Patton's (1990, pp. 169–86) strategies and offered examples of how they might be applied in education studies in which interviewing is the data collection strategy of choice:

- *Extreme or deviant case samples* include individuals who demonstrate highly unusual manifestations of the phenomenon of interest (e.g., interviewing state Teachers of the Year).

- *Intensity samples* are made up of individuals who manifest the phenomenon intensely but not extremely (e.g., interviewing students identified as "hyperactive").

- *Maximum variation samples* seek to include individuals with different perspectives on the same phenomenon (e.g., interviewing representatives of all of the stakeholders in a full-service school).

- *Homogeneous samples* are made up of individuals with similar characteristics or experiences (e.g., interviewing a cohort of graduates from a specialized doctoral program).

- *Typical case samples* include individuals who represent what is considered typical (e.g., interviewing middle-school students nominated by teachers as typical adolescents).

- *Stratified purposeful samples* are those that include individuals selected to represent particular subgroups of interest (e.g., interviews of elementary, middle, and high school teachers on their homework practices).

- *Critical case samples* include individuals who represent dramatic examples of or are of critical importance to the phenomenon of interest (e.g., interviewing principals of highly successful inner-city schools).

- *Snowball or chain samples* are created when one informant identifies the next as someone who would be good to interview (e.g., interviewing a chain of high school students who identify each other as individuals who know about being popular with peers).

- *Criterion samples* are made up of individuals who fit particular pre‹ mined criteria (e.g., interviewing all district administrators who wer‗ ‗‗ mer coaches).

- *Theory-based or operational construct samples* include individuals who manifest a theoretical construct of interest (e.g., interviewing primary teachers who teach reading via "direct instruction").

- *Confirming and disconfirming samples* are made up of individuals who can shed light on tentative findings that researchers have put together (e.g., interviewing college students to confirm or disconfirm interpretations from a study of dorm life).

- *Opportunistic samples* develop fortuitously from other interviews, leading researchers to new informants (e.g., interviews with more parents of children with autism become part of your study when an informant tells you she is a member of a special-child support group).

- *Politically important case samples* are those that strategically include or eliminate individuals who represent certain political positions (e.g., interviewing teachers who openly teach creationism in high school).

- *Convenience samples* select individuals because they are easy to access (e.g., interviewing the students in your math methods course).

- *Combination or mixed purposeful samples* are combinations of the sampling strategies above (e.g., interviewing supervisors, principals, and teachers responsible for kindergarten instruction in districts selected to represent rural, suburban, or urban categories across a state).

I do not think it is necessary for qualitative interviewers to announce to their readers (or doctoral committees) that they have used one particular sampling strategy or another. I do think it is essential that they are able to justify the inclusion of those they interview, and these strategies will be conceptually helpful in making such justifications. It should also be remembered that Patton (1990) and I agree that convenience samples are the *most common and least desirable* of the strategies described. Their inclusion here should not be taken as permission to study individuals because they are familiar and easy to access.

At the next level of preparation, researchers should attend to making decisions about issues such as contacting potential informants, gaining informed consent, arranging interview times and locations, and selecting/preparing recording equipment. Strategies for contacting participants are addressed in chapter 2, as are methods for acquiring informed consent and making research bargains. When informal and formal interviews are planned along with observations, potential informants should have a clear understanding of the ground rules for informal interviews (when and where they will and will not take place, how they will be recorded, if all conversations will be "on the record"), and they should know what to expect from planned formal interviews (when, how many, for how long, will they be recorded, will they review transcriptions). In interview only studies, informants need to know all of the information about formal interviews just listed and have a clear sense of what the study is about and why they have been selected to participate. Initial contacts are likely to be made over the telephone and are often followed up with a letter describing the study, an outline of the research bargain, and a copy of the informed consent form. I think it is acceptable to have informants in qualitative interview studies sign informed consent forms at the first interview but before it actually begins. It is not acceptable for informants to have no information ahead of time, then have to decide whether or not to participate with the researcher sitting in front of them with a tape recorder at the ready.

Nuts and bolts issues like where to do interviews and what kind of recording equipment to use should be taken on before interviews begin, whenever possible. I have done studies in which I drove into cities, found schools or administration buildings, met informants who had agreed to be interviewed, and then conducted interviews wherever space was available. When explaining and setting up such interviews over the phone, I always asked for an appropriate area for an interview, but we sometimes ended up in hallways, open office spaces, or occasionally a restaurant. In order to get good quality recording, you will need a quiet space in which you and your informant are close to the microphone. Interview spaces need to be private so that you are comfortable asking for sensitive information and your informants are comfortable giving it.

Recording equipment should be reliable and of sufficient quality that you are assured it will make a clear record of your interviews. For interviews, I like microsized recorders that run on batteries because they are easily transported, unobtrusive, and do not require an electrical outlet. The downside is that microphones built into such devices are small and usually one-directional, and batteries tend to run out at the worst times. Whatever kinds of recorders and microphones are used, they must be tested *in the interview setting* prior to doing an interview. I always say, "Just let me test this to be sure it's working" before starting the actual interview. I always carry extra batteries and tapes and sometimes have an extra recorder. Once you lose an interview or have to face a transcriptionist who cannot make out what's on a tape, you will become very careful about your equipment. It will also save time to make careful notations on the tapes themselves of what is recorded and in what order multiple tapes are to be played back.

Developing questions is the final level of interview preparation to be discussed here—and the most important. Qualitative researchers from different paradigms and different methodological camps disagree about what kinds questions to bring to their interviews. Some researchers, including many constructivists and critical/feminists, believe that interviewers take too much control of the interview situation when they have preplanned interview schedules. In formal interviews, they prefer to introduce a topic area or ask one or two broad-based questions, then encourage informants to talk about the topic or create a conversation around the questions. The emphasis is on getting the informants' stories without imposing the researchers' perspectives or authority (see Van Manen, 1990). Others, including most postpositivists, take the position that, without some preplanning and structure, interviews can wander away from the topic under investigation and end up wasting both the researcher's and the informant's time. Recognizing that some approaches will dictate more or less structured questions, I encourage a middle ground for most interviews, recommending that researchers enter interviews with guiding questions and then be prepared to follow the leads that are generated in the interview context.

The discussion to follow is concentrated on developing questions for formal interviews. Most questions for informal interviews are created in context and on the spot; that is, researchers take advantage of opportunities to ask participants to reflect on what they were thinking when they did things observed by the researcher. Sometimes researchers have questions in mind for certain visits to the research scene, and they work these into informal interview conversations when opportunities arise, but usually questions develop from what is observed. It would be very unusual for researchers to pull out an interview schedule and start going through it as he or she is chatting with a participant—that would make it an unannounced formal interview. In contrast, standardized interviews are always prepared ahead of time, always administered in structured settings, and rarely leave room for spontaneous exploration (see Mishler, 1986). I see their utility as limited for most qualitative researchers and recommend reference to texts that emphasize their use to those interested in standardized interview development. Bernard's (1994) chapter on structured interviewing is an excellent resource.

I call the questions I bring to formal interviews *guiding questions*. They are questions I have prepared in anticipation of the interview and are designed to guide the conversation that I anticipate will take place. Guiding questions for studies that include observation and interviewing use ongoing analyses of observational data as a basis for constructing questions. Formal interviews in such studies are opportunities to get participants talking about the phenomena under investigation, so questions should build from observations. It is common for final formal interviews to become an opportunity for member checking, giving participants opportunities to react to tentative findings generated by the researcher.

Guiding questions for studies using interviewing as the primary data source require researchers to develop questions based on their research purposes, knowledge of their informants, and hunches about the phenomena they are studying (which may or may not be informed by the theoretical and research literature in that area). When multiple interviews are scheduled for the same individuals, then analysis of early contacts will inform later interviews, and spontaneous conversation will develop out of researcher-informant rapport. However, when multiple informants are interviewed only once, more carefully designed research questions will be needed. While it is still to be expected that interviews will be dynamic and follow the leads of informants, guiding questions for one-shot interviews with many individuals will be ordered in certain ways and include certain question areas that all informants should address. Such studies are designed to capture a number of perspectives on particular topics, so it is essential that each participant has the chance to discuss each topic. While guiding questions will look different for different kinds of studies, some general suggestions for developing a variety of questions, wording questions effectively, and ordering questions may be helpful for those learning the process.

Qualitative researchers seek to capture participant perspectives, so formal interview questions need to be open-ended. They should be designed to get informants talking about their experiences and understandings. When informants think that "correct" answers exist to the questions they are asked, the interview becomes a game of finding the right answers. Because of how they are socialized in school, young children are especially likely to try to find the answers they think the researcher is looking for (Hatch, 1995). Researchers should stress that there are no right or wrong answers, and they should construct questions that invite informants to talk from their own perspectives and experiences. Even when multiple informants are interviewed on the same topics, questions should encourage elaboration and leave room for moving along pathways that open during the interview. The emphasis must be on understanding participant points of view, not getting through the questions (see Bogdan & Biklen, 1992).

Berg (1998) divides interview questions into four types: essential, extra, throw-away, and probing questions. Essential questions are those concerned with the central focus of the investigation. These are rarely asked at the beginning of an interview but may be asked together or scattered throughout. Extra questions are related to essential questions but come at the topic from a slightly different angle or ask the same questions using different wording. They serve the purpose of going more deeply into areas of importance. Throw-away questions are often asked at the beginning of an interview and usually include information about demographics, background, or context. These are designed to put the informant at ease and get the conversation started. They are sometimes used to provide a break when interviews become intense or tedious. Prompts and probes provide researchers with means for getting informants to talk more about particular subjects that arise in the interviews. While some standard probes are often at the ready (see below), it is difficult and probably unwise to write probing questions as part of interview preparation.

The first three question types in Berg's (1998) organizer are useful for thinking about creating formal interview guides. Obviously, developing high-quality essential questions is most important to the data collection purposes of the interview. If the content-related questions do not get at the phenomena under investigation, the rest of the guiding questions will have little meaning. Extra questions need to be carefully planned so that they encourage informants to be reflective without being repetitive or appearing to challenge what they have already said. When used with appropriate probing questions, they can add to the depth and richness of interview data. I don't think much of the term *throw-away* for questions designed to gather important background information and warm up reluctant informants, but the concept is important to developing high-quality formal interviews. I prefer the term *background questions*, which I will use in the following discussion.

Background questions are often used to start formal interviews. They are framed as questions that get the informants talking about familiar information, get them used to the interview context and recorder, and ease their concerns about what the interview might be like. They often include information that helps distinguish one informant from another in multisite studies. They invite informants to share demographic information that may be useful in putting together analyses and final reports as the study progresses. Opening background questions usually ask about age, education, experience, mobility, and the like. In school studies, questions are likely to take the form: "Why don't you start by telling me a little about yourself—where you're from, how you got into education, how long you've been with this system?" I don't recommend a series of short-answer questions such as, "How old are you? Where did you go to college? How long have you been teaching?" Terse questions get terse answers and set the wrong tone for the interview you hope will follow. It is better to ask a broad, "Tell me about your background" question then listen for places where you can follow up with more specific questions (e.g., "Oh, so you started teaching after your children were older?") that show your interest and start a pattern of conversation as opposed to recitation.

Essential questions are essential because they get at the core of the research; they generate the central data of the study. They are the most important and the most difficult to write. I was trained using Spradley's (1979) ethnographic interview model, and I still find the model useful for generating interview questions even when ethnographic research is not the methodology being used. Spradley identifies three kinds of "ethnographic questions" (p. 60) that I try to build into every formal interview I conduct. For me, these provide a taxonomy that gives structure to the writing of essential questions. My adaptation of Spradley's descriptive, structural, and contrast questions is outlined next.

Descriptive questions are designed to get informants talking about the particulars of a social scene with which they are familiar. They are a way to begin to get inside how participants talk about what they do. Informants are selected for interviews because they have some special knowledge that the researcher hopes to capture in his or her data. Descriptive questions ask informants to put that knowledge into words. Qualitative researchers studying school people will ask them to describe what it's like to be student, teacher, principal, custodian, or whatever. Such questions will ask for descriptions, not analyses or critiques, and they will always ask for the informant's perspective. They begin with phrases such as the following: *Can you describe . . .* , *Tell me about a time when . . .* , or *Could you give me an example . . . ?* In a study of teacher, administrator, and supervisor perspectives on kindergarten philosophies and practices, a colleague and I included the following descriptive questions in our interview guide for teachers:

- "Could you describe a typical day in your kindergarten?"
- "Could you give an example of a reading readiness or early literacy lesson that you've used recently in your classroom?"
- "How are children grouped for activities or instruction in your classroom?" (Hatch & Freeman, 1988, p. 165).

Structural questions invite informants to demonstrate how they organize their cultural knowledge. They ask informants to put their knowledge into categories or domains. They are a way to get some understanding of how informants think about what they do. They provide questioning tools for going beyond descriptive information into exploring what relationships informants see in their cultural experiences. Structural questions usually take form in questions that begin: *What are the kinds of . . .* , *What are the steps in . . .* , or *What characteristics typify. . . .* Structural questions are never used in place of descriptive questions, but most often are used concurrently with them. When used in participant observation studies or multiple interviews with the same informants, they can be used to verify hypothetical domains discovered by the researcher. In any interview study, they provide ways to study how individuals make sense of the social phenomena under investigation. In the study mentioned above, the following were some of our structural questions for kindergarten teachers:

- "What are the steps involved in deciding what you will mark on a particular kindergarten child's report card?"
- "What qualities, characteristics, or abilities typify a successful kindergarten student?"
- "When you're talking to parents about your kindergarten program, what do you stress as its most positive qualities?" (Hatch & Freeman, 1988, pp. 165–66).

Contrast questions are tools for exploring how informants make meaning in their social worlds. By asking informants questions that include phrases such as, *What's the difference between . . .* or *Can you compare . . .* , researchers are able to "discover the dimensions of meaning which informants employ to distinguish objects and events" (Spradley, 1979, p. 69). Used along with descriptive and structural questions, contrast questions provide another angle from which to approach the perspectives of informants. Examples from the kindergarten study included the following:

- "How would you characterize the differences between the developmental level of kindergartners and first graders?"
- "Can you compare your kindergarten program with kindergarten programs five years ago?"
- "What's different about kindergarten teachers in relation to teachers in other grades?" (Hatch & Freeman, 1988, pp. 165–66).

Essential questions have to get at the purposes of the study, especially if the data of the study are primarily interview-based. Descriptive, structural, and contrast are types of questions that give researchers an organizer for thinking about how to frame questions, but the substance comes from the unique focus of each study. In the study from which the example questions have been given, we were interested in getting school people talking about what they thought kindergarten ought to be (their philosophies) and what they thought it actually was (their practices). We didn't directly ask, "What's your philosophy?" or "What's your practice?" but we designed questions that we thought would reveal how they thought and what they did. Spradley's (1979) question types gave us a guide for generating questions that served our purposes and helped us accomplish our research ends (appendix D is an edited transcript of an interview done as part of this study, and it includes examples of each type of question and how they were actually asked in an interview setting).

How questions are worded is another important consideration. The ways words are used in questions can make a great deal of difference in the kinds of answers informants will give. Even though, except for standardized interviews, questions are almost never read verbatim from interview guides, it is important to write guiding questions using words that frame them in ways that respect informants and generate the kinds of responses that make good data. Several generalizations are offered as a guide for writing effective questions:

- *Questions should be open-ended.* The power of qualitative interviewing is that it gives informants opportunities to share their unique perspectives in their own words. When questions are set up in dichotomous terms so that yes or no answers are possible (e.g., "Is your reading program effective?"), or if questions are framed in ways that presume unstated categories ("How effective is your reading program?"), they are little better than mailed questionnaires. Even though researchers may plan to probe beyond initial responses, the tone of such an interview can become more like an interrogation than a conversation.

- *Questions should use language that is familiar to informants.* It is the responsibility of researchers to account for differences in language between themselves and their informants. Unless two-way communication is established, data will be of questionable value, and interviews will be awkward, at the least. This issue goes beyond obvious concerns when native languages are different; it includes dealing with differences in dialect and taking into account specialized vocabularies used in distinct subcultures and occupational groups.

- *Questions should be clear.* In addition to using familiar language, questions should clearly communicate what the researcher expects from the informant. Informants should be able to understand questions so that they can feel comfortable sharing their perspectives. Complex questions that ask too much, multiple questions that overwhelm, or obliquely asked questions that confuse tend to make informants uncomfortable and shut down interview interactions.

- *Questions should be neutral.* It is unfair and unwise to use leading questions. While Kvale (1996) argues that leading questions are useful for "checking the reliability of interviewees' answers" (p. 158), I do not believe it is the researcher's place to act as police officer, lawyer, or psychoanalyst. Framing questions in ways designed to trip participants up or point the interview in directions that favor the perspective of the researcher (e.g., "It's easy to see why kids love working in small groups, what's your experience using small groups?") disrespects informants and generates bad data. Similarly, it is unethical to value some responses over others in the course of interviews. Researchers should signal their empathy and understanding in an effort to build and maintain rapport, but avoid judging responses because doing so may lead informants to try to please rather than inform (see Patton, 1990).

• *Questions should respect informants and presume they have valuable knowledge.* The researchers' stance in relation to informants should be one of students who hope to learn from their informant teachers. While questions need to be clear and stated in familiar language, they need not be simplistic or condescending. The reason individuals are selected for interviews is that they have special knowledge that is valuable to the researcher. Asking questions that invite informants to teach the researcher what they know and asking them in a way that presumes special insight is a good strategy. For example, a researcher should expect different responses from questions such as, "Do you know what your district's policy is on corporal punishment?" and "Tell me about the corporal punishment policy in your district." The latter signals the informant that the researcher assumes he or she has important knowledge.

• *Questions should generate answers related to the objectives of the research.* Guiding questions should reflect the purposes of the interview, and the interview ought to be undertaken because it helps accomplish the purposes of the research. Every interview need not provide an avenue into all of the research questions that frame a study, but every interview should address some portion of the research questions. I give this apparently self-evident advice because I have critiqued many interview guides that I had a hard time connecting to the purposes of the proposed research. Great questions get informants talking, but unless they are talking about the topics under investigation, the talk is of little use to the project.

Doing Qualitative Interviews. Informal interviews are often sidebars to the action of the research, and these require the ability to engage participants in reflective conversation about that action. Establishing relationships that facilitate comfortable and productive sidebars is important, and relationships will grow and change depending on how researchers behave during informal interview opportunities. Formal interviews often do not allow opportunities for developing relationships over time; they require other skills and sensitivities in order to build rapport and generate useful data.

In any interview setting, certain qualities will make interviews more effective. Good qualitative interviews are characterized by respect, interest, attention, good manners, and encouragement on the part of researchers (see Bogdan & Biklen, 1992; Seidman, 1998). They often begin with small talk that serves to get the informant talking and to make human connections between researchers and informants. The purposes of the research should be made clear, and researchers should reassure informants that there are no right or wrong answers, but that informants' honest perspectives are the most desirable outcome of the conversation about to take place. This will often lead into background questions that continue to set the tone for the interview (it may be helpful for readers to refer to the interview transcript in appendix D for examples of the elements discussed in this section).

Some informants will be ill at ease or feel as if they have nothing important to say. It is the researcher's job to help put informants at ease and to assure them that their perspectives are vital to the goals of the study. Some informants will give abbreviated or guarded responses. Researchers should work to get them talking by showing interest in their comments and asking for clarification and detail. Body language, facial expressions, and verbal prompts signal informants that the researcher is engaged and interested in what they have to say. Prompts should not challenge what informants have said but let them know that their comments are important and that you want to know more (e.g., Can you tell me more about that? or I'm not sure I know exactly what you mean. Can you give me an example?).

Learning to listen like a researcher is a skill that will improve the quality of interviews. I have learned to recognize that when I am doing observations or interviews, a part of my brain is constantly monitoring what I do or say *as researcher*. Acknowledging this metacognitive awareness of acting *qua* researcher, for me, is parallel to taking on what Berger and Kellner (1981) call a "sociological perspective," which forces researchers to process experience from "both inside and outside the situation" (p. 34). They participate in the external conversation of the interview but carry on a simultaneous inner conversation, "which is a crucial *sotto voce* accompaniment to the verbal exchange" (Berger & Kellner, 1981, p. 21). When I enter the research setting, I am still Amos, still a husband and father, still a professor, but I am operating within the awareness that I am there to do research. Part of that awareness has me listening like a researcher.

As researcher, I listen to informants in ways that I think will facilitate their ability to teach me about the topic at hand. I am listening (and watching) for clues that certain topics are sensitive to informants, and I may probe more gently or return later to such topics as I sense informants' discomfort or willingness to go further. I am listening for key words or phrases that may give me opportunities for unlocking the special knowledge of the informants. An easy and effective probe is always, "Tell you what you mean by _____."

I am listening for what informants take for granted. I have learned that the most powerful cultural knowledge for participants is made up of understandings that they assume everyone shares. When I hear informants make "of course statements" (Lynd & Lynd, 1937, p. 402) that signal the taken-for-granted nature of what they are saying, I "play dumb" (often convincingly) and ask informants to let me in on these understandings that everyone else seems to have.

I am also listening to my questions and keeping track of where the interview is headed. I want to balance valuing the informants' desire to talk about certain subjects with using the interview time to get at information directly tied to the research project. When we seem to be going down a path that has limited use to the research, I will be listening for opportunities to tactfully bring the conversation back around to the topic of interest. Listening like a researcher is hard work, and it takes practice to do it well. Practicing interviews with colleagues or friends is a good idea. Studying transcripts once interviews are completed is another way to improve interviewing skills.

Listening is also important because the quality of good interviews depends so heavily on generating effective prompts or asking timely probing questions based on what happens during the interview. Only standardized interviews run from beginning to end without the need for careful adjustments and shaping by the researcher. Several prompts and probes have been used as illustrations above. Prompts are verbal and nonverbal signals that researchers use to keep the informants talking. They include strategies for active listening such as making eye contact, nodding, leaning forward, making positive verbalizations like "uh-huh" or "I see," paraphrasing back, and asking for clarification. Sometimes prompts take the form of silences or questioning looks. In the interview context, or in almost all speech events, silence often makes for discomfort. By waiting a few seconds after an informant stops speaking, or by responding with a quizzical expression, informants will often break the silence themselves, expanding or clarifying what they have been talking about (see Kvale, 1996).

Probing questions are designed to encourage informants to go more deeply into a topic, and they can be used to reshape the direction of an interview segment. At another level, they let the informant know what depth of response the researcher desires (Patton, 1990). Probes are not prepared ahead of time but are created as follow-up questions during the give and take of the interview. This means that I have to listen like a researcher, paying careful attention to what is mentioned and what is not mentioned (see Loftland & Loftland, 1984). Probes are used to fill in details (e.g., When did that happen?), encourage elaboration (Can you tell me more about that?), get clarification (I'm not sure I understand what you mean), and generate examples (Can you tell me about a time when you felt that way?).

Probes can also be used to shape the direction of the interview when informants tend to move away from the subject at hand. I said in an earlier chapter that we need to teach informants how to teach us. We should be telling them what we are interested in directly, but the kinds of things the researcher follows up on let the informant know where the researcher wants the interview to go and what level of understanding is being sought. Probes can bring the informant back around to the topic, but they will shut down the interaction if the informant perceives that what's important to him or her is of no interest to the researcher. So such redirections should be gentle and acknowledge the inherent value of all the informant has to say (e.g., "I'd like to spend more time talking about that, but let me ask you about something you said earlier").

Some researchers recommend avoiding "Why?" questions as probes because such questions have a negative connotation in Western discourse (e.g., Why did you do that?), assume a cause-and-effect relationship that may not exist, and put the informant on the spot because asking "Why" can infer that their preceding response was inappropriate (Berg, 1998; Patton, 1990). I think it is important to be aware of any "loaded" words or phrases that may sound accusatory or confrontational, and asking "Why?" in some instances will come across as loaded. Still, there will be situations in which asking, "Why do you say that?" will be a neutral and effective probe. Being in touch with informants' reactions to the interview experience and keeping research objectives in mind will help guide the use of this and other prompts and probes.

Self-disclosure is an issue in qualitative interviewing. Students often wonder, "How much of my self and my experiences should I share with informants?" Researchers want to establish connections with informants, and offering personal information or telling stories that demonstrate affinity with informants will often serve to improve rapport. But, some researchers are concerned that individuals can be manipulated by researchers and seduced into revealing sensitive information by individuals they have come to trust (see Bogdan & Biklen, 1992; Finch, 1984).

Researchers never want to exploit their research participants by using their vulnerabilities to gain an advantage, but the assumptions of different research approaches will logically lead to different relationships within interview dyads. As a pattern, it is more likely that postpositivist researchers will have less personal contact and do less self-disclosure than other qualitative researchers. It will be their goal to gather data that are relatively free of influence from the researcher. Constructivists see their role as to coconstruct data with their informants, so their interviews will likely include more participation, more control of research processes, and more active sharing by informants than those of postpositivists (see Mishler, 1986). Critical/feminists emphasize the importance of self-disclosure in interview settings (DeVault, 1990; Lather, 1988), the logic being that both sides should be honest and take risks in order to move to shared understandings of oppression and explore possibilities for empowerment. Poststructuralists are interested in the stories that individuals tell to make sense of their lives, and they understand that interviews are special contexts that generate not "the story" but "a story." When researchers disclose their own stories to informants, they understand that those stories will influence the ways their informants' stories are told.

Finally, good interviewers have a sense of when interviews have gone on long enough. Informants need to know ahead of time about how long interviews are expected to last. My rule of thumb is that about an hour will usually be required, and going longer than 90 minutes will require special circumstances. The audiotapes I use are usually 30 minutes per side, and once I have moved to the second tape (about 60 minutes in) I become very aware of my informant's and my own comfort level. Seidman (1998) argues convincingly for 90-minute interviews, but perhaps because my experience is with interviewing busy educators and children in education settings, I recommend aiming for about an hour. Of course, some interviews will run long, and some will last for less time than anticipated. Again, part of listening like a researcher is keeping track of time in relation to how much the informant is willing to share, how tired or fatigued you both may become, and how well the guiding questions are being addressed.

When thinking about how anticipated interviews will actually go, I like to remind students that all social occasions in Western society have beginnings, middles, and ends. Interviews are special kinds of social or speech events that follow the same pattern. It is sometimes helpful to think of interviews as having an introductory and concluding phase, with the body of the interview in between. The introductory phase includes small talk to help make informants comfortable and used to talking into a microphone; explanations reminding informants of the purposes of the interview, their importance as the "teachers" of the researcher, and that confidentiality is guaranteed; and background questions that provide context and demographic information and set the tone for the interactive nature of the interview.

The body of the interview is the place where the essential descriptive, structural, and contrast questions are woven into the interchange. The idea is to get the informant talking about issues of importance to the purposes of the study. Guiding questions guide but do not determine the direction of the interview. The researcher is attentive to the comfort level of the informants and mixes in prompts and probes to keep the interview moving and to follow up on the important elements that emerge. The overall pattern is to move from general to specific discussions based on guiding questions and informant responses. The researcher is constantly watching for opportunities to take the conversation to a deeper level of meaning and understanding by listening to responses and inviting reflection, examples, and details.

Interviews, like all speech events in our culture, feel incomplete without a sense of closure. Again, it is important for researchers to be attuned to the

CLOSURE

affective dimensions of the interchange so that they know when informants are becoming uncomfortable, fatigued, or defensive. They also need to monitor the substantive progress of the interview, taking note of how well the guiding questions have been addressed. Signaling that the interview is about to end is important to giving a sense of completeness to the interview speech event. One way is just to say, "Let me ask you just one (or a few) more question(s) before we stop." Another is to summarize what you see as the major points of the exchange and to ask for feedback (Lincoln & Guba, 1985). Another is ask, "Is there anything you'd like to say that we haven't covered in the interview?" If plans are in place for further contact, in the form of future interviews, a chance to review transcriptions of the interview just completed, or for informal follow-up, arrangements for these should be made clear. If informants will have a chance to read and correct/edit interview transcripts, that should be established in the research bargain, but the procedures and a timeline for completing it should be reviewed. If research bargains call for sharing final reports with informants (in summary or complete form), arrangements for doing so should be reviewed. Finally, informants should be thanked for giving up their time, congratulated for their candor and insights, and reminded of their importance to the study. The goal is to be sure that informants leave the interview setting with a sense of closure, an understanding of what to expect in the future, the impression that their time was well spent, and the feeling that they have been treated with respect.

Processing Interview Data. During interviews, I keep a copy of the interview guide in front of me on a clipboard, and I make notes directly on the guide as the interview proceeds. These notes help me keep track of what guiding questions have been addressed and where I want to go next with the interview. I also try to write down key words or phrases that I want to ask about either in this interview or later, depending on the study. I sometimes write down questions that I don't want to forget to ask. If I notice nonverbal indicators or contextual influences that will not be picked up on tape, I try to make a record of them, and I also make bracketed notes of impressions that come to mind during the interview. These notes become part of the data of the study. They can be included as "raw data" and stored as is. They can be written up as part of research journals or even recorded at the end of interview tapes for transcriptions. If recording equipment ever fails, such notes can be the source for reconstructing as much of the interview as possible from memory.

These and all other data from interviews should be processed as soon as possible following the interview. I always check the tape immediately to be sure everything was working, especially when tapes were turned over or multiple tapes were used. If something went wrong, I can at least write up all I can remember from the interview (see Patton, 1990). Depending on the study, I try to get the tape transcribed right away. If I am doing a participant observation study, interview data will be useful for directing future observations. If I am doing interview only studies with multiple informants or a series of interviews with a small number of individuals, having transcribed data will help shape subsequent interviews. In many studies, starting analysis procedures along with early data collection is important (see discussion above), and this, of course, will require transcription. However, even when data analysis will be delayed, it is important to review transcripts (or at least listen to interview tapes) as interviews are completed.

Transcribing is often difficult and tedious work. Patton (1990) estimates that it takes about four hours of transcription time for every hour of interview. I have transcribed my own interviews and paid to have it done. On the one hand, there are advantages to doing the transcribing yourself in that you will be able to add context, nonverbal information, and bracketed notations from your notes and memory as the interview is typed up (see Woods, 1986). You will be able to recognize words that a transcriber will not be able to understand, and you will learn things about your informants, the substance of the interview, and yourself as interviewer that will be missed in the transcript alone. And you will save lots of money. On the other hand, transcribing takes forever, even with sophisticated transcribing machines, and university campuses often have experienced transcriptionists who do a good job for a reasonable price. If others are hired (or friends or family are coerced) to transcribe for you, it is still important to listen to the complete tape while going through the typed transcript. This will be the time for you to correct problems in the transcript, fill in elements the transcriptionist could not make out, and add contextual information from your interview notes and impressions (see Lapadat & Lindsay, 1999). Paying attention to punctuation is especially important. Seidman (1998) points out that punctuating transcripts is a kind of analysis that can alter the meanings associated with informants' words. It will be helpful to give those transcribing for you clear and consistent directions about the format you want the interviews to have. Putting such directions in writing will help, as will being sure that word processing programs can be transferred between your transcriber's computer and your own.

Students want to know if they have to transcribe all of their interview data, noting that some of the conversation in the interviews does not really apply to their studies. Some researchers (e.g., Woods, 1986) recommend that interviewers listen to tapes and decide if the whole conversation needs to be transcribed. I understand the suggestion, but I worry that making such decisions will involve judgments about what's important that ought to be made more systematically later on as data analysis begins (see Seidman, 1998). Again, it's my training that "everything is data" that leads me to tell students to transcribe everything and save data reduction for later in the research process.

Qualitative researchers should keep a research log no matter what kind of study is done. Such logs for pure interview studies will include records of where, when, with whom, and for how long interviews were held. Research journals should also be kept, either along with logs or separately. Journals are places to evaluate how interviews went, to record impressions about informant reactions, to judge the quality of certain guiding questions, and to critique interviewer performance during the interview. Research journals are important places to reflect on the research process and keep track of the human side of the research experience. Entries should be made as soon as possible after leaving the interview setting and again as transcripts are typed or filled in.

The best way to get better at doing interviews is to study transcripts of your early interviews (see interview transcript example in appendix D). Examining what you said and what kinds of responses resulted from what you said can be very revealing. Many students are surprised at how much they talked during interview and often wonder, "Why didn't I ask her about that?" You will always find places where you will wish you had asked another question or probed in another way, but studying what you have done will help you improve your interviewing skills. Keeping track of impressions and making plans for change in writing (in a research journal or some other format) will help you get better faster.

Summary: Tips for Successful Interviews

To summarize this section on qualitative interviewing, I have synthesized suggestions from several authors who have written about qualitative interviews with my own observations and experiences. I characterize these as tips for successful interviews:

- *Follow the rules of polite conversation.* Interviews are a special kind of conversation, but it is important that informants be invited to participate in a two-way conversation that treats them with respect and dignity. Interviewers should signal this respect by never starting an interview without some small talk or without explanations of research purposes and the importance of the informant to the research process (Berg, 1998; Spradley, 1979). Researchers should ask "real questions" that acknowledge and value knowledge that informants have and researchers need, and researchers should give informants ample opportunity to respond without interruption (Seidman, 1998). Questions should be open-ended and framed in ways that do not lead informants in particular directions. Answers should be received without judgment; that is, the informant should be reinforced for responding, not for answering in certain ways. And researchers should bring closure to interviews, thanking informants for their participation and contribution.

- *Interview in a comfortable place.* If informants are uncomfortable because of the physical setup of the interview setting or because they are concerned that their comments will be overheard by others, interviews will be negatively affected (Berg, 1998). Whenever possible, check out interview spaces and try out recording equipment prior to beginning an interview.

- *Plan well before the interview begins.* Not all researchers agree that a well-developed interview guide is necessary for successful interviews, but I believe going into the interview with carefully thought out guiding questions is essential for new researchers. If researchers do not have questions in mind and have not thought through the beginning, middle, and end of how they hope an interview will go, they may be fine; but they run the risk of wasting their informants' time or worse. Berg (1998) recommends that researchers remember their research purpose. I agree that this is important. Having that purpose in mind before the interview begins will help keep the interview on track and productive.

- *Learn how to listen.* Both Wolcott (1995) and Seidman (1998) recommend that researchers talk less and listen more. This is a good general rule that ought to guide all interviewers, but learning how to listen is just as important as spending more time listening. I discussed using active listening strategies and listening like a researcher above. Wolcott (1995) describes what he calls "creative listeners," or those who are "able to play an interactive role, thereby making a more effective speaker of out of the person talking" (p. 111). Being aware of the importance of listening is vital, and practicing creative listening in other social contexts is useful, but doing interviews and studying the transcripts of your own performance as listener and questioner is the best way to improve listening and asking skills.

- *Explore informants' understandings.* Or, stated in the negative, don't prod them for information. Good qualitative interviews are dynamic, interactive, social events. Even though a set of guiding questions will frame the interview, researchers must be attentive to informants' responses so that they can generate appropriate prompts to encourage more detail and ask effective probing questions to request more depth and reflection. Seidman (1998) makes several suggestions for exploring informant understandings, including the following: follow up on what informants say, tolerate silence, ask for details, ask for more information, and ask questions when you don't understand (pp. 69–77). The trick is to make the informant aware that you are listening and interested without bombarding him or her with questions that make the interview feel like a cross-examination. I think the key is to be genuinely interested in what the informant has to say and to signal that interest in the way answers are received and questions are asked.

- *Invite informants to help you be a better researcher.* This suggestion from Wolcott (1995) goes beyond the discussion above of inviting informants to teach you about the social phenomena you are studying. Here we are talking about asking informants to give you feedback about the research process itself. This should be more than an opportunity for self-congratulation or fishing for compliments, informants should be asked for their perspectives in the research process, not an evaluation of you as an interviewer. Wolcott (1995) recommends direct questions such as, "Do you have any suggestions about these interviews?" (p. 115) and "Are there topics we should explore that I haven't asked about?" (p. 116). Asking such questions values informant perspectives and creates the opportunity to find out more about your interviews and your subject matter.

- *Transcribe your interviews right away.* Students find this difficult advice to take; they are often involved in ongoing data collection and don't have the time or energy to stop to transcribe interviews. Even if they are fortunate enough to have someone else to type up taped interviews, they are often too busy to study interviews with great care. There are good reasons to transcribe and do some initial analysis of interviews as soon as possible. Done well, early analyses shape the direction of future interviews and observations. They give a sense of confidence to researchers as they continue data collection or create a sense of disequilibrium that ought to lead to changes in research implementation. In addition, as mentioned above, reading completed interviews will give immediate feedback about the effectiveness of certain questions, prompts, and probes. Finally, transcribing and analyzing as the research unfolds reduces the chances of finding major gaps in the data set of the study after it is too late to do anything about it.

COLLECTING UNOBTRUSIVE DATA

The third primary data collecting strategy in qualitative studies is the collection of unobtrusive data. Unobtrusive data provide insight into the social phenomenon under investigation without interfering with the enactment of that social phenomenon. Unobtrusive data are said to be nonreactive in the sense that they are not filtered through the perceptions, interpretations, and biases of research participants (Webb et al., 1981). While there are several kinds of such data, what binds them together is that they are gathered without the direct involvement of research participants; they are unobtrusive because their collection does not interfere with the ongoing events of everyday life.

Kinds of Unobtrusive Data

Some of the kinds of unobtrusive data are artifacts, traces, documents, personal communications, records, photographs, and archives. While there is overlap among these types, I will describe each and give examples of what such data might look like in education settings. While some anthropologists might count all of the types of unobtrusive data listed as artifacts, here I will use the term to stand for "material objects that represent the culture at [a particular] site" (Chiseri-Strater & Sunstein, 1997, p. 78). Artifacts are objects that participants use in the everyday activity of the contexts under examination. Gathering and studying these artifacts can give alternative insights into the ways people think and act (Hodder, 1994). For field anthropologists, artifacts include objects such as clothing, tools, toys, jewelry, and musical instruments. For educational researchers, examples might include samples of children's work, copies of teacher plans, collections and/or descriptions of classroom tools (from crayons to computers), descriptions of furniture and decorations found in teachers' lounges, or accounts of objects children bring for "show and tell."

Traces are the unintended residues of human activity. They provide physical evidence of how participants operate in their settings. The classic study using this kind of unobtrusive measure was an evaluation of the Natural History Museum at the Smithsonian Institute in which "wear spots" on rugs were studied as indicators of how frequently certain exhibits were visited (Wolf & Tymitz, 1978). Trace analysis allows researchers to study patterns of behavior without interfering with the flow of that behavior. In school studies, traces that may provide insight include wear spots on grass playgrounds, signs of wear and tear on library books, dust on science equipment, or the condition of school restrooms.

Documents are powerful indicators of the value systems operating within institutions. I am making a distinction between official written communication, which I call "documents," and unofficial or personal communication, which I take up later. All modern institutions generate documents that create a written record of official activity within the institution. Documents can provide a behind-the-scenes look at institutional processes and how they came into being (Patton, 1990). They can give the researcher a sense of history related to the contexts being studied. In education settings, this kind of unobtrusive data can range from public documents such as state curriculum guides, district policy statements, and school codes of conduct to internal communications such as policy interpretations, letters of reprimand, and memos of understanding. Other documents, such as news releases and parent newsletters, are prepared specifically to communicate directly with the public.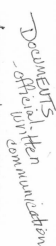

PERSONAL COMMUNICATION

Personal communications are another type of unobtrusive data that can be collected as part of qualitative studies. Personal communications are written without the intent of representing the official positions of institutions. They may be unofficial communications between colleagues or take the form of individual diaries or journals that are usually not written with an audience in mind. These kinds of data are unobtrusive only if they have been produced as part of the participants' natural experience, not in response to requests from the researcher. We will discuss the use of journaling as a data gathering technique later in this chapter. Here it is assumed diaries or journals have been kept by participants prior to the study, then voluntarily shared with researchers. In addition to journals or diaries that school folks may share with researchers, other kinds of personal communication may include notes between teachers, unofficial letters between school personnel, interactive journals that teachers sometimes share with students or parents, and the usually clandestine notes passed among students.

RECORDS

Records are an additional kind of unobtrusive data that can add significantly to many qualitative studies. Records are special kind of documents on which notations are made in an effort to keep track of certain facets of school life. Records are kept on all kinds of activities within institutions, and just knowing what kinds of records are kept tells a great deal about institutional values and practices. Personnel, financial, and performance records are just some of the general types of records institutions keep. Schools are large bureaucratic institutions that keep vast records at all levels. An example from some of the levels will indicate the possibilities: at the national level, records are kept of state performance on achievement indicators such as the National Assessment of Educational Progress; at the state level, pupil attendance records are kept for each district; at the district level, personnel records are kept for each employee; at the school level, cumulative records are kept of each child's progress from year to year; and at the classroom level, report card records are generated several times throughout each year. Other kinds of records might include valuable information but not come to mind immediately, for example, at the school level, records of copy machine use per month, records of parent volunteer time, records of teacher absenteeism, or records of how parent teacher organizations spend their money.

PHOTOS

Photographs that have been taken by participants or collected by institutions are another valuable kind of unobtrusive data. As with personal communications, if these are produced *for the researcher* or made *by the researcher,* they might be useful and appropriate, but they do not qualify as unobtrusive. Many organizations keep photographic records of important events in their histories, newspapers often maintain photo collections, and sometimes individuals keep photo albums or scrapbooks. While there are limitations to what can be learned from photographs, as there are with all unobtrusive data (see below), photos can provide a sense of what the setting was like in the past, provide specific factual information about who was where when, and present anomalies that do not fit with other data in the study (see Bogdan & Biklen, 1992). Schools sometimes keep photographic records, many schools have class pictures made from year to year, and districts often have some kind of archival system that may include photos. Many teachers use photography as part of their instruction. Teachers of young children, in particular, often photograph individual children and make photographic records of important events. Finally, yearbooks produced at most middle and high schools can be rich sources of unobtrusive photographic (and textual) data.

Historical research is a particular type of qualitative study identified in chapter 1. Often, studies of this type rely heavily on archival data. Many of the kinds of unobtrusive data outlined in this section will be collected in archives, and such collections can be of use to researchers other than historiographers. Institutional archives often include documents, records, and photographs that tell the story of the institution. My experience is that school archives are seldom carefully organized or cataloged. They are likely to be old files or boxes of materials that are stored in multiple places. In studies that depend on historical grounding, searching through archives, no matter what their state, can be an essential step.

Working with Unobtrusive Data

Including unobtrusive data collection as part of research design offers several advantages. Again, unobtrusive data are nonreactive. They can tell their own story independent of the interpretations of participants, and they can be gathered without disturbing the natural flow of human activity. This makes them an especially useful point from which to make comparisons with data from other sources such as observation and interviewing—a process usually called "triangulation." For example, teachers' descriptions of learning objectives can be compared to the actual products of student work, or field-note records of an exchange between a superintendent and her school board can be checked against the official minutes of that meeting. Triangulation is an important concept that is discussed in the next chapter and throughout this book. Unobtrusive data are useful to triangulation processes because their nonreactive nature makes them one step removed from participants' intervening interpretations, they provide an alternative perspective on the phenomenon being studied, and they are relatively easy to acquire—often someone else has collected the data (see Marshall & Rossman, 1995).

In direct contrast, another use of unobtrusive data is as a stimulus in interview interactions. Anthropologists often ask informants to explain the histories, uses, and significance of artifacts gathered in the field (Chiseri-Strater &

Sunstein, 1997). Used in this way, unobtrusive data invite and stimulate participant reflection and interpretation. In both formal and informal interviews, asking participants to talk about how they use certain artifacts (e.g., getting teachers to talk about textbooks, bulletin boards, plan books) can get at important dimensions of school life. Other kinds of unobtrusive data can be used in similar ways. Bogdan and Biklen (1992) offer the example of a child development researcher asking parents to discuss their children's development while looking through family photo albums in the parents' homes. I have asked teachers to talk about evaluation practices while looking at examples of their districts' student cumulative record folders.

Another basic contribution that unobtrusive data can make is to help establish history and context in which to ground findings generated from other data. Quantitative social science research is often criticized because it attempts to study human behavior in controlled, artificial circumstances (see Hatch, 1998). The assumptions of the positivist paradigm lead to research that leaves out the idiosyncratic nature of each setting's context, participants, and history. Qualitative researchers worry about "contextualizing" their studies as well, that is, placing them in sufficient historical, political, and cultural context that readers have a rich sense of where and how they fit (see Graue & Walsh, 1998). Some elements of this context can be captured in interview interactions, but researchers should always be aware that they are getting participants' perspectives on history and context in such data. Describing settings is important in qualitative work, and unobtrusive data from archives and other sources can help researchers pull these descriptions together.

Researchers should also be aware of the potential weaknesses of unobtrusive data. Used in isolation, they can offer a distorted view of events and social contexts. For example, using only the minutes of a school board meeting on school desegregation may present a condensed and "edited" version of the interactions that actually took place, or collecting records that show how much money has been spent on classroom computers may not reveal much about how computers are actually used. Relatedly, it is often hard to establish what Lincoln and Guba (1985, p. 281) call the "trustworthiness" of particular pieces of unobtrusive data. As Hodder (1994) points out, "objects cannot speak back; . . . there are no 'member checks' because the artifacts themselves are mute" (pp. 398–99). Interpreting meanings and significance of unobtrusive data is, therefore, heavily inferential, and it is incumbent on researchers to go about making interpretations carefully. Hodder (1994) recommends that such interpretations include the following: (a) identifying the contexts within which artifacts had meaning; (b) recognizing meaningful similarities and differences within contexts, and (c) judging the relevance of theories to the data at hand (p. 399).

Another concern with unobtrusive data is that they are most often gathered piecemeal, so it is difficult to know what parts of the incomplete picture are represented in the data at hand. Archived materials are often poorly organized and inconsistently maintained, complete sets of documents and records are hard to find, and collections of personal communications and photographs will often be uneven and skewed in certain directions. In his discussion of the limitations of archival research, Bernard (1994) notes that "while *your* examination of archival data has no reactive effect, there is no guarantee that the data were collected nonreactively in the first place" (p. 336, emphasis in original). This warning holds for other kinds of unobtrusive data as well; part of your interpretation should include an awareness of the positionings and potential motives of those collecting the data in the first place. Even local newspaper accounts and national reports on school progress should be considered within the historical, social, and political contexts that surround them.

Triangulating unobtrusive data with data from other sources is one way to improve confidence in reporting findings based on such information. In historical studies or other research projects that rely heavily on unobtrusive data, triangulation can be accomplished through using multiple sources of unobtrusive data. For example, a study of the history of an alternative school may include the school's own records, local newspaper accounts, parts of the archives of the local historical society, and personal communications and photographs collected by individuals working in or attending the school. Including interviews with teachers, students, administrators, and community members will strengthen the study even further. In any study, researchers must carefully describe their data and data sources so that readers can make their own judgments about the trustworthiness of the accounts in the study, but this is especially important when unobtrusive data are used.

It should be made clear to gatekeepers and participants on the front end exactly what unobtrusive data the researcher expects to be collecting. The research bargain should specify as much as possible what data will be collected, including unobtrusive data. This is especially true when sensitive information that might be kept in personal diaries or school records is involved. In most systems, researchers will not be allowed access to children's school records without permission from parents, so this needs to be built into research bargains and informed consent agreements. "Sunshine laws" in many states guarantee open access to records of public meetings, but it is ethical and prudent to inform gatekeepers of your intentions to use such records as part of gaining access. When the researcher knows at the outset that he or she wants to include specific records (e.g., teachers' grade books), documents (e.g., administrative memos), or artifacts (e.g., samples of children's math homework) in the analysis, these should be named directly in the research bargain and informed consent. When it is anticipated that unobtrusive data will be collected, but the researcher may not be certain of all of the specifics, the language should stipulate what the researcher knows he or she wants and indicate the intent to gather, describe, photocopy, or photograph other indicators related to the purposes of the study *with the permission of participants.* The idea is to set up a situation in which the researcher can ethically add unanticipated unobtrusive data after the study is underway. It should be clear in such language that the participants have the final say in whether or not data that are not specifically named in original agreements will be added.

ABLE TO ADD

Collecting and Processing Unobtrusive Data

Different kinds of unobtrusive data will require different methods of collection. Some artifacts, such as student work, might be gathered directly, placed in folders or boxes, and labeled in such a way that figuring out who produced them, when, and in what context will be possible. At other times, student work and other artifacts in school settings will need to be returned or remain in the setting. These can be carefully described as part of field notes or records can be made and kept in separate files. Sometimes paper-based artifacts, such as teachers' plans or a principal's meeting notes can be photocopied with the participants' permission. Making photographs of classroom objects, such as bulletin boards or computer stations can be a useful tool for collecting some kinds of artifact data. In a study of children's social and creative development in a preschool, a colleague and I used still photography and videotaping to make a record of art objects that children created in various media (Johnson & Hatch, 1990). As these and other kinds of unobtrusive data are collected, it is imperative that researchers develop a system for labeling and keeping track of what the objects are, where they came from, and why they have been gathered. In the study mentioned, we were interested in observing the interactions and creations of specific "target children," so keeping track of who produced what under what circumstances was important to interpreting the data later on.

Need for labeling / storage + system

Trace data can be captured in written descriptions and/or photographs. Again, written descriptions can become part of field notes or be kept separate, and photographs should be processed quickly and written notes used to supplement the photographic record. Research logs are a good place to keep track of this and any other kinds of data that are collected. As notations are made to log the observations or interviews done on a particular day, describing any trace descriptions or photos will help researchers keep track of how those data fit into their studies.

Documents are paper-based by definition and, wherever possible, should be collected directly or photocopied to ensure accuracy and completeness. This must be done with the knowledge and permission of participants and gatekeepers. Extra copies of some documents will be available when they are first distributed, but those kept in files or stored in other ways should be photocopied whenever possible. When this is not possible, careful written descriptions of what is included in documents can be made. This is the time to record what is in documents, not to interpret and analyze. Impressions can be bracketed within descriptions as with any other data, but getting the actual language in the document is essential.

Collecting personal communications from research participants requires care and sensitivity. Some individuals will feel perfectly comfortable sharing their diaries, letters, and other personal communications; others will feel vulnerable and self-protective. When studies are designed to make personal communications the primary data source for the research, participants will be selected because they are willing to share such communications. When personal communications are supplementary data or even data that are not anticipated, researchers should tread lightly to be sure that participants feel secure in sharing what is sometimes very sensitive information. Informed consent requires giving participants the right to withdraw from a study at any time without penalty. Similarly, participants should understand that they have the right to withdraw permission to use any or all personal communications if they change their minds as studies progress. Photocopying, with permission, is best, and some kind of system for organizing these data is essential.

It is often the case that certain records cannot be photocopied and/or cannot be removed from their place of storage. I have sat in school vaults taking down information from students' cumulative folders because district policy did not allow me to photocopy such records or take them from their secure storage place. As with documents, photocopies are best, but written descriptions of information from records can be valuable data. School systems are rightly concerned about how their records are to be accessed and used, and it is important to be clear about these issues as research bargains are negotiated.

Photographs that count as unobtrusive data are those taken by individuals other than the researcher and for purposes other than the research at hand. These are treated differently from the photos described above as secondary records of artifacts or traces. Photographs collected by institutions or newspapers or saved by individuals have value to their owners and cannot be added directly to research files. As with other data, it is preferred, where possible, to make copies of photographs. Developments in photocopying make copying color photos more feasible and affordable. Written descriptions of photos that cannot be copied are second best but will do when copying is impossible. Some photographs will be fragile and require special handling, and all should be processed with care so that they are returned in as good a shape as they were received.

Archival research involves a specialized kind of data collection that will be reviewed only briefly here. Individuals doing extensive work with archival records should consult sources specifically designed to guide such research (e.g., Hill, 1993; Scott, 1990). Qualitative researchers supplementing other data with archived materials collected by school systems, schools, newspapers, or institutions such as professional organizations or historical societies should follow the guidelines for collecting other kinds of unobtrusive data noted above. Archival records will likely include materials such as documents, records, and photographs and may include some personal communications. It is an advantage that these materials have been gathered together by someone else, but researchers should be aware that materials may have been collected with specific purposes in mind so that information that might be important to the research at hand may be over- or underrepresented in archival collections. Therefore, it is important to examine the history and purposes of archives being examined as data are collected and analyzed. It is also important not to assume that data collected in archives are error free (Bernard, 1994). Just because information found its way into archives does not mean it was systematically gathered, was free of bias, or was checked for accuracy. In sum, archives offer a valuable source for unobtrusive data, but researchers should use such data with care.

As has been mentioned, no matter what type of unobtrusive data are being collected, developing and consistently using some kind of organizing or indexing system is very important. Records of the nature of data collected and when and where they were collected should be part of research logs, but some way to identify and store materials and descriptions also needs to be created. Some records, documents, and personal communications will include dates as part of their text, but an accounting of how, when, why, and from whom these were collected may be important to their interpretation. Artifact data, the objects themselves, or photos or descriptions of objects should be identified with such information as where and when they were collected, the contexts in which they were used, who used them, and how they were used. It should not be assumed that the objects themselves will remind the researcher of their importance to the study. Descriptions or photographs of trace data should also be accompanied with descriptive information reminding researchers of where and when such data were collected and why they were included. Making notes that included bracketed impressions as artifacts and other unobtrusive data are collected will help a great deal when analysis processes are begun.

Some researchers assign numbers to individual pieces of unobtrusive data, then keep a separate record describing each numbered object, photo, description, document, or record. Others write brief notes and attach them directly to the unobtrusive data. Some develop elaborate cataloging systems, organizing files by date, site, type of data, or emerging themes. Others rely on less sophisticated organization schemes such as making piles in their offices (you should see my office when I am in the middle of a complex study). Individual style and the centrality of unobtrusive data to the research at hand will determine what kinds of systems will be used. The point here is that some kind of record keeping and organizing system is important in any study using unobtrusive data. The more central this type of data is to the accomplishment of the study, the more important it is to have a consistent way to keep track of what data are there and how they fit together.

There is nothing in the nature of unobtrusive data that makes them fit or not fit within any of the research paradigms outlined in chapter 1. How they might be used, of course, will be different in different kinds of studies. Postpositivist researchers will likely see unobtrusive data as a tool for verifying findings based on other data sources through systematic triangulation processes. Constructivists will likely see unobtrusive data as sources for generating other stories, constructing other realities, and, with participants, coconstructing other levels of meaning that add to the richness of their studies. Critical/feminist researchers will likely use unobtrusive data to expose the unequal distribution of resources and influence in the social groups they are studying and to trace the material consequences of that inequality in terms of race, gender, and/or class. Poststructuralists will likely use text-based unobtrusive data as sources for deconstructive analysis, searching for inconsistencies, aporia, or gaps that reveal the subjective, transitory, and power-infused nature of the supposed truth at the core of texts under examination.

So, for example, education researchers from any of these paradigmatic orientations might do a study of retention practices in a large urban school district. As part of their data, each might see the district's policy statement on retention as an important document to include, but each is likely to use this piece of unobtrusive data in very different ways. The postpositivist researcher might compare the statement with school-based informants' interview statements about how they make retention decisions. The constructivist might ask informants to discuss what the policy document means to them. Critical/feminists might look at other unobtrusive data, such as school records, to determine if district policy is being applied differently in schools with different racial and/or socioeconomic characteristics. Poststructuralists might systematically deconstruct the policy statement in terms of what it says about knowledge/power relationships. Unobtrusive data can be a powerful source of insight in many kinds of qualitative studies. Collecting them carefully and processing them systematically will improve the quality of unobtrusive data's contribution to any study.

COLLECTING OTHER TYPES OF DATA

In this section, I discuss three other types of data collection that are often used in qualitative studies: video recording, focus group interviewing, and participant journaling. These are not all of the possibilities that might be included, but they do represent data collection strategies that many of my students have found useful in their initial research efforts. My goal here is to give beginning researchers a sense of what is possible using these kinds of data collection. References provided throughout the discussion will lead those interested in learning more about particular strategies to sources of information and direction.

Using Video in Qualitative Studies

Visual anthropology, visual sociology, and other genres of image-based research have made important contributions to our understandings of how photography, film, video, and other visual media can be used in qualitative research. In this section, I will focus on uses of video recording as a data collection tool in qualitative educational studies. My own experiences, those of my students, and accounts in the literature lead me to believe that video recording can provide a powerful means for capturing data that can improve the quality of many studies. My approach here, as with my students, is to recommend that video recording be used along with, not instead of, other data collection approaches described in this chapter. I know that it is fully possible to do high-quality studies based only on video or other image-based data (see Prosser, 1998), but my view is that these should be undertaken only after specialized training. What follows are guidelines for using video data collection strategies as primary or secondary means of gathering qualitative data.

At one level, video recording can be thought of as having a documentary function, as a way of preserving a record in the same way a historian might make a written record. Such records are treated essentially as a special kind of unobtrusive data. At another level, video recording provides a way of capturing contextualized face-to-face social behavior in greater detail than can be accomplished using other means. These two aims are characterized by Erickson and Wilson (1982, p. 41) as, "to tell a summary story of what happened, or to make an exhaustive record that permits analysis of what happened." The later aim is our principal interest in this discussion.

Videotaping a science lesson using high-quality equipment can produce a record that can be used to produce very detailed transcripts of what occurred, be replayed over and over again to ensure accuracy and to pick up subtle details, document elements of context within the visual frame of the lens, and be analyzed in fine-grained ways that would not be possible with field-note records of the same event. Events such as science lessons are complex and fast moving, and video recordings provide ways to supplement and/or fill in field-note records in ways that improve the chances of capturing the complexity in spite of the speed. Facial expressions, nonverbal communications, and emotions that are often missed in field-note records can be captured on videotape. In addition, research teams or other researchers can "validate" individual interpretations by going back to the original recorded data (Marshall & Rossman, 1995).

Microethnographic studies offer the best examples of using video data to accomplish fine-grained analysis of everyday social interactions in classrooms (see Erickson, 1977; Erickson & Wilson, 1982; and discussion in chapter 1). Microethnographic work depends on a combination of field-note and videotape data that allows microanalysis processes "to identify the fundamental principles of social organization, and cultural patterning of that organization, according to which people make sense of the actions they and others take in the conduct of everyday life" (Erickson & Wilson, 1982, p. 43). In these studies, video records are the primary data source. That means they must contain as complete a record as possible of the continuous sequence of action involved in the events of interest. Written field-note records supplement video data.

Other kinds of studies also rely on videotaping as their primary data source. In some studies, videotapes of classroom action are played back for participants or others, and the discussions around the playback are recorded as an additional layer of video data (e.g., Silvers, 1977; Tobin, Wu, & Davidson, 1989). Such studies use the initial taped data to capture aspects of classroom life in the same ways that traditional field-work methods might be used, but they also provide a powerful stimulus to get individuals talking about their own perspectives and interpretations of behavior on the tape. Tobin, Wu, and Davidson (1989) taped classroom events in China, Japan, and the United States, then played the tapes from all three cultures to participants (including children) and other early childhood educators from all three cultures. They made video records of these viewing sessions, and information from the second layer of video data was the primary source for their "multivocal ethnography" (p. 4) of preschool in three cultures.

Videotaped data can also be used to supplement observation, interviewing, and unobtrusive data collection. They can be used to document one-time events such as plays, classroom visitors, or field trips, in which case they would be processed as a kind of unobtrusive record. They can also be used to capture a small number of events that are thought to represent other frequently occurring events that are recorded in field notes. For example, in a study of remedial reading programs, the researcher might observe teacher-child interactions in such programs over a period of months, then videotape a few instructional sessions in an effort to supplement the field-note analysis with the detailed analysis possible with video records. Also, video data can be collected simultaneously with field-note data then used to fill in protocols, making it possible to create a much more detailed record of classroom action.

Video data offer obvious advantages, but their collection has technical, economic, and ethical limitations. Even though advancing video technologies are more user friendly all the time, using video equipment effectively requires some technical skill. The better the equipment is for making clear video and audio recording, the more complex the technology involved. Putting wireless microphones on multiple children in a classroom or using more than one camera to capture the same event are examples of how technological issues can quickly go beyond the expertise of the ordinary researcher. Also, I have learned from my own limited experience with video recording that playback equipment for filling in field-note data or doing microanalysis needs to be more sophisticated than ordinary VCRs, or processing data will slow to a near halt. Buying or renting video equipment of the quality needed will be very expensive, as will hiring individuals with specialized technical expertise. Most graduate students and many new researchers will not have outside funding or personal resources to acquire state-of-the-art equipment or hire technical expertise.

Confidentiality is a key concept in agreements of informed consent. It is much more difficult to ensure confidentiality to participants when their faces, voices, and actions are recorded on videotape. Since it will be impossible to disguise participant identities, the handling of video data will be of great concern as research bargains are struck. In an age where television news programs broadcast scenes from everyday life every night of the week, participants deserve guarantees that records of their lives will be used for research purposes only. Exactly how data will be used, how they will be stored, and who will have access must be spelled out as part of informed consent. Long- and short-term usage should be specified as well. If there is a chance that any part of the video footage might be used for purposes other than data analysis (e.g., as part of presentations, training films, or coursework examples), participants must be aware of this possibility at the outset and have the chance to veto such uses after they have had the opportunity to view the footage in question (see Erickson & Wilson, 1982).

Another limitation that has technical and ethical implications is the obtrusiveness of video taping in educational settings. Again, the more complex the equipment, the more likely the intrusion. My experience is that individuals, particularly children, soon get used to having microphones, video cameras, and even technicians around, but the impact of their presence on settings, events, and actions should not be underestimated (Marshall & Rossman, 1995). As suggestions for collecting video data are outlined below, technical ways to limit obtrusiveness will be discussed. In terms of the ethical concerns associated with intruding in the lives of others, I agree with Erickson and Wilson's (1982) general approach that rapport is more important than data when obtrusiveness becomes an issue. In their words,

If any technical maneuver that is convenient for you is obtrusive or inter-feres with the action of the setting—a route for stringing a power cord, the placement of a camera, the timing of your movement to correct camera focus—sacrifice the technical matter rather than inconvenience the people you are filming. (P. 47)

I will conclude this section with tips for collecting and processing video data as part of qualitative studies in education settings. The suggestions are made in an effort to optimize the effectiveness of using this type of data, and it is understood that adjustments will need to be made based on the particulars of individual studies and circumstances.

- *Make decisions about what to video based on research design.* Video data are difficult and expensive to collect and cumbersome to process. Just setting a camera on a tripod and taping continuously is likely to be ineffective as well as inefficient. It is better to think carefully about what is to be recorded, when, and why. As studies are designed, the place of video (and all types of qualitative data) should be carefully considered, and decisions about what to video should follow from the research questions at the base of the design (see Marshall & Rossman, 1995). More is not necessarily better when it comes to video data. It is wiser and more effi-cient to be strategic about using video as primary or secondary data. As with observation and interviewing, analyzing data as they are gathered will help shape the selection of what to tape as studies proceed.

- *Select equipment carefully.* Knowing what you want your video data to do for you will help you decide what to buy or rent. If you want to record conver-sations between children on a playground, you will need different micro-phones and cameras than if you are taping parent-child interactions in their home. Classrooms are busy and often noisy places. My experience in early childhood classrooms is that it is virtually impossible to get good sound quality from microphones built into video cameras and that clarity is diffi-cult even with external microphones because background noise often makes understanding individual comments problematic. Special vests with built-in microphones have been used in studies involving children, and teachers are sometimes willing to wear wireless microphones with battery packs that can be placed in a pocket. Standard video cameras with tripods and zoom lenses meet the needs of most educational researchers, but special studies may require higher-quality cameras and lenses. Most universities have individuals with the technical expertise necessary to informing good decisions about equipment selection and utilization.

- *Become familiar with equipment and procedures before going into the field.* The first morning of data collection is not the time to learn how to set up microphones and operate cameras. Researchers and/or technicians should practice setting up equipment ahead of time and rehearse anticipated taping strategies prior to going to the field (see Erickson & Wilson, 1982). The practice will be an opportunity to be sure that equipment is working properly and that operators are comfortable and confident working with it. Obtrusiveness is increased greatly when research staff does not have specific routines for setting up and breaking down recording equipment. Whenever possible, set-up and break-down should happen before and after participants are present in the setting. Taping strategies and locations should be scripted ahead of time as much as possible and reviewed just before data collection is to begin so that confusion and disruption during taping are kept to a minimum. It's a good idea to test equipment on site to be sure everything is working properly.

- *Build in time for participants to get used to being videotaped.* Erickson and Wilson (1982) recommend a period of adjustment wherein data collection takes second place to helping participants get used to being taped. They suggest showing samples of taped segments to participants, so they can see themselves "acting in mundane events in competent ways" (p. 46). These researchers contend that this playback will quickly become boring to adults and children because they will already know what happened, and it will serve to reduce their anxiety about being recorded.

- *Keep movement and conversation to a minimum while in the research setting.* This is good general advice for gathering any kind of data directly from the setting, but it is especially important when taping. While adults and children become used to having microphones hanging from the ceiling or from their necks and forget that a camera is recording their every action, when researchers/technicians move microphones, zoom lenses, or adjust camera angles, attention is drawn back on them and the equipment. That does not mean that taking these actions is prohibited; they may be prudent and necessary. It does mean that changes should be minimized and that, whenever possible, they should be made during natural transitions in the setting being studied. In addition, conversation between researchers and/or technicians should be keep to a minimum. This calls for planning ahead of time and the development of special nonverbal signals to facilitate making necessary changes with minimum disruption.

- *Create a system for keeping track of what has been taped.* As with all of the data collection strategies described, ways to make a record of what video has been collected in what settings need to be initiated from the outset of data collection. For me, this is another dimension of a research log, but others may have other means of keeping up with their data. In any case, a record that shows the dates, times, settings, and circumstances of video taping needs to be kept. If field notes have been taken along with video recording, real time notations should be kept in the field notes as well as a record of what times video recording started and stopped. In addition, field notes should identify key individuals and describe particular elements of context that will help with analysis of taped events. A system of marking and indexing tapes is also essential. Most video cameras have a mechanism for marking the tape itself with date and time. This should be used, but tape cartridges and boxes should also be marked with sufficient information that the particulars of the session will be clear later on. Having dates, times, and places may be sufficient on the tapes themselves, as long as more detailed information is included in the research log under the same date, time, and place. It is also a good idea to make copies of tapes and carefully index these copies before analysis processes begin. You can imagine the nightmare of losing data that have not been backed up.

In sum, video recording can provide a powerful data source for qualitative studies. The use of video cameras can provide detailed and accurate information about what was said and done in particular social settings that other data collection strategies cannot match. When used carefully alongside other data collection strategies, video recording can be a valuable tool for improving the quality of qualitative studies.

Doing Focus Group Interviews

Focus group interviewing was described in chapter 1 as a distinct kind of qualitative research that has its own history and literature (see Berg, 1998; Morgan, 1997). While it is possible to apply focus group methods developed in sociology and marketing to self-contained studies in education settings, many qualitative researchers adapt focus group techniques as supplemental sources of data. In these studies, focus group data are collected along with other kinds of data that might include observations, individual interviews, and unobtrusive data. As with the other strategies in this section, focus group interviewing will be discussed here as a secondary data source that can be useful in enriching the overall data sets of qualitative studies. Other sources should be consulted if focus groups are to be used as free-standing qualitative data (e.g., Greenbaum, 1998; Krueger, 1994; Merton, Fiske, & Kendall, 1990; Morgan, 1993, 1997; Stewart & Shamdasani, 1990; Vaughn, Schumm, & Sinagub, 1996).

I considered calling the methods discussed in this section just "group interviews" instead of focus group interviews. But, as Morgan (1997) points out, focus group interviews are more than just interviewers asking questions of informants in a group setting. Focus group interviews rely on the interactions that take place among participants in the group to generate data. The interviewer typically acts as a moderator who encourages participants to generate discussion around particular topics. The goal of focus groups is to create conversation that allows participants to explore a topic in depth (Vaughn, Schumm, & Sinagub, 1996). It is the interaction among those participating that gives focus group data their unique character.

What are some of the advantages and disadvantages of focus group data collection? The major advantage of focus groups is their capacity to produce "concentrated data on precisely the topic of interest" (Morgan, 1997, p. 13). They are called "focus groups" because they are designed to focus on a particular topic. Such a focus can generate a lot of data in a relatively short period of time as compared to observations and individual interviews. Another strength is that they have the capacity to capture the dynamics of group interaction that are unavailable in individual interviews and may be few and far between in observation studies. A record of how meaning is negotiated in groups is powerful data that is hard to come by using other strategies. In addition, being interviewed in groups gives informants a sense of security and comfort that may lead to more candid and reflective responses than in individual interviews (Hillebrandt, 1979). Being in a group may make participants more willing to express opinions that they perceive might not fit with researcher expectations. And finally, focus groups offer the advantage of giving participants a say in how the direction of the interview ought to go. While moderators are prepared with specific questions, they are sensitive to going where the group wants to go with particular topics, and this opens the opportunity for richer, more meaningful data (Byers & Wilcox, 1991).

Each of these advantages has a potential dark side. For the sake of efficiency, focus group moderators may take too much control of the interview and limit the range of responses that participants make. The issue of control is central in focus group research. The more control the researcher has, the less natural the conversation is likely to be (Morgan, 1997). Similarly, group interaction in the special circumstances of the focus group interview may not represent how such interaction might take place in more natural settings. So, the group dynamics information available really only tells you about social interaction *in focus groups*. Not all participants will feel comfortable and secure speaking up in group settings. Some may be reluctant to be candid with a group of strangers, and some will be reticent about speaking at all in group situations. This may lead to findings that are biased in the direction of those who talk more or are more assertive in making their points to the rest of the group. Allowing groups too much flexibility, obviously, could lead to interview sessions that produce little useful data on the topic at hand.

It is clear that focus group strategies offer advantages and disadvantages for qualitative researchers. Understanding these strengths and weaknesses can help researchers decide if focus group methods are appropriate for their studies and help them take steps to monitor and adjust to issues of control, efficiency, naturalness, candor, participation, and researcher/moderator influence.

How should focus group techniques be used in qualitative studies in education settings? It depends on research purposes and questions. They can be the only data source for some studies, but here we are more interested in looking at how focus groups can be used to supplement and enrich data from other sources. In traditional marketing research, focus groups are often used in preliminary stages as a basis for refining other data collection tools such as structured interviews or questionnaires. While this may have a place in some qualitative studies, preliminary focus group work would more often lead to helping qualitative researchers develop individual open-ended interviews or shape plans for observation. For example, a researcher interested in studying campus fraternity issues might start with focus group interviews to get a sense of what those issues might be, then use interviewing and/or observation to capture more in-depth insights into particular issues.

Focus groups can also be used to follow up on observations or individual interviews. I am currently working with a student who is doing individual interviews with selected beginning teachers in an effort to identify areas of focus for a planned series of group interviews. She is interested in how new teachers are socialized into the profession and how they share, reflect, and offer support in the group setting. This student plans to follow up in the other direction as well. Teachers will be interviewed one-on-one again after the focus group cycle to explore individual perspectives that may be underrepresented in the group interviews (see Morgan, 1997). A pattern of following up observations with focus groups (and vice versa) is also possible. Observations can produce topics for focus group discussion, and discussions can give direction to future observations. Using focus groups and other data collection strategies "in series" can be an effective strategy for exploring topics from different perspectives.

In some studies, focus group data can be a valuable source for research triangulation. When particular social phenomena are under investigation, having data from a variety of sources can be very powerful. Here the intent may not be to explicitly follow up on one source with data from another but to collect data on the same phenomenon from a variety of sources. In a study of community attitudes about charter schools, for example, data from individual interviews; observations from public hearings; and unobtrusive data such as minutes from public meetings, internal communications, and newspaper accounts may be triangulated with data from focus groups made up of individuals who represent multiple community perspectives.

Decisions about when and how to use focus groups should be made based on the particulars of the setting, the goals of the study, and the research questions at hand (Stewart & Shamdasani, 1990). Not all studies will be improved with focus group methods. There will be times when focus groups are inappropriate, unnecessary, or not feasible. Vaughn and her colleagues (Vaughn, Schumm, & Sinagub, 1996) recommend that focus groups are most appropriate for studies that are "exploratory or explanatory in nature" (p. 34). For me, focus groups work best when research questions are set up to explore the perspectives of particular groups on particular topics. These groups need not be homogeneous, but they do need to be describable; that is, readers of the research will need to know the makeup of the groups whose perspectives are being reported. Adding insights from focus group interviews to individual interviews, observations, and/or unobtrusive data collection can improve the depth and richness of understandings gained. As outlined in the focus group section in chapter 1, focus group methods will be used in different ways by researchers coming from different paradigms. Understanding the assumptions at the base of those paradigms is as essential to designing focus group strategies as any other methodological tool.

What do I need to do to prepare for focus group interviews? Selection of participants is a key issue in this kind of work. To take full advantage of the strengths of focus group techniques, the general rule is to select strangers with some shared characteristics or experiences. Individuals who are familiar with each other engage in conversations based on what they assume they already know about one another and one another's perspectives. They take things for granted in group interactions that will have to be explicated among strangers, and what they take for granted is often the stuff of interest to the interviewer, so using participants who know each other is usually avoided.

Having shared characteristics or experiences means that participants, who will likely be strangers, will have something to say about the focus of the study and be willing to talk about it. If gathering opinions from a random sample of the population is the goal, other methods will be much more efficient. Here we are interested in going more deeply into people's perspectives, and focus groups are often put together in ways designed to get at the understandings of identifiable groups. Segmenting groups by such characteristics as sex, age, race, class, and socioeconomic status is a common practice in focus group interviewing (Morgan, 1997). Some individuals will be uncomfortable talking about some subjects with others having different characteristics. For example, individuals from backgrounds in which English is a second language may not feel comfortable speaking up about language arts curriculum issues in a group that includes native English speakers. While interesting interactions might be possible in a mixed group, putting together multiple homogeneous groups so that the groups

[handwritten marginal notes, left side, rotated:] select strangers with some shared experience / ~ characteristics

[handwritten marginal notes, left side, rotated:] will have something to say about topic and willing to talk

represent a variety of backgrounds might be a better strategy for encouraging candid and balanced participation.

Most texts on focus group interviewing recommend that group size be kept in the six to 12 range. The idea is to have enough individuals to generate and maintain a discussion but not so many that some individuals will have a hard time getting the floor. I like Morgan's (1997) recommendation that size issues be decided based on the purposes of the research and the kinds of questions being asked. On the one hand, if the participants have strong connections to intense issues, then having fewer in the group will make sense. Small numbers will give individuals room for going more deeply into a topic than will be possible with many participants. On the other hand, if issues are more general and are likely to raise less strong emotional reactions, then larger numbers may be better so that more individuals will be there to share in keeping the discussion going.

Issues of how many interviews to have are also related to research questions and goals. If the researcher is using a purposive sampling procedure (Vaughn, Schumm, & Sinagub, 1996) to identify groups with different characteristics (as suggested in the language arts example above), then several group sessions will be needed. Morgan (1997) says that three to five group sessions is the rule of thumb for most studies, but that this should be taken as a starting place, not a hard and fast rule. For example, if there are many differences of opinion within groups as discussions take place, more sessions will be needed; and if the meetings are more open-ended than "standardized," more sessions will be needed. Unless strict timelines prohibit flexibility, I recommend proposing a range rather than a set number of focus groups as research proposals are put together. Committees and potential participants can understand that decisions about how many focus groups to have may change as studies unfold.

A basic question that must be addressed at the planning stage is who will lead the focus group interviews. In marketing research, trained moderators are usually hired to lead discussions, while researchers help design the focus groups, develop questions, and analyze data. This is a tricky issue in educational research, where questions are usually different and budgets are usually small. The advantages of a moderator are that this person is primarily interested in facilitating group processes and does not have a particular interest in the outcomes of the discussion. When researchers act as group leaders, it may be difficult for them not to subtly interject their own perspectives into the conversation or to ask questions that may lead the discussion in ways that might be biased toward getting certain kinds of data. In addition, the skills of group facilitation are complex, and not all researchers will be adept a leading groups. However, knowing the subject well and having a good idea of what kinds of data will be useful can be positive attributes of researchers as moderators. Whatever the decision, the study will be changed because of it, and this will become an important feature that needs to be made clear in final reports. I am not against students leading their own focus groups so long as they clearly acknowledge the limitations of such an approach and do all they can to monitor the possible effects of doing so.

Deciding where to hold focus group interviews is also an important consideration. At the least, they must be held in places that are comfortable and allow for accurate audio recording (Morgan, 1997). The ideal is probably a conference room with a large oval table. If rooms are too large, it is hard to develop a sense of connectedness among participants and sound quality is often a problem. If it's too small, the space may cramp participants and make them feel confined. Rectangular tables will make it difficult for leaders and group members to make eye contact with other participants. Places should be accessible to all participants, and accommodations for parking should be taken into account. In order to encourage comfort and candor, it may also be a good idea to move the interviews away from the workplaces of participants. Places where interruptions can be kept to an absolute minimum are preferred. Many large cities and some universities have spaces designed specifically for doing such interviews; however the costs of renting such spaces will be prohibitive for most students.

Recording equipment should be of high quality, and microphones designed to capture sounds from many directions should be used. The researcher should be thoroughly familiar with equipment operation before coming to the research setting, equipment should be tested in the setting prior to beginning sessions, and back-up equipment should be at the ready. Individuals with expertise in using recording equipment should be consulted as decisions are made about what to use, how to place it, and what to do if things don't work as expected. If ten people are giving their time, it is imperative that the researcher be ready to go ahead with an interview. Having the right equipment and having it in good working order are essential to recording data in the focus group.

I recommend using audio recording for focus groups and staying away from videotaping. Assuring confidentiality becomes an issue when video is used, and participants will be less comfortable and less likely to share sensitive information when they know a video camera is running. In addition, it is difficult to place a camera in a room set up for focus groups. If the goal is for all participants to be able to see one another, it will be hard to place a camera where it will be able to focus on each participant's face. The advantages of using video (e.g., to capture facial expressions, body language, and other nonverbal behaviors) are usually outweighed by the disadvantages listed above. While there may be cases where this is the exception, for most focus group studies, high-quality audiotaping is sufficient.

As with individual interviews, guiding questions should be written in preparation for focus groups. The rationale is the same. Even though the discussion will take on a life of its own once the session begins, the researcher/moderator needs to have a road map of where he or she wants the discussion to go. Guiding questions will give group leaders a way to keep track of the progress of the group and steer discussions in desirable directions. Like guiding questions discussed above, these are likely to begin with warm-up questions to introduce the group and orient participants to the topic at hand, move to more focused questions as the session proceeds, and give opportunities near the end for individuals to summarize their perspectives. Questions should be open-ended, should not lead participants in certain directions, and should encourage the airing of different points of view. Bringing guiding questions to the interview will give the researcher/moderator a sense of security and a way to go if things don't play out as planned.

How do I lead a focus group interview? In this discussion, I will assume the researcher will be leading the interviews. In cases where moderators are utilized, it will be important to work closely with these individuals so that they understand their role in relation to the research process and that researcher and moderator have a shared understanding of how the groups will be conducted (see Vaughn, Schumm, & Sinagub, 1996). What follows are some tips for conducting focus group interviews for researchers who are also acting as moderators:

- *Allow some time before interviews begin to meet each participant and to give participants the chance to meet each other.* Light refreshments and soft drinks and coffee are often made available so that participants have a chance to relax and chat before interviews start. Still, a specific starting time should be specified so that the time will be well spent.

- *Give participants a brief overview of what your expectations are for the focus group and review some ground rules for participation.* Remind everyone of the purposes of the research, give them a general overview of the topic(s) to be discussed, and thank them for agreeing to help out. Tell the group how the session will proceed and estimate how long it will last. Explain that there are no "right answers" to any of the questions, that each person's point of view is valued, and that everyone's participation is valued. Encourage them to listen to each other and talk one at a time. It is acceptable to disagree with other participants' ideas but not acceptable to attack them personally.

- *Start with an "icebreaker."* Rather than going directly to the topic, give participants a chance to introduce themselves and perhaps share a little background information. This can range from just telling where they are from and where they work to asking about their direct experience with the topic at hand. For instance, if the topic is posttenure review and participants are invited from various local institutions of higher education, they might quickly say what the policy is at their college or university.

• *Get a meaningful opening statement from each participant.* This strategy is designed as a discussion starter. It's a way to get folks talking about the topic and signals the group that everyone's input is desired. Morgan (1997) recommends that the questions designed to get discussion started be interesting and easy to answer. He also suggests that individuals be given thinking time before answering and that it be stressed that further discussion (not consensus) is the desired outcome.

• *Build on the opening statements as guiding questions are addressed.* Here is a place where considerable skill will be required. The goal is to guide conversation among participants around the topic without making the interview a recitation activity—each participant answering the researcher's questions in series. Listening carefully and making notes of individual comments and then tying these to the guiding questions will make the group move more smoothly and encourage more interaction among participants.

• *Keep the conversation focused on the topic.* It is hard to encourage spontaneous conversation and stay on the topic, but this is part of the moderator role. People may leave the focus group feeling good, but unless the topic under investigation was discussed in some depth, the interview may produce data that are not helpful to the researcher. When the conversation wanders, bringing it back to the topic needs to be done delicately. People are interested in how they are doing during the interview (Vaughn, Schumm, & Sinagub, 1996), so praising individuals for their comments is important (and putting them down is unacceptable). It is acceptable to say, "Let's get back to the issue of posttenure review. Bill what have your experiences been like?" And it is acceptable to say, "Let's move on to my next question" as a way to move back to the topic. The trick is to not let the conversation go too far astray without making someone feel uncomfortable when you bring the talk back to the area of focus.

• *Encourage participants to be specific and use examples.* Guiding questions should be set up in a pattern that moves from generalizations to more specific instances and examples. As with individual interviews, stories of specific examples make powerful data. In addition, being specific forces individuals with different experiences and perspectives to confront differences that may be masked by general statements (Merton, Fiske, & Kendall, 1990). Using prompts and probes can be a useful tool for encouraging participants to go more deeply and give specific examples. For example, two universities may both have posttenure review policies, but the details and enactment of those policies are likely to be very different. By probing responses from representatives from those institutions, those differences can be drawn out.

- *Monitor and balance participation.* In most groups, some individuals will have more to say than others. It is my experience that there is little relationship between the willingness of a person to speak and the value of what he or she has to say. Monitoring who is speaking and who is not is an important part of doing focus group interviewing. There are ways to balance participation by how you attend to responses, how you organize interactions, and how you direct questions. Individuals who dominate conversation to the point that others are not being heard can be asked directly (and with good humor) to allow others to go first so that everyone gets a chance to be heard. Moderators can also use hand signals and eye contact as ways to limit talking that has gone on too long (see Langer, 1992). Individuals who have not participated much can be encouraged directly ("What do you think about that, Mary?"), or questions can be framed so that everyone has a chance to respond ("Let's start by having everyone answer this question in a sentence or two"). If ground rules have been established, referring back to these in a gentle way can be a way to remind participants that everyone's ideas are important.

- *Give closure to the session.* As the session winds down, let participants know that there are only a few minutes left. It is often a good idea to give each a chance to make a closing statement. This can be framed as a chance for them to summarize their perspective, to add something they left out, or to express their feelings about the experience. In any case, the idea is for each member and the group at large to gain a sense of closure. Researchers should take this opportunity as well to congratulate participants on their group process skills, to acknowledge their importance to the study, and to thank them for their participation.

How do I process focus group data? Once focus groups are completed, the first step is to make a duplicate copy of the audiotape, then to transcribe it or have it transcribed by others. It is expected that researchers will have taken notes during the interviews, and these will be helpful in making a rich and accurate transcription. If others are doing the transcriptions, researchers should listen to the tape and check it against the typed transcript and notes taken during the interview. A complete record of the particulars of each interview should be carefully recorded in the research log. It is vital to know who the participants where, what was discussed, and when and where the interviews took place. Following the procedures for handing individual interview data detailed above will be a good guide for focus group work as well.

In sum, focus group interviews can be a valuable tool for qualitative researchers in education. They can be especially useful as supplementary data in studies using observation and individual interviewing. They provide a way to capture group processes around a topic of interest and generate concentrated data on areas of particular focus. Considerable planning and skill are required to use focus groups effectively, but these are worth the trouble to researchers interested in understanding group perspectives on particular social phenomena.

Using Participant Journaling as Data

A final supplementary data source to be discussed in this chapter is the use of journals kept by participants at the request of researchers. These journals are different from the diaries and journals discussed above as unobtrusive data. Individual diaries or personally initiated journals are unobtrusive data because they would have been produced even if the research were not done. Participant journaling is a strategic data collection strategy that researchers build into their studies. As part of research bargains, participants agree to keep some kind of written record of their experiences and reflections during the research process. These records are shared with researchers and become data for their studies. While I am sure studies have been done using this as the sole data source, the discussion here will assume journaling of this type will be supplementary to other qualitative data collection strategies.

The act of writing things down encourages individuals to process and reflect on experiences in different ways than thinking about them or discussing them with others (Johnstone, 1994). This is one of the reasons why so many individuals keep their own diaries and journals, why reflective writing is a part of many action research projects (Newman, 1998), and why instructors often assign journal writing as part of course requirements when they are trying to encourage students to become more reflective (Emig, 1977; Fulwiler, 1987). Qualitative researchers are especially interested in how individuals understand the social circumstances in which they operate, and asking them to make written reflections on their experiences can be a powerful way to get another take on participant perspectives.

Journaling can be used along with any other types of qualitative data collection. Researchers doing observation studies sometimes ask those being observed to keep a record of their perspectives during the research cycle. For example, one of my students observed interactions between interns and mentoring teachers throughout the cycle of a year-long internship, asking teachers and interns to make weekly journal entries in which they reflected on their interactions with each other during the week. Journal keeping can be used as part of interview studies as well. A doctoral student from Australia I advised designed a study of teachers' professional development that included interviews and journal keeping as important data. In the focus group discussion above, I mentioned a student doing a study of new teachers using focus group and individual interviews. That student is also planning to ask participants to write reflections using email following each focus group session as a way to capture individual perspectives on what happened in the group. A wide variety of studies that seek to capture participant perspectives from the inside out can benefit from using journaling, but an examination of the strengths and weaknesses will help determine if this strategy is a good fit for particular studies.

The most obvious strength of journals as data is that they can provide a direct path into the insights of participants. Some individuals are comfortable expressing their feelings, ideas, and insights in writing, and these can be powerful data that reveal how they are understanding the phenomena under investigation. These data have a slightly different nature because they are not processed through a researcher; they come directly from the participant. Of course, researchers still have to interpret these data as analyses are made, and participants are aware as they write that entries will be read by researchers. Still, the quality of data is different because it flows directly from the participant to the page (or computer screen) without passing through a researcher who is making a record of the data in some way.

Another strength is the flexibility of journaling. Participants can make entries at their leisure. Special interviews do not need to be scheduled and organized, observations do not need to be made, and unobtrusive data do not need to be found and gathered. Entries can be written whenever the participant gets the chance and feels comfortable doing so.

An additional strength is the usefulness of journal data in guiding the direction of other data collection methods. If informants write in their journals that individual or group interviews are missing some important facet of the research, adjustments can be made for future interviews. If journal entries reveal that participants are uncomfortable with observation patterns, efforts to improve the quality of researcher-participant relations with them can be undertaken. It is possible to make journaling an interactive process, in which the researcher writes back in response to the participants' revelations. This can be a powerful tool for generating data and for making adjustments as the study progresses, but it changes the nature of the data, and procedures should be carefully reported so that readers understand the different qualities of such data in comparison to one-way journaling.

My students have found the biggest drawback of using journals as a data collection tool is the time and effort required of participants to keep up with doing journals. School people are busy, and finding time to sit down and write about their experiences and feelings is difficult. While many are inclined to reflect in writing and enjoy the task, others find it difficult and burdensome. Another problem is that some individuals are adept at putting their ideas and feelings into words, and others are not. So the quality of reflexive thinking that is desirable in qualitative data collection of this type (Hammersley & Atkinson, 1983) varies from writer to writer. Related to this problem is the issue of writing *for* the researcher. Some participants will feel constrained because they feel they have to write something even if they don't want to, and some will shape their reflections based on trying to meet the expectations of the researcher. The negative effects of these drawbacks can be reduced by clearly communicating the expectation that the participants' genuine perspectives and reactions are what the researcher is interested in, that whatever level of reflexivity participants are capable of is just fine, and that entries do not have to be of a certain length. This will mean that the researcher will have to engage in yet another balancing act, trying to make reluctant journal keepers comfortable and still get useful data. Other suggestions for using this type of data collection include the following:

- *Be clear about writing expectations when participants are selected.* If journal writing is a key element to the data of the study, selecting participants who are willing and able to write useful entries is important. It is possible to use the ability to reflect in writing as a selection criterion in some studies, in which case experience doing personal journals or evidence of written reflections might be appropriate. In any case, participants must know that writing will be expected, and how much writing, how often, and for what purposes must be spelled out before they agree to join the study.

- *Give clear directions about journal topics.* Individuals have difficulty with journal tasks that are global or undefined. If they are told to just write about anything, they will likely write about nothing. While the researcher may not want to dictate exact topics, it will work out better if participants are invited to write about their experiences, thoughts, and feelings about a particular incident ("Pick something that stands out in your mind about student misbehavior"), a particular time period ("Write about something that happened in reading group this week"), or a particular topic ("How do you feel about athletics and academics?"). Some studies will be set up so that informants know that they are to write about their experiences dealing with the substance of the research but may still need direction and support as the time passes. Other studies will not have such clear objectives for journal writing. In either case, care needs to be taken to be clear about expectations initially and as the study progresses.

- *Process journal data in an ongoing way.* Don't wait until the end of the study to collect journal entries. If you wait, you may be surprised at what you get, and it will be too late to do anything about it. If individuals are not keeping up with their journal writing, write very little, or are writing off the topic, your data will be thin or worse. By setting up regular intervals at which time journal entries will be collected and processed, you will be able to monitor what kind of data you are getting and help shape the quality of data from that point on. The point is not to threaten participants so that they will do a better job, but to let them know that journals will be collected at certain times so that they can plan their time accordingly. Setting up journaling as an interactive venture between participant and researcher is a way to shape responses and encourage reflection, but as above, this does change the nature of the data.

- *Give participants credit for keeping up with their journals.* Journal writing takes time and energy, and participants should be praised for their efforts and congratulated for their contributions to your research. Acknowledging the efforts required of busy people to participate in any data collection effort is important to maintaining positive participant-researcher relations. It is especially important to recognize the discipline and effort it takes to sit down and write when the researcher is not there and so many other important things wait to be done. Honest expressions of appreciation go a long way to making participants feel like their contributions are valued.

Video recording, focus group interviewing, and participant journaling can be useful strategies for collecting supplementary qualitative data. Each strategy has its own special strengths and weaknesses that should be weighed carefully before researchers make decisions about applications. These decisions should be made on the basis of how the strategy will help researchers answer their research questions within the framework of their research assumptions. Deciding to use videotape, focus groups, or journals, then looking for a topic to study turns the logic of sound research on its head. All decisions about data collection should be based on how well certain choices provide data that will allow researchers to address the purposes and questions that drive their studies. This section has highlighted the possibilities of using three alternatives that may be useful in doing just that.

CRITERIA FOR ASSESSING DATA COLLECTION ADEQUACY

The questions in this section offer a guide for making judgments about the adequacy of data collection in qualitative studies. The questions are organized into a set of general questions that parallel questions concerning data collection design from Chapter 2 and separate sets of questions from each section of this chapter—one set each for observation, interviewing, unobtrusive data collection, and other types of data (video, focus groups, and participant journals). As judgments are being made, it is important to keep the special nature of each research project in mind. Once again, students must have an answer to each question that applies to their studies—not *the* answer, but an answer that fits within the internal logic of their research paradigm and that addresses the special circumstances of their study. Every qualitative researcher must answer the general questions. Specific methodological choices will dictate which other question sets will need to be addressed.

General Questions for Assessing Data Collection Adequacy

1. Are the data of the study described?
2. Is it clear how and when the data were collected?
3. Do the data make sense given the paradigmatic assumptions of the study?
4. Are the research questions answerable given the data described?

Questions for Assessing Observation Data Adequacy

1. Is the researcher's level of involvement in the research scene described and justified?
2. Are procedures for taking raw field notes clearly described?
3. Do field notes represent an accurate descriptive account of participants' words and actions?
4. Are the contexts of the study well described?
5. Are procedures for filling in research protocols from raw field notes well described?
6. Were field notes filled in as soon as possible after leaving the field?
7. Are impressions, feelings, and initial interpretations bracketed in field notes and protocols?
8. Was a research journal kept to record the affective experience of doing the research?
9. Was a research log kept to record exactly what data were collected, where, and when during the study?
10. Do the data of the study cover a full cycle of the activity under investigation?

Questions for Assessing Interview Data Adequacy

1. Are the kinds of qualitative interviews used in the study described and justified?
2. Are procedures for selecting interview informants described and justified?

3. Were appropriate guiding questions written in preparation for interviews?
   A. Were they open-ended?
   B. Were they clear and understandable to informants?
   C. Were they neutral (i.e., nonleading)?
   D. Did they reflect the purposes of the research?
4. Were appropriate prompts and probes used during the interviews?
5. Were taped interviews transcribed and transcriptions checked against the original recordings as soon as possible following the interviews?
6. Was a research journal kept to record the affective experience of doing the research?
7. Was a research log kept to record exactly what data were collected, where, when, and from whom during the study?

Questions for Assessing Unobtrusive Data Adequacy

1. Are the kinds of unobtrusive data used in the study described and justified?
2. Are the procedures for collecting unobtrusive data clearly described and justified?
3. Do the unobtrusive data collected help answer the research questions and accomplish the research purposes?
4. Was a systematic record keeping or cataloging system established to keep track of unobtrusive data?

Questions for Assessing Video Data Adequacy

1. Are the ways video data are used in the study described and justified?
2. Are procedures for collecting video data clearly described and justified?
3. Was video data collection kept as unobtrusive as possible in the research setting?
4. Do the video data collected help answer the research questions and accomplish the research purposes?
5. Was a system for keeping track of video data established and followed?

Questions for Assessing Focus Group Data Adequacy

1. Are the ways focus group data are used in the study described and justified?
2. Are procedures for selecting interview participants described and justified?
3. Are the size of groups and number of group interviews described and justified?
4. Is the role of the moderator clearly described and justified?
5. Are focus group contexts described, and were settings appropriate for facilitating group discussion?

6. Were appropriate guiding questions written in preparation for interviews?
7. Were taped focus group interviews transcribed and transcriptions checked against the original recordings as soon as possible following the focus groups?
8. Was a research log kept to record exactly what data were collected, where, when, and from whom during the study?

Questions for Assessing Participant Journal Data Adequacy

1. Are the ways participant journaling are used in the study described and justified?
2. Are procedures for selecting participants to keep journals described and justified?
3. Were participants clearly informed about journal writing expectations, and were they given clear directions about journal topics?
4. Do the journal data collected help answer the research questions and accomplish the research purposes?

CHAPTER FOUR

Analyzing Qualitative Data

How do I make sense of the mountain of data I have collected? How do I start to analyze my data? How will I know when I am finished? How exactly do I do data analysis? This last question is one I hear all the time. Even students who have taken the courses and read the books still ask, "How do I analyze my data?" As someone who teaches some of the courses and recommends many of the books, I am sometimes frustrated that they seem genuinely to have no clue.

While acknowledging the complex and idiosyncratic nature of data analysis processes, one of my objectives in writing this book was to provide first-time qualitative researchers with frameworks that would provide enough guidance to actually allow them to do qualitative data analysis. Looking at the books I had been recommending left me with the sense that, with few exceptions, data analysis processes have not been well described in the literature. In volumes of 300 pages, as few as 9 or 10 pages have been devoted to data analysis. When full chapters are devoted to data analysis, the information provided is often general and abstract, leaving new researchers without much concrete guidance. Data analysis is portrayed as messy, cumbersome, inductive, creative, challenging, subjective, nonlinear, labor-intensive, exhilarating, and time-consuming; but analysis processes are seldom spelled out with sufficient clarity that novice researchers are confident at getting started.

Postpositivist researchers get the most guidance from the literature (e.g., Glaser & Strauss, 1967; Miles & Huberman, 1994; Spradley, 1980). This makes sense since research methods in this paradigm are characterized by much more structure than procedures used in other approaches. Constructivist researchers often adapt data analysis procedures developed by postpositivists (e.g., Goetz & LeCompte, 1984; Lincoln & Guba, 1985; Van Manen, 1990), and this makes sense as well, given that both are interested in uncovering "reality"—one, the reality presumed to exist in nature, and the other, the realities constructed by social participants. Critical/feminist researchers often use data collection methods adapted from postpositivist approaches, but their emphasis on the political nature of knowledge leads them to analyses that are undertaken within particular political frames of reference (e.g., Carr, 1995; DeVault, 1990, Reinharz, 1992). Data analysis is more difficult to characterize for poststructuralist researchers. Those who gather data using methods adapted from other paradigms will adapt analysis procedures as well; those doing deconstructive or genealogical work have their own analytic approaches that have closer connections to continental philosophy and postmodern literary criticism than traditional qualitative research (see Flax, 1990; Graham, Doherty, & Malek, 1992; Sarap, 1993). I will try to make paradigmatic similarities and differences in relation to data analysis clearer as the chapter unfolds.

Data analysis is a systematic search for meaning. It is a way to process qualitative data so that what has been learned can be communicated to others. Analysis means organizing and interrogating data in ways that allow researchers to see patterns, identify themes, discover relationships, develop explanations, make interpretations, mount critiques, or generate theories. It often involves synthesis, evaluation, interpretation, categorization, hypothesizing, comparison, and pattern finding. It always involves what Wolcott calls "mindwork" (1995, p. 233). Researchers always engage their own intellectual capacities to make sense of qualitative data. Even when computer programs are used to assist in the mechanics of sorting data, only the intelligence, creativity, and reflexivity of the human mind can bring meaning to those data.

I conceptualize the general data analysis process as *asking questions of data.* What kinds of questions are asked is related to what kind of research is being done within what set of paradigmatic assumptions. Postpositivist researchers doing interview studies will likely start analysis with different questions than critical/feminist researchers doing case studies. For example, the former may read their data with a question such as this in mind: What are the criteria my informants use to make judgments about promoting or retaining students? The latter may ask: How does race influence decision making about promotion and retention in this school?

Different approaches and paradigms lead to different analysis strategies, but the general approach I am proposing is built on the assumption that important information is in the data, and by systematically asking the right questions of the data, that information can be revealed. Much of the rest of this chapter describes alternative models based on this assumption. Obviously, the approach falls apart if the data lack sufficient depth to support careful analysis, if questions are ill-suited to the data, or if question strategies are haphazard, inadequate, or biased. Before taking up specific data analysis models, I address issues related to beginning and ending qualitative data analysis.

When to start data analysis will, of course, depend on the study, but I recommend starting soon after data collection has begun. At an informal, but essential, level, analysis is happening from the first moments of data collection. During observation, decisions are made about where to be, what to attend to, what to record, and so on. In interviews, decisions are made about what to ask, what to follow up on, and what to probe. Decisions are also made about what unobtrusive data to include and what to ignore. These decisions involve an informal kind of data analysis. They shape the study based on analytic judgments about what data are desirable. In addition, I have recommended that researchers keep track of their impressions, reactions, reflections, and tentative interpretations in field notes and/or research journals (see example in appendix C) as studies unfold; and these are forms of informal data analysis as well.

Beginning more structured, formal data analysis early in data collection is also desirable in most studies (Bogdan & Biklen, 1992; Glesne & Peshkin, 1992; Spradley, 1979, 1980). Starting early allows researchers to shape the direction of future data collection based on what they are actually finding or not finding. It is common for qualitative researchers to change the focus of their studies once they are in the field, but such changes will be haphazard unless they are based on careful analysis of the data that have been collected to that point. Some kinds of research, ethnographies for example, call for a recursive cycle of data collection and analysis designed so that, from the beginning, data collection and analysis inform each other (see LeCompte & Schensul, 1999; Spradley, 1980). In most other qualitative studies, beginning formal data analysis early will improve the quality of the research.

The design or timing of some studies will require that data analysis wait until after a complete cycle of data analysis is completed. For example, an interview study with fairly narrow research questions will be less affected by waiting to start data analysis than a focus group study based on relatively open-ended questions. An intense examination of a short-term event may require so much energy focused on collecting data that formal analysis will have to wait. An example might be a school district crisis involving measures for the quick removal of a principal. While there are times when starting analysis right away will not be feasible or imperative, as a general rule, earlier is better.

It is not an exaggeration to say that no qualitative analysis is ever complete. There are always more data than can be adequately processed, more levels of understanding than can be explored, and more stories than can be told. Data analysis is like teaching—there is always more you could do. Knowing when to stop data analysis is a judgment call that can be as perplexing as deciding how to start. For every study I have done, I am left with the feeling that only a part of what was in the data was ever reported. For virtually every qualitative dissertation I've helped students get through, I have advised students to focus on parts of their data and "let go" of others, saving them for another day, another analysis, another article or book.

New researchers will have the most trouble deciding when to stop. My basic advice will not surprise those who have been reading carefully: You cannot stop until you have answered your research questions. No matter how interesting or important your other findings may be, you have made a contract in your proposal to answer your research questions. Another reason to start data analysis early is that research questions sometimes change during the course of the study. When that happens, it must be justified with the data and made clear to the committee. Early data analysis will confirm the answerability of the research questions and shape data collection so that data provide ways to answer them. In the end, data analysis cannot stop until research questions are answered.

Other criteria that signal that data analysis is complete are suggested in the following questions:

1. RESEARCH Qs ARE ANSWERED
2. Are all deviant cases and disconfirming data accounted for?
3. Can the analysis be explained and justified?
4. Can a complete story be told?
5. Can the analysis be organized into coherent written findings?

An axiom related to the final question is that writing up findings is another stage of data analysis. Analysis is ongoing throughout the writing process. Much more on writing up findings will be presented in chapter 5, but for now, it is important to understand that putting the products of data analysis into the narratives that characterize qualitative research reports involves intellectual processing and decisions that are decidedly analytical. Making findings make sense to others means creating textual representations that are true to the data and organized in ways that communicate clearly. In a very real sense, no data analysis is complete until the final report is written.

DOING QUALITATIVE DATA ANALYSIS

I want to provide models of doing data analysis that novice qualitative researchers can adapt for their individual projects. Here I am treading on the

(margin note: CRITERIA - DATA ANALYSIS IS COMPLETE)

toes of many qualitative researchers who worry that providing models runs against the open-ended nature of qualitative work. They believe that too much structure makes qualitative data analysis too much like the formulaic procedures used by quantitative types. They are concerned that the thoughtful interpretive dimensions of data analysis will be lost if prescribed modes are "plugged in." Some believe that models are fine for postpositivist work but just don't fit for the other paradigms I have identified.

I am concerned about each of these issues. My way of justifying the models proposed is to present them as frameworks for designing data analysis strategies. They are less prescriptive than exemplary. They are not meant to make the analysis process closed-ended but offer examples of ways to systematically follow data where they lead. They are quite different from the quantitative models into which statistical data are "punched." These models suggest steps that can be adapted to the contexts, research questions, and data of individual qualitative studies. They do not short circuit the interpretive process but provide a framework within which interpretation can grow from asking questions of the data. The same question-asking approach makes these models applicable to studies undertaken in the constructivist, critical/feminist, and poststructuralist paradigms. The questions will be very different, but having a model that provides a framework for organizing analysis neither prohibits nor necessarily inhibits researchers in any of the qualitative paradigms from applying their special perspectives to making sense of their data.

The sections that follow present five models of qualitative data analysis that I have labeled "typological," "inductive," "interpretive," "political," and "polyvocal." In a rough sense, they move along a continuum that parallels my organization of qualitative paradigms. For example, typological analysis will fit most easily with postpositivist assumptions and polyvocal analysis has apparent applicability to data-based poststructuralist studies. But the intent is not to assign particular analysis models to particular paradigms. The idea is to present the models as frameworks for thinking about data analysis across paradigms. Some will fit more easily than others, but I believe adaptations are possible so that the models can be useful for certain studies undertaken in any qualitative paradigm.

I also want to be clear that I do not believe these are the only appropriate ways to do qualitative data analysis. I have learned a great deal from other researchers who have described data analysis approaches. Indeed, I will attempt to acknowledge the thinking of others as I present the models. I encourage readers to search out the sources cited here and to learn all they can about alternative ways to organize and process data. What this is about is providing a starting place for approaching the daunting task of making sense of the overwhelming mass of data usually associated with qualitative research, giving new researchers frameworks for thinking about what's possible, and sharing models for organizing the work that provide enough structure to demystify the processes of qualitative data analysis.

TYPOLOGICAL ANALYSIS

I first came across the term *typological analysis* in the 1984 edition of Goetz and LeCompte's *Ethnography and Qualitative Design in Educational Research*. In their second edition (LeCompte & Preissle, 1993), these researchers describe typological analysis as "dividing everything observed into groups or categories on the basis of some canon for disaggregating the whole phenomenon under study" (p. 257). That means that data analysis starts by dividing the overall data set into categories or groups based on predetermined typologies. Typologies are generated from theory, common sense, and/or research objectives, and initial data processing happens within those typological groupings. As we will see, this is very different from the inductive approach described later. In an inductive analysis, categories emerge from the analysis of the data set as a whole. In typological analysis, an early step is to read through the data set and divide it into elements (i.e., disaggregate it from the whole) based on predetermined categories.

I have developed typological strategies that have been especially useful in helping me and my students analyze data from interview and focus group studies. I will present the typological model and give a detailed example of applying it to interview data, then discuss its applicability to other types of data. The basic typological model is presented in figure 4.1.

 Identify Typologies to Be Analyzed. Obviously, selecting the typologies that are going to be used to frame the rest of the analysis is a key step in this process. If typological analysis is the appropriate data analysis strategy for a study, the selection of typologies should be fairly obvious as well. This is the wrong approach if the researcher does not begin the analysis with a good idea of what topics are addressed in the data. In fact, typological analysis only has utility when initial groupings of data and beginning categories for analysis are easy to identify and justify.

Studies that rely on interviewing as the sole or primary data collection tool are often undertaken with a fairly focused purpose, a fairly narrow set of research questions, and a fairly well-structured data set in terms of its organization around a set of fairly consistent guiding questions. When the study was designed, the researcher had as his or her goal to capture the perspectives of a group of individuals around particular topics. If the study was well designed and implemented, data from the interviews ought to provide lots of evidence

Typological analysis [handwritten margin note]

FIGURE 4.1
Steps in Typological Analysis

1. Identify typologies to be analyzed

2. Read the data, marking entries related to your typologies

3. Read entries by typology, recording the main ideas in entries on a summary sheet

4. Look for patterns, relationships, themes within typologies

5. Read data., coding entries according to patterns identified and keeping a record of what entries go with which elements of your patterns

6. Decide if your patterns are supported by the data, and search the data for nonexamples of your patterns

7. Look for relationships among the patterns identified

8. Write your patterns as one-sentence generalizations

9. Select data excerpts that support your generalizations

related to participants' perspectives on the topics of interest. So the topics that the researcher had in mind when the study was designed will often be logical places to start looking for typologies on which to anchor further analysis.

[handwritten margin note: topics researcher had in mind often logical starting places]

This will become clearer with a concrete example. As mentioned in earlier chapters, Evelyn Freeman and I conducted an interview study of Ohio educators' perspectives on kindergarten curriculum and teaching (Hatch & Freeman, 1988). We were interested in the relationship between what our informants believed (their philosophies) and what they did in their jobs (their practices). We didn't ask directly: "What is your philosophy of kindergarten curriculum and teaching?" Instead, we designed a series of guiding questions that gave them opportunities to discuss the thinking behind their work, in addition to asking them to describe the work itself. When it came time to analyze the interview transcripts, it was logical for us to start with our major topics, so the first two typologies identified for analysis were "educators' philosophies" and "educators' practices." Other typological areas identified for analysis in this study included "purposes of kindergarten," "classroom organization," "goals and objectives," "children's tasks," "instructional delivery," and "approaches to literacy." As I explain the rest of the typological model, I will use this study as an ongoing example.

Read the Data, Marking Entries Related to Your Typologies. Once an initial set of typologies has been identified, I recommend that the data be read through completely with one typology in mind. The idea is to find and mark those places in the data where evidence related to that particular typology is found. At this point, the level of interpretation is limited to asking, Does this information relate to my typology? If it does, have some kind of way to mark that portion of the data so that you can go back to it later for closer examination. If you are working from hard copies, highlighting in a particular color data portions that fit is one strategy. If you are working on a word processing program, data excerpts can be copied to another file. If you are working with data processing programs designed to assist in data management, each program will have a way to identify and separate data by categories (more on computer assisted analysis later in this chapter). In any case, as parts are separated from the whole, it is imperative that the whole be left intact because data excerpts will virtually always include elements related to multiple typologies, and, if they are lifted from their original context within the protocols, it will be difficult to process them later. In this step, you are simply separating the larger data set into smaller sets based on your predetermined typologies. The result will be large chunks of raw data related to particular typologies drawn from across the original data set.

In the interview study of kindergarten educators' philosophies and practices, we began by reading the data asking, Where are all the places that informants' philosophies about learning and development are evident? We read through each of the 36 interview protocols bracketing all the places with a yellow highlighter where anything indicated an individual educator's assumptions about teaching and learning. We didn't stop to try to characterize what the statement might indicate, only marked it for later analysis. Next, we searched the entire data set for evidence related to actual practices, marking those places in green, and so on.

Read Entries by Typology, Recording the Main Ideas in Each Entry on a Summary Sheet. At this point, you want to begin to process the information within the entries marked as being related to your typology. This time only the data within the typology of interest will be read. A summary sheet should be created for each informant, and as the data excerpts are read, you should write a brief statement of the main idea of the excerpt on the summary sheet. The objective is to create a summary of what will often be a large amount of data. It is hard enough to process the summaries; trying to make sense of large chunks of raw data is nearly impossible. These summaries should be just that: summaries. This is not the place to try to interpret the significance or to guess what informants really meant—just summarize their words as best you can. It is important to make note on the summary sheet of the place in the data that is being summarized. This will give you a quick way to refer back to the original data as analysis continues.

In the kindergarten analysis, we created summary sheets for each informant, keeping track of these by research site. We were interviewing a teacher, a principal, and a supervisor at each of 12 sites, so we assigned a number to each site and used different colored pens to write the data summaries for this step. For "educators' philosophies," we ended up with 36 summary sheets divided into 12 sets, but we were able to easily pull out all of the teachers and look at those together because they were written in red pen. Obviously, electronic tools could be used to do this task. The key is to have solid summaries that can be easily located, identified, and manipulated.

④ *Look for Patterns, Relationships, Themes within Typologies.* Now is the time to start to look for meaning within the data from your typology. Because we are doing typological analysis, it is likely that you will have a good idea going into this step what patterns, relationships, or themes might be present in the data. As you designed research questions and guiding questions for interviews, you were thinking about getting certain kinds of information. The typologies you selected for this type of analysis will likely lead you to be looking for certain dimensions in the data. As you read the data, selected excepts by typology, and did your summaries, it is also likely that certain patterns were evident. This is the point at which you try out your hypothetical patterns, relationships, and themes using the summary data from the last step. Brief explanations of what I mean by patterns, relationships, and themes will give you a sense of how to focus your work.

Patterns are regularities. They come in several forms, including similarity (things happen the same way), difference (they happen in predictably different ways), frequency (they happen often or seldom), sequence (they happen in a certain order), correspondence (they happen in relation to other activities or events), and causation (one appears to cause another). It may be, for example, that as you read you see that your informants seem to answer certain questions in a similar way based on some common characteristic. There may be a patterned difference between the ways high school and elementary school guidance counselors think about their relationships with students, for example. LeCompte and Schensul (1999) provide a useful discussion of pattern-level analysis that can be applied to this and other models to follow.

Relationships are links. Spradley (1979, pp. 111) identifies many semantic relationships that can become the tools for identifying links between data elements (see the inductive model discussion below). Some examples are strict inclusion (X is a kind of Y), rationale (X is a reason for doing Y), cause-effect (X is a result of Y), and means-end (X is a way to do Y). As you start searching for relationships, it is possible that the research literature suggests relationships that may or may not be evident in your data. For example, new teachers are thought to be operating at a "survival" level during their first few years in the field; that is, being new causes teachers to operate at a survival level. You may have data that will bring new light to understanding or questioning such a relationship. Spradley's semantic relationships will have a major part in our discussion of inductive analysis in the next section of this chapter.

Themes are integrating concepts. They can be defined as statements of meaning that run through all or most of the pertinent data (Ely et al., 1991). One searches for themes by asking: What broad statements can be made that meaningfully bring all of these data together? Dissatisfaction with pay is a theme thought to pervade the psyches of teachers who leave the field, but you may have data that indicate that other themes are also important. Again, searching for themes will be part of the models to follow.

In typological analysis, you will probably come to this stage with some idea of how you want your search for patterns, relationships, or themes to go. Now is the time to read the summary statements, searching for your anticipated patterns, relationships, and themes, and watching for others that may be unexpected. At this point, you are not trying to "verify" that the pattern, relationship, or theme is worth reporting. This is the stage for identifying possibilities to be checked out later.

In our study, Freeman and I came to the analysis of educators' philosophies of learning and development with a theoretical framework in mind. We used a widely agreed upon classification of early childhood theories to organize our analysis of educators' philosophies. We looked closely at the summary statements using three categories identified by Schickedanz, York, Stewart, and White (1983): maturationist, behaviorist, and interactionist. We read each informant's summary statements and determined that it was possible to classify educators' assumptions using these theoretical categories. Even without the theoretical framework, it would have been possible to look for patterns, relationships, and themes around our question: What are our informants' philosophies of kindergarten teaching? Exploring the assumptions summarized from their interview responses provided a rich source for analysis with or without the predetermined categories. Again, the acceptability of using predetermined categories is what makes typological analysis distinct. Our search for patterns, relationships, and themes was more inductive within the other typologies of this study.

Read Data, Coding Entries according to Patterns Identified and Keeping a Record of What Entries Go with What Elements of Your Patterns. Now we go back to the marked protocols and read through all of the data marked for inclusion in the typology under investigation. The product of the previous step will be hypothetical patterns, relationships, or themes. For example, a researcher studying relationships between guidance counselors and students may hypothesize four kinds of relationship patterns: psychologist-client, counselor-student, mentor-mentee, and parent-child. He or she will read all of the data highlighted for this category and code each entry using the patterns identified. Data excerpts that indicate psychologist-client relationships will get coded with some kind of mark that distinguishes it from the other categories. At the same time, I recommend making a simultaneous record of where elements related to that category are found in the data. So when I mark the data excerpt with a special code, I also have a sheet on which I make a record of all the places in the data where I coded that category. As I mentioned in the last chapter, protocol pages need to be numbered. This makes it possible to record the place in the data by noting the interview name or assigned number, the date, and the page number.

Our coding of the kindergarten data meant reading through all of the data in the sections highlighted in yellow with our three categories in mind. We studied each excerpt for evidence that teachers' assumptions fit one or more of the three theories that framed this part of the analysis. As statements were coded as maturationist, behaviorist, or interactionist, separate records were made of where those statements were found in the data. Because we were examining statements from three groups, again we used colors to distinguish one from the other. At the end of this stage, we had coded the data for philosophy and made records of where that data could be found, organized into sets by teachers, principals, and supervisors.

Decide If Patterns Are Supported by the Data, and Search Data for Nonexamples of Your Patterns. As the data are re-read and coded, it will probably become evident that not all excerpts will neatly fit into your categories. Having coded all that you could, it is now necessary to make a judgment about whether or not your categories are justified by the data. On the one hand, your judgment will be based on how well the data that are coded fit into the categories you have tried. Another side of the issue is deciding if the data not coded contain insights that are different or contradictory to what you have proposed. In the first instance, it's a matter of deciding if the evidence is strong enough to support your case. In the second, it's about asking if there is evidence upon which other cases, even competing cases, can be made. Overall, decisions ought to be driven by the data. If, in a study of new teacher adjustments, data indicate that while some teachers operate in ways that look like "survival," others behave very much like seasoned professionals, then new categories of adjustment will need to be explored.

Searching for nonexamples of your patterns is a systematic measure that should be undertaken in any qualitative study, including those using typological analysis. This will mean rereading all of the data set, not just the portions highlighted for this part of the analysis, purposefully asking: Is there anything in the data that contradicts my findings? This process takes time and discipline. When data are discovered that run counter to findings, they must be satisfactorily explained, or findings must be changed. The best rationale for such work and the most elaborate system for ensuring completeness are included in what Glaser and Strauss (1967) call the "constant comparative method." The spirit of such an approach is called for here and in the analysis models that follow.

In our study, we found that educators talked in ways that indicated that most borrowed assumptions from more than one of the theoretical bases we were using. We decided to classify them according to the "philosophy" that seemed to dominate their thinking, but this required an especially careful reading of each statement in order to be able to justify our decisions to ourselves and have confidence that our readers could trust our judgments. While we did not claim to use constant comparative techniques in this study, we were careful to search the data for nonexamples of the patterns we reported.

Look for Relationships among the Patterns Identified. The procedures above will be carried out with all of the initial categories identified in the first step. The result will be a set of patterns, relationships, and themes that have, to this point, been analyzed separately. The task now is to step back from the individual analyses that have been completed and look for connections across what has been found. This process can often be helped along by making some kind of visual representation of the categories explored so far, then looking to see what relationships might exist between or among categories. Miles and Huberman (1994) describe such visual representations as "data displays . . . that present information systematically, so the user can draw valid conclusions and take needed action" (p. 91). For example, in a study of individuals who leave teaching before retirement age, making boxes for categories such as low pay, low status, low sense of efficacy, and low sense of autonomy might lead to the discovery of connections that give a much richer sense of why teachers leave than reporting elements separately.

For Freeman and me, this level of analysis led us to our most powerful finding: many educators in our study were experiencing what we called "philosophy-reality conflicts" (Hatch & Freeman, 1988, p. 151); they were implementing practices that ran counter to what they believed was best for young children. As we tracked down teacher philosophies and analyzed practices, we were able to identify this conflict as a powerful theme that ran across the data. Our final report emphasized the experience of philosophy-reality conflicts for teachers, principals, and supervisors.

Write Your Patterns as One-Sentence Generalizations. While experienced researchers may see this as limiting and/or unnecessary, this strategy has been very useful for my students just learning to do qualitative data analysis. Making yourself construct sentences forces you to organize your thinking into a form that can be understood by yourself and others. It turns out to be invaluable as you begin to write up your findings, but it serves the purpose of giving closure to your analyses. A generalization expresses a relationship between two or more concepts. Expressing findings as generalizations provides a syntactic device for ensuring that what has been found can be communicated to others. If findings cannot be expressed as generalizations, chances are data analysis is incomplete. I hope it is clear by now that I am not talking about general statements that imply "generalizability." Generalizations are special kinds of statements that express relationships found in the particular contexts under investigation. Of course, the generalizations will follow from your analysis within and across categories.

We used two generalizations to organize the findings section of the kindergarten study. These generalizations are examples of the kind of sentences that might come from looking across categories near the conclusion of a typological analysis: "Kindergartens are increasingly academic and skill oriented; Individuals who implement kindergarten programs may not believe that these programs best serve the needs of young children" (Hatch & Freeman, 1988, p. 154). These sentences capture generalizations that pull the whole study together. Many subgeneralizations were generated from analyses within categories, and these make up the meat of the report; "Teachers' modes of instruction were direct as opposed to incidental or child-initiated"(p. 157); "All programs used a skill-based approach to evaluating reading progress" (p. 158). Writing specific generalizations from each category examined and bringing them together under more general statements exemplifies the typological analysis process described here.

Select Data Excerpts That Support Your Generalizations. In preparation for writing up findings, the last step in the typological model is to go back to the data to select powerful examples that can be used to make your generalizations come alive for your readers. In qualitative reports, it is usual to include data excerpts that take readers inside the contexts and allow them to hear the voices of participants. It is better to select potential quotes from the protocols at this point in the process rather than to go back to the data when you are involved in your writing and the data are cold. This is a place where you can go back to the record you made when you were coding the data. If you followed the suggestions above and made a note of where excerpts related to categories were located, finding salient quotes will not be difficult.

When I am processing data, I make a star next to powerful quotes both in the protocol and in my record of where excerpts are located. When it's time to identify potential data to be included as examples, I start with the starred excerpts. But even knowing that some items are starred does not keep me from looking carefully at each excerpt associated with my findings. In the kindergarten study, we used quotes from teachers, principals, and supervisors to illustrate our generalizations. An example of a quote from a principal demonstrates the power of excerpting informants' own words:

> The paper-pencil orientation is disturbing to me. The fact that we want to regiment and put school on a real competitive academic achievement basis disturbs me a bunch. I see firsthand experiences going out the window that way. I see muscular growth and development ignored that way. I see very little attention to language development and appreciation of language per se. What I see as distressing is that we are ignoring what we know about how young children learn. (Hatch & Freeman, 1988, p. 161)

It is worth noting that finding quotations that accurately and clearly convey your ideas is a final check on your analysis. If you have too many good examples to report, that's a sign that your findings are well supported. If you have difficulty finding quotations that make a compelling case for your generalizations, it will be worth your time to go back to the analysis process to be sure that your findings are indeed supported by your data.

The kindergarten study example used to illustrate typological analysis procedures is an interview study, and this type of data analysis works well for interview data when research questions are fairly narrow in focus. Typological analysis will also work well for processing artifact data that are gathered with specific purposes in mind. Observational data are more problematic. As a general rule, I do not recommend typological analysis for studies where observations are the only or primary data collection strategy. The nature and richness of such data make it hard for me to picture a case where starting analysis with predetermined categories would be a good idea. There are exceptions to every rule, and I've broken a few rules myself, but in order to justify applying typological techniques to the analysis of observation data, you may have to circumscribe observations to the point that they would look more like those done by positivists than qualitative researchers.

While there is generally a bad fit between typological analysis and studies that rely on observation, I see no inherent conflicts between this analytic approach and postpositivist, constructivist, critical/feminist, or poststructuralist assumptions. The categories used to start the analysis and the questions asked of the data throughout will be decidedly different, but the steps outlined should work within all of the qualitative paradigms. This is not the same as saying that typological analysis is appropriate for all types of studies. I noted above that studies relying heavily on observation are not good candidates for typological analysis. Several of the approaches listed in chapter 1 are not natural matches because of their emphasis on observation (i.e., ethnography, microethnography, naturalistic inquiry, and educational criticism). Other approaches that often emphasize interviewing are also not good candidates for typological analysis because they depend on more inductive strategies to get at informants' meaning structures (e.g., grounded theory, narrative studies, and phenomenological studies).

The primary strength of typological analysis is its efficiency. Starting with predetermined typologies takes much less time than "discovering" categories inductively. The potential weakness is that applying predetermined categories will blind the researcher to other important dimensions in the data. I agree with LeCompte and Schensul (1999) that all analysis involves both deductive and inductive thinking. That typological analysis starts with a deductive step does not preclude the researcher's being aware that other important categories are likely to be in the data or prevent the researcher from searching for them. Some unexpected patterns, relationships, or themes will jump out of the data as they are read and reread by the researcher. Others will be discovered as searches for disconfirming evidence are completed. But if there is a sense that not all important data are accounted for by a typological analysis, I recommend that inductive analyis procedures be applied to fill in the gaps. Those procedures are detailed next.

| INDUCTIVE ANALYSIS |

proceeds from the SPECIFIC to the GENERAL

All qualitative research is characterized by an emphasis on inductive rather than deductive information processing. Even the typological model, which starts deductively, depends on inductive thinking within several of its steps. Calling the model described here "inductive analysis" may be misleading if it is understood to be a universal model of qualitative analysis or even *the* inductive model of qualitative analysis. Other decidedly inductive approaches have been well described in the literature (e.g., Glaser & Strauss, 1967; Spradley, 1979, 1980), and this model is meant only to provide a framework to guide novice researchers through the steps of a basic kind of inductive analysis. I call it "inductive" analysis to signal its distinct nature in relation to the other models described.

Inductive thinking proceeds from the specific to the general. Understandings are generated by starting with specific elements and finding connections among them. To argue inductively is to begin with particular pieces of evidence, then pull them together into a meaningful whole. Inductive data analysis is a search for patterns of meaning in data so that general statements about phenomena under investigation can be made. Inductive analysis begins with an examination of the particulars within data, moves to "looking for patterns across individual observations, then arguing for those patterns as having the status of general explanatory statements" (Potter, 1996, p. 151).

examination of particulars within data – moves to looking for patterns across

Rather than following the deductive logic of traditional positivistic research, in which theory guides the development of hypotheses to be tested, in this model, theory is derived inductively from the careful study of a contextualized phenomenon. In their description of grounded theory, the most widely known inductive approach, Strauss and Corbin (1998) describe theory as "discovered, developed, and provisionally verified through systematic data collection and analysis" (p. 23). While the inductive model presented below is influenced by the important work in grounded theory, my goal is to provide a more general inductive model that can be utilized for more than the discovery of data-based theory. In addition, I believe my model will be adaptable to other qualitative research approaches across multiple qualitative paradigms, while grounded theory and other important inductive models (e.g., Miles & Huberman, 1994; Spradley, 1979, 1980) are less flexible and fit most comfortably within postpositivist assumptions. An outline of the inductive model is found in figure 4.2.

Read the Data and Identify Frames of Analysis. I start with reading the data because all inductive analysis must begin with a solid sense of what is included in the data set. As the analysis moves forward, as different questions are asked of the data, and as decisions are made about how to make sense of what's there, the data will be read over and over. Each reading will bring new insights (and often new concerns), but without a thorough sense of what's

FIGURE 4.2
Steps in Inductive Analysis

1. Read the data and identify frames of analysis

2. Create domains based on semantic relationships discovered within frames of analysis

3. Identify salient domains, assign them a code, and put others aside

4. Reread data, refining salient domains and keeping a record of where relationships are found in the data

5. Decide if your domains are supported by the data and search data for examples that do not fit with or run counter to the relationships in your domains

6. Complete an analysis within domains

7. Search for themes across domains

8. Create a master outline expressing relationships within and among domains

9. Select data excerpts to support the elements of your outline

included in the overall data set at the outset, the direction of early analysis may be off the mark and lead to a great deal of frustration and wasted time and energy. If, as recommended here, data analysis begins while data collection is going on, this means that whenever new data are added to the data set, all of the data should be read before analysis continues.

Early reading of the data should be done with a key initial question in mind: What will be my frames of analysis? Once you have become familiar with the dimensions of your data set, you will have to make an important decision about how you will break your data into analyzable parts. I call these analyzable parts "frames of analysis." As you read your data, you will see many possible ways to frame your analysis, and deciding how to do so will have major implications for how your analysis happens and how it turns out.

Frames of analysis are essentially levels of specificity within which data will be examined. Tesch (1990) notes that qualitative researchers identify smaller parts of their data that she describes as "segments, items, incidents, meaning units, or analysis units." Her definition of such a unit is "a segment of text that is comprehensible by itself and contains one idea, episode, or piece of information" (p. 116). My notion of frames of analysis fits within this definition.

If you are working with observation data, you will have a range of options that runs from framing your analysis around particular words to looking at descriptions of entire events. Sociolinguists, microethnographers, and ethnomethodologists are often interested in examining how meaning is constructed in everyday social settings, and their analyses are often framed very tightly around specific individual utterances. They often analyze their observational protocols line by line, word by word. Other researchers may choose to examine their data more broadly, framing their analysis by blocking off complete interchanges between interactants or complete social events involving a specific group. So someone using participant observation to study peer social relations in high school may frame his or her analysis by looking at conversations that have a beginning and an end, while an ethnographer studying rituals in a parochial school may frame analysis around events that have the qualities of ritual.

Interview and artifact data need to be handled the same way. Decisions will have to be made about how tightly to focus the analysis. It may be easier with interview data because they are already organized into a question-answer format, but "answers" will rarely be an adequate frame of analysis for processing high-quality interviews. It is much more likely that something like "comments on specific topics" will be a starting frame. Some unobtrusive data will be objects that can be analyzed as free-standing pieces, but many will be more complex or text-based and require careful framing to be sure all important dimensions are explored.

Frames of analysis will shift and change as analysis proceeds, but initial decisions about the level at which data are to be studied are necessary, or there will be no way to begin to search for meaning in a mass of data. Obviously, the purposes of the study, the research questions, the nature of the study, and the kinds of data will influence decisions about frames of analysis. The argument throughout this book has been that studies should be designed so that research steps follow logically one after the other. If the study is well designed, and data collection is solid, then deciding how to frame the analysis should follow logically as well. For example, a researcher interested in understanding the experience of student athletes in university tutoring programs might interview athletes, tutors, coaches, and/or professors and observe interactions among these individuals in a variety of settings on campus. Frames of analysis for the interview protocols might start with "comments related to tutoring programs," and the observation analysis might begin with frames such as "conversations related to tutoring" or "events related to tutoring."

The object of identifying frames of analysis is not to do the analyis but to put rough parameters on how you will start looking closely at the data. As initial readings of the data are done, asking yourself how you will frame your beginning analysis is important. This early decision will shape the analyses that follow. It is possible that initial frames will prove unworkable or ill-suited to the data; that will become apparent as you proceed through the following steps. If your frames of analysis don't work, they will not work for a reason, and that should lead you to identifying frames that better suit your purposes.

I *do not* recommend going through the data and marking off the frames identified as a next step. I am afraid such a strategy will put more structure on the data than I am comfortable with at this stage. The next step involves the most inductive thinking in this form of analysis, and confining these processes with too much structure may limit what is discovered in the data. So frames of analysis are conceptual categories that help researchers look at data and make it possible to move to the next step of creating domains.

(2) *Create Domains Based on Semantic Relationships Discovered within Frames of Analysis.* In this step, I borrow heavily from Spradley (1979, 1980) in terms of language and process. The object of this step is to develop a set of categories of meaning or domains that reflects relationships represented in the data. Creating domains is the key inductive element in this model; the data are read searching for particulars that can be put into categories because of their relation to other particulars. The process described here gives researchers a systematic way to develop domains by exploring relationships among particulars within frames of analysis.

Spradley (1979, 1980) uses domain analysis as the first analytic step in his Developmental Research Sequence. For Spradley (1979), "Any symbolic

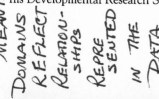

(Handwritten margin notes:)
IDENTIFYING FRAMES OF REFERENCE OR HOW YOU FRAME ANALYSIS

TO PUT ROUGH PARAMETERS ON YOUR BEGINNING

DEVELOP A SET OF CATEGORIES OF MEANINGS OR

DOMAINS REFLECT RELATION-SHIPS REPRESENTED IN THE DATA

category that includes other categories is a domain. All the members of a domain share at least one feature of meaning" (p. 100). All the knowledge that individuals use to make sense of their worlds can be organized into domains. Domains can be categories that are understood by large numbers of people with common cultural understandings, or they can be categories that are developed within smaller groups with specialized interests and needs. For example, mammals, fish, and birds are categories that fit among other categories under a domain called "animals." Positivist, postpositivist, constructivist, critical/feminist, and poststructuralist are categories that fit under research paradigms. Discovering domains gives researchers a way of getting at how participants organize their understandings and operate in their worlds.

Domains are structured in ways that make their discovery possible. Categories can only be categories when specific elements are related to other elements. Domains are categories organized around relationships that can be expressed semantically. As mentioned in the discussion of typological analysis, Spradley (1979, p. 111) identifies nine semantic relationships that are especially useful for accomplishing domain analysis. The first and most common is strict inclusion, which can be expressed as X is a kind of Y. The following is an example from a school context: a secretary is a kind of noncertified school worker. Second is spatial (X is a place in Y): the teachers' lounge is a place in school where students are not allowed. Third is cause-effect (X is a result of Y): larger class sizes are a result of not passing the tax increase. Fourth is rationale (X is a reason for doing Y): helping children manage their behavior is a reason for prescribing Ritalin. Fifth is location for action (X is a place for doing Y): the bar at the Holiday Inn is a place for teachers to get together away from school. Sixth is function (X is used for Y): school newsletters are used to communicate with parents. Seventh is means-end (X is a way to do Y): in-school suspension is a way to hold students accountable. Eighth is sequence (X is a step in Y): an interview with the principal is a step in getting a teaching job. Ninth is attribution (X is a characteristic of Y): curiosity is a characteristic of gifted students.

Domains can be represented by identifying "included terms" and "cover terms" that are linked by a semantic relationship (Spradley, 1979, p. 114). Included terms name the members of the category and a cover term names the category into which all the included terms fit. From the examples above, a researcher looking at discipline practices in elementary school might discover a means-end domain that could be called "Ways to hold students accountable" (cover term) that consisted of the following elements: "In-school suspension," "Time out," "Missing recess," "Notes to parents," "Vice-principal's office," "Suspension," "Expulsion," "Paddling" (included terms). It is possible to express this and any domain graphically by listing all the included terms and linking them with the cover term using the semantic relationship. For the example domain, such a graphic might look like figure 4.3.

FIGURE 4.3
Domain Example

Included Terms	Semantic Relationship	Cover Term
In-school suspension		
Time out		
Missing recess		hold
Notes to parents	are ways to	students
Vice-principal's office		accountable
Suspension		
Expulsion		
Paddling		

The basic idea behind creating domains is to find categories by reading the data with specific semantic relationships in mind. The questions that drive this step in the analysis will depend on the semantic relationship one is searching for. I agree with Spradley that it is a good idea to pick one semantic relationship, then search through the data for examples of that relationship—for example, strict inclusion. Now is the time to look to your frames of analysis, reading through them asking: What are the examples of strict inclusion in this piece of data? What are examples of X being a kind of Y in this comment, conversation, event, or whatever? As you are reading the data, you will be creating domain sheets based on the model in figure 4.3. It's a good idea to copy many blank sheets with space for multiple included terms and to have those in hand before starting domain analysis.

This step is the most time consuming and, for me, the most fun. If you are doing an inductive analysis, it is likely that, while you have some general idea of what might be going on in your data, you are really looking to the data to tell you what you have. For example, as you have been observing or interviewing, you may have made note in your brackets or research journal that there seem to be some relationships in the data that you want to explore. You may have noted that there are a variety of ways to hold students accountable and believe that such a domain will be important. You will go into your domain analysis with such hunches in mind, but I recommend that you resist starting with them. It will become too easy to shift into a deductive mode of thinking and risk missing other important categories that you will find if you stick to a more inductive approach.

As I mentioned, I like to start with a specific semantic relationship in mind, then read each frame, asking myself if there is an instance of that relationship happening within the frame being examined. Once an included term is associated with a cover term and a domain sheet is created, reading from that point includes a search for other examples of that domain, as well as the ongoing search for new domains. The complexity of the task increases with each newly discovered domain possibility. It is a slow process, especially at first. Keeping track of where you are and what you are doing will help you stay on target. You may want to make a separate record of potential domains as you discover them. I have taken up two full library tables doing domain analysis, ordering newly created domain sheets in a way that I could visually see my growing set of categories in a glance.

My experience is that you will find many more domains than will actually be reported in your study; most will be put aside as unimportant, or they will turn out not to be domains at all. But you will not know that going into the analysis. I would resist making decisions about the centrality of domains to the study until later in the analysis process. It is much easier to eliminate domains later based on all available evidence than to discover that important information has been missed, and early analytic steps will have to be repeated.

After you have read all of your data for a specific semantic relationship, that process needs to be repeated for the other relationships listed. You will find that having read carefully for one kind of domain, the process will go much faster for the succeeding semantic relationships. In fact, with practice you will start to see different kinds of relationships as you are searching for another. Once I became comfortable with domain analysis, I was able to look for more than one semantic relationship at a time. This increases the complexity of keeping track of what you are finding, but as your mind learns the thinking processes involved, it will be natural for you to see different types of relationships in your data frames. This is acceptable, but go slowly. It's exhilarating to discover interesting and fairly obvious domains, and the temptation will be to stop looking closely at what else is going on in the data. This can lead to a surface-level analysis that lacks the depth that makes this kind of work different and important.

The final products of this step will be stacks of domain sheets that will likely include multiple domains from each of the semantic relationships described. These represent just the beginning of the inductive analysis process, but without a thorough domain analysis, nothing that follows will make any sense.

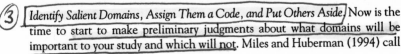

(3) *Identify Salient Domains, Assign Them a Code, and Put Others Aside.* Now is the time to start to make preliminary judgments about what domains will be important to your study and which will not. Miles and Huberman (1994) call

this general process "data reduction" (p. 10). Your goal is to narrow the focus of your analysis by studying the categories that emerged from your domain analysis and deciding which domains will be salient to the project underway. As you look through your domain sheets, it is probable that several of the domains you started did not play out in the data. There may be several domains that have only one or two included terms. It is hard to think of a category with only one element, so eliminating these should be easy. Still, it is worth the time to ask: Could this relationship be linked to other domains discovered in the data?

Domains with small numbers of included terms are more difficult. The questions to ask here include: Are these included terms important to understanding what's going on in the data? Are these the only included terms in this domain? Are there more included terms that I may have missed or that will show up in later data? Small domains should be looked at carefully, but they should not be set aside just because the number of included terms is small. If the domain seems important to the study, future data collection could include a systematic effort to gather information related to the domain.

Just because some domains are large does not mean that they are salient to the study at hand. Here is another place to refer back to research purposes and questions. You may have a lot of data related to a mundane topic, or you may have powerful data related to an important topic that is not related to your study. For example, in a study of elementary school discipline, you may find a large domain that shows teachers ways of taking attendance, and you may decide that this is not important enough to pursue. Or you may have a provocative domain showing how kids categorize each other into status groups that you decide will have to wait for another analysis because it does not tie to the thrust of this particular study. Again, be careful when you put such domains aside. If there is any doubt about their potential importance to the study, keep them active. If not, set them aside, but do not forget they are there. As you move on to the next steps in inductive analysis, you will not be handling the domains you have set aside directly, but saving the domain sheets will allow you to go back to them if necessary.

Once salient domains are identified, it will save time if you create some kind of code to help you keep track of your domains. I find it easiest to set up such codes using an outline format. I assign a Roman numeral to each domain and a capital letter to each included term. That allows me to have a handy record of my domains to that point and to be able to add included terms as they are discovered. So, for the example being used here, the domain "Ways to hold students accountable" would be identified with "I," and IA would be "In-school suspension," IB "Time out," and so on. At this point, I would just mark these codes directly on the domain sheets, although you may find it useful to create a list that includes all your domains and included terms in the form of an outline.

CREATE A CODE TO KEEP TRACK OF YOUR DOMAINS

The products of this step will be a set of domain sheets that include categories that offer potential for further exploration. These will have a code for keeping track of the domains as analysis continues. These will not be all of the domains of importance to your study. If you are continuing data collection at this point, domain analysis and this step will have to be repeated as new data are added. In addition, as further analysis takes you deeper into the data, new domains will be discovered and old ones refined.

4. *Reread Data, Refining Salient Domains and Keeping a Record of Where Relationships Are Found in the Data.* The data will be read and reread no matter what the analyis model used. Here, you will be reading the data with specific domains in mind. The idea is to be confident that the data support the existence of the domain and that all of the important included terms within a domain have been identified. Once salient domains have been selected, the process is to pick one or two and read all of the data, searching for examples of where the relationships that make up the domain are found in the data. Most will have been discovered during domain analysis, but, often, other included terms will be discovered during this careful reading.

When the elements of the domain (i.e., included terms, semantic relationships, and cover terms) are found in the data, it is a good idea to make a record of where they are located both in the data and on the domain sheets. So when an analysis frame includes an example that fits a domain such as "Ways students are held accountable" (e.g., a child is put into time out), you will identify that place in the data in some way (I often just make a dark bracket in the margin) and mark that place by writing the code assigned to that domain (in this case, IB). On the domain sheet next to the "Time out" included term, you should write down the number of the page in the data where the example was found. I do this each time I see an example of my included term. That means that at the end of this step, I will have marked all the places in the data where examples of time out were found, and I will have a record on my domain sheets of each frame of analysis where that semantic relationship was located.

The process of searching and coding within salient domains will lead you to look more closely at your data and give you a better sense of the richness and importance of the domains you are finding. As this process proceeds, it is important to be open to discovering new domains or discovering that existing domains need modification. It will not be unusual throughout inductive analysis for you to find that you need to return to earlier steps in the model. Going back is not a sign that you have done a bad job, only that you are trying to do a comprehensive job. In the next step, we will systematically decide if the domains discovered are supported by the data. If they are not, that just means going back to the data in an effort to search out what the data will support.

⑤ EXAMINING THE QUALITY OF THE DATA USED TO CONSTRUCT DOMAINS

Decide If Your Domains Are Supported by the Data and Search Data for Examples That Do Not Fit with or Run Counter to the Relationships in Your Domains. Up to now, all domains have been hypothetical and tentative. It is at this point that deductive reasoning is fully employed to decide if the hypothetical categories identified hold up. While it is advisable to do a preliminary version of this step as part of a recursive cycle of data collection and analysis, it is essential at this stage of data analysis. This step involves examining the quality of the data that have been included in constructing your domains. In this step, you will be asking questions such as the following: Is there enough data to support the existence of this domain in the setting being studied? Are the data strong enough to make the case for including this domain? Are there other data that do not fit with or run counter to the relationships expressed in my domains?

Deciding if there is enough data is tricky business. Early in my publishing career, I was forced by editors to do frequency counts within my domains in order to have articles published. That turned out to be more annoying than difficult because I had followed the coding and recording procedures described above; but I am generally against relying on counting the times examples supporting certain included terms are found in the data as a way to judge the efficacy of a finding. The notion of counting and calculating percentages assumes a kind of standardization in data collection that is rarely found in qualitative work.

Glaser and Strauss (1967) describe reaching what they call "saturation," a point at which "no additional data are being found whereby the sociologist can develop properties of the category" (p. 61). You will rarely reach a place you might characterize as data saturation, but if your analysis indicates that the elements in your domains are repeated over and over again, that is good evidence that the relationships expressed are "really" in the data.

But, it is also possible that examples of your relationships will not appear frequently in the data set but be important to understanding the setting under investigation. Here, I am talking about data that are powerful because they make a strong case without appearing frequently. It may be, for example, that in some schools paddling is a way students are disciplined. Paddling may happen infrequently, may be impossible to observe, or may not get talked about much in interviews with school personnel, but one or two persons' descriptions of such events could be powerful enough to merit including it as part of the ways students are held accountable domain. The power of data I am describing need not be as dramatic as uncovering corporal punishment. Powerful can also mean that it connects other pieces of data or has explanatory properties that get at important elements of the study. To push this example a little, it is possible that the discovery that some personnel are paddling children turns out to be powerful evidence of the existence of two behavioral accountability systems in a school, one official and one unofficial.

The search for counterevidence is vital to any qualitative study. In order for domains to be reported, researchers must have taken the time to read all of the data in a systematic effort to uncover data that disconfirm the domains discovered. As mentioned under typological analysis, the constant comparative method (Glaser & Strauss, 1967) is the archetype for looking for "negative cases, cases which do not confirm the current formulation" (p. 104). Constant comparison starts when the first hypothetical categories are identified and continues throughout the analysis (that's what makes it constant). My experience as a researcher, editor, and doctoral advisor is that the constant comparison done in most studies is rarely as constant as described by Glaser and Strauss. I prefer to be more precise (and honest) in characterizing my own search for negative examples by framing it as the application of principles of "analytic induction" (Denzin, 1978; Lindesmith, 1952; Robinson, 1951). This approach emphasizes the interplay of inductive and deductive processing in data analysis and provides a general model of forming rough initial definitions and categories inductively, then modifying or discarding hypotheses as dissonant cases are examined.

The basic process for me is to lay out all the domains that I think will be important to my findings, then read the data, specifically asking of each analysis frame: What is going on here that does not fit with what I have included in my domains? Sometimes domains are altered because of confrontations with such data, sometimes what appear to be contradictions can be explained away, and sometimes domains will have to be abandoned. These are difficult decisions, but making them allows you to look yourself (and your critics) in the eye and say with confidence that your findings are supported by your data. It should also be noted that even though I have placed the search for negative evidence within a particular step in the inductive model, it is your obligation to be alert continually to disconfirming evidence throughout the analysis process.

 Complete an Analysis within Domains. Many qualitative dissertations report findings that appear to be generated following procedures that stop with what has been described so far. While this is often sufficient for reporting findings that emphasize description, such studies rarely go beyond description to other levels of reporting that Wolcott (1994) describes as analysis and interpretation. These reports often appear to be thin on depth or insight, staying mostly on the surface of the phenomena being studied. This and the step to follow are designed to help new researchers move their analyses to deeper, richer levels. The interpretive model described in the next section will detail how to move toward interpretation.

This step is about looking *within* the domains identified for complexity, richness, and depth; the next step provides ways to search for themes by looking *across* domains for the same qualities. Both these steps treat the products of the analysis so far as data. The object is to study the data that have been organized into domains in ways that allow the discovery of new links, new relationships, new domains. In the first case, we will be looking inward, and in the other, out. In both cases, we must be ready (and willing) to go back to the data upon which the original domains were constructed.

Completing an analysis within domains means revisiting included terms, semantic relationships, and cover terms in a search for other possible ways to organize what's there. It means playing out the idea that there may be categories (or subdomains) that could be organized under each included term. It means considering the possibility that some of the included terms in the domain may have connections to each other that other included terms do not have. It means exploring the idea that one or more of the included terms could be developed into freestanding domains not related to or in a different relation to the original domain.

A simple way to conceptualize this process is to think about it as filling in and modifying an outline. I have recommended above that domains be organized as outlines—Roman numerals for the domain name and capital letters for each included term. In the most basic element of this step, you will examine the data for each included term, looking for subcategories (which can be represented as subheadings). So within the ways students are held accountable domain, the process of analyzing the included term *In-school suspension* might lead the identification of several kinds of in-school suspension that can be represented in a portion of an overall outline that looks like this:

I. Ways students are held accountable
   A. In-school suspension
      1. In-class suspension
      2. Suspension in another teacher's classroom
      3. Suspension in the vice-principal's office
      4. Suspension in the suspension room.

While this example is mundane in some ways, you can see the possibilities for going much deeper into the data by looking beneath the surface of included terms for richer representations of what's going on.

Another strategy of looking within domains is to search for special relations between or among certain included terms. Finding such relationships may cause you to reconceptualize the structure of your domain (and modify your outline). Here you are asking: Do any of my included terms fit together because of some common thread? Looking at the domain example in figure 4.3, one link may be that "Time out," "Missing recess," and "Notes to parents" are all classroom-level actions, while the others are school-level. So part of a modified outline might look like the following:

I. Ways students are held accountable
   A. Classroom-level actions
      1. Time out
      2. Missing recess
      3. Notes to parents
   B. School-level actions . . .

You can see from these simple examples how the complexity of the outline will increase during this process. That complexity reflects the increased richness that will be represented in the analyses and findings of the study.

A third way to analyze within domains is to study expanded domains to determine if any categories have a different relation to the rest of the domain that merits considering the formation of a new domain. I am pushing the limits of my example, but I can imagine a situation in which a careful look at suspension might reveal that some students do not perceive being sent home to be a deterrent. From the school's and most students' perspectives, this is indeed a way to hold children accountable, but a new domain might be suggested that could be called something like "Ways students react to accountability actions."

The big idea for this step is to make a fine-grained examination of each domain that has made it thus far in your analysis. You want to enrich your analysis by getting a more complex understanding of what's going on within each domain. Some domains will not change much as a result of applying the strategies suggested, but others will change dramatically. Failure to take this step and the next may lead to findings that only catch the surface-level understandings that participants use to make sense of their social surroundings.

7. *Search for Themes across Domains.* After looking inward at previously identified domains, the next step is to step back from individual domains and look for connections among them. This step might be characterized as a search for themes (see Ely et al., 1991; Seidman, 1998; Spradley, 1979, 1980). Here we are looking across the data for broad elements that bring the pieces together. We are studying our domains to see what connections can be found among them. We are searching for patterns that repeat in the data and for patterns that show linkages among different parts of data. We are reading our data in ways that parallel how students of literature are trained to search novels for underlying themes about human existence that authors are addressing in their work (Ely et al., 1991). We are looking for relationships among the relationships we have outlined in our domain analysis.

The analytic questions for this step are: What does all this mean? How does all this fit together? How are the pieces related to the whole? Others suggest, and I agree, that searching for themes requires an intimate knowledge of the raw data (e.g., Ely et al., 1991; Spradley, 1979). This means once again immersing oneself in a careful reading of the original data set. But this time you are not searching within frames of analysis for particular relationships; you are reading with a broader focus, keeping the "What does all this mean?" question in mind. As you read, you should make note of possible themes that may run throughout the data and the places where evidence for these themes is found. These themes will be initially tentative, but keeping track of all potentially important patterns will help you stay "on task" (i.e., pay attention to what you are reading for) and help you process what you found when you finish.

It is likely that you will start this step with potential themes in mind—tentative themes discovered during data collection and previous analyses. Reading for these and searching for new potential themes can be done simultaneously with some careful self-monitoring. It is also possible that certain "universal themes" may become evident in the data. These themes are universal in that they are found among all or most humans groups. These are the themes that drive high-quality literary works and are found across studies in all the social science disciplines. Some examples are conflict, status and power, social control, and managing interpersonal social relations (see Opler, 1945; Patton, 1990; Spradley, 1979). Being well read will give your mind an extra set of resources on which to base your examination of the data, but the data must still tell you if the themes are evident or not.

Another strategy for identifying themes is to do a systematic comparison among the domains identified so far. Here you are asking: How does all this fit together? In Spradley's (1979) terms you are looking for general semantic relationships among your domains. A straightforward way to start such an analysis is to look across domains for commonalties, asking, What's the same or similar about these domains? Here you are treating the analyses you have done so far as data. You are examining the elements of your domains for ways to explain how it is possible for both domains to be salient in the experience of those you are studying. What threads connect the domains in positive ways? How are they similar? How are they linked?

Comparison always involves looking for similarities *and* differences. You should also undertake an analysis of what's different among your domains. Here you want to tease out relationships that can be expressed in other than positive terms. The cognitive processes involved in playing with what's the same and what's different have the capacity to generate general statements about the connections among data parts that may lead to the identification of overarching themes.

How are the pieces related to the whole? This question drives a third way to search for themes across domains. The strategy here is to make yourself construct a meaningful whole that fairly represents all of the parts of your

CREATE A DATA DISPLAY

analysis so far. This process can be facilitated in several ways. One is to represent the whole graphically, and the other is to write a summary overview of what you have found. By making yourself describe the whole in one of these ways, you will have to account for how the pieces (domains) fit together in relation to that whole.

Miles and Huberman (1994) make "data displays" (p. 91) an important part of the analytic processes they describe. They recommend putting data into visual formats that present information graphically and systematically. Creating a data display of the type Miles and Huberman recommend can be a useful tool for getting a sense for the whole of the data set being analyzed. They describe two major families of data displays: "*matrices*, with defined rows and columns, and *networks*, with a series of 'nodes' with links between them" (p. 93). Many of my students are attracted to the idea of organizing their data graphically, and Miles and Huberman's ideas are useful for representing the whole data set in a way that forces them to see relationships between the parts and the entirety. Some also like to create such displays using widely available and easy-to-use software programs.

For me personally, data displays are often busy and hard to follow. I am more likely to summarize the whole by making myself write a summary statement that describes what my study is all about. Organizing such a statement means processing all the parts in order to create a whole that makes sense. Wolcott (1995) recommends that such summaries be written all along the data collection/analysis process, and Spradley (1979) lists writing summary overviews as one process for discovering cultural themes. Both are probably right, but the emphasis here is on Spradley's approach to condensing "everything you know down to the bare essentials" (1979, p. 201). The overview should be only a few pages, and organizing its construction and writing it should lead you to the discovery or "verification" of themes that tie the parts to the whole.

My own dissertation offers an example of how searching for themes across domains might be implemented in a real study. I did a participant observation study in a kindergarten classroom (Hatch, 1984). I focused on children's peer interactions in settings without direct adult supervision. The process of searching for themes across domains turned out to be a difficult process, but successfully identifying themes that organized what was going on in children's face-to-face social interactions was a breakthrough that made the rest of the analyses and write-up of the study possible.

I came to this point in my analysis with many domains that described behavior patterns discovered in observations of children's peer interactions. For example, I had domains describing ways children put other children down and ways children demonstrated academic competence to peers. Immersing myself in the data, I became fascinated with trying to understand why children were acting the ways they did in relation to the other five and six year olds in the room. I asked, What are children gaining from these interactions? I hypothesized that children had what I eventually called "social goals" that they tried to fulfill in peer interactions.

I played out the notion of social goals by looking across the data to see relationships among domains. This process led me to new analyses that took the general form of ways children acted toward each other and ways they responded to those actions. So I eventually developed domains in pairs such as "Ways to practice self-promotion" and "Ways to respond to self-promotions." The social goals theme also worked for bringing the parts together under a meaningful whole. I identified three main dimensions of social goals that I labeled "affiliation," "competence," and "status goals." These three dimensions effectively organized the data of my study and provided a framework for developing my findings (the complete master outline for the study is included in appendix E).

As my example demonstrates, using a combination of the strategies suggested in this section should lead you to a fairly well developed sense of what your data mean, how they relate across domains, and how the parts fit the whole. Themes should emerge that provide a basic framework for understanding the social setting being studied and for writing up your description and analysis of that setting. In the next step, we will see how to formalize that basic framework into a master outline from which your findings can be written.

Create a Master Outline Expressing Relationships within and among Domains. If you have followed the suggestions above (especially the previous step), creating a master outline should follow logically from what you have done so far. Here we are after a comprehensive outline that concisely represents all of the analyses completed to this point. In the previous two steps, relationships were explored within and among domains. Now is the time to create a comprehensive representation of how the overall analysis fits together. Such a representation will provide processes for putting final refinements on analyses and bringing closure to this part of the study. Just as important, it will become the guide for writing up findings.

In earlier steps in the inductive model, I recommended using an outline format to organize the expression of relationships within domains. There are other ways to represent the whole. Miles and Huberman's (1994) data displays and Spradley's (1979, 1980) taxonomies are examples of other ways to express relationships among all the elements of the analysis. It will be a matter of personal preference. One is not inherently better than the other, but I like outlines because of their familiarity (we are used to organizing knowledge this way), their relative flexibility (you can add complexity and depth by adding elements and levels to the outline), and because they lead naturally to the writing phase of research (many of us write from outlines).

My way of constructing master outlines is to find an empty classroom with lots of blackboard (or dry erase board) space. I have also used large sheets of paper spread on the floor. I then take the pieces of outline that I have created so far and put them together into a single, comprehensive outline. If I have done a good job all the way along, especially in terms of identifying themes, this process will be mostly a matter of putting together the pieces of a puzzle. You should have created a "whole" in the last step that took all the pieces into account. If that process was successful, making a master outline should be a mostly organizational task of making it all make sense in outline form (see appendix E). *(p 273)*

If you had problems with any of the steps, this process will provide the opportunity to go back and refine the analysis done to this point. If you had difficulties reducing data to salient domains, and these are still in the data set, it will be likely that they will not fit into an outline that makes good sense. Here is another chance to decide exactly what needs to be reported and what can wait for another day. If some domains seem "thin" in relation to other more robust findings, here is another decision point where you need to determine if reporting such domains is necessary for representing the social phenomenon being studied. If your themes do not account for all of your data, this is the time to reconsider what holds your analysis together.

I make my students do a master outline in some form to bring closure to their analyses. For some, usually those who have followed procedures like those described above, this is a routine step that's just a matter of putting what they have known for some time into a final form. For others, this step is more difficult. It often means giving up dimensions of their work that they have "fallen in love with," even though these elements don't really fit into the studies they designed. Having to construct a comprehensive outline of findings forces the elements that don't fit to stand out. Others sometimes resist the idea of finalizing their analyses. My guess (from my own feelings and talks with others) is that part of this reluctance to making an end is the nagging fear that finally there may not be much to report. For me, there is a kind of emotional bouncing back and forth between "this is awesome stuff" and "this is pure crap."

I can testify that even though it is sometimes traumatic for students to have to pull their analyses into some understandable final form, there is great relief associated with finally having a "product" from so much labor and anxiety. A master outline does not mean analysis is complete, but it signals the researcher that something of meaning has come from the mass of data, hours of mindwork, and tons of energy associated with most qualitative projects. It organizes the work to this point and provides tangible evidence that all of the effort actually leads somewhere. Just as important, it provides a ready-made option for organizing the writing of the final report. Even if final versions of research findings turn out to be organized in ways different than the master outline, the relationships evident in the outline will have a major influence on how findings are reported.

Select Data Excerpts to Support Elements in Your Outline. As a final check on the analysis done so far and as further preparation for writing, data need to be read yet again to search for examples that can be used in the text of the findings to support the elements that make up the outline. As with typological analysis and the models to follow, including data excerpts to support findings is essential in qualitative reports. Identifying potential quotes in the data is important to getting ready to write, but it is also a good final check to see if sufficient data are evident to give you confidence in making your final report.

I recommended above that powerful or prescient quotes be starred in the data and on the domain sheets. Tracking down these quotes will be easy if careful records have been made; still, it is important to read all of the data within domains when searching for excerpts. As studies evolve and analyses are finalized, subtle shifts in emphases may require different quotes to make different points. When the actual writing begins, you will find that analyses become even more refined, and new quotes will be sought, but searching these out at this point gives more closure to the analysis, prepares you to write, and gives you confidence in what you have found.

Inductive analysis can take many forms. The model described here is one framework from which inductive analysis can be undertaken. Steps can be modified to fit the particulars of individual studies and particularities of individual researchers. The processes described here work well with observation data and can be used comfortably with most interview and unobtrusive data as well. This model does not make sense for data that have been collected with a narrow focus in mind, especially interview data that have been collected using structured guiding questions. Typological analysis has been described as appropriate for such data, and applying inductive procedures does not make good sense.

Inductive analysis as described here fits naturally within studies based on postpositivist and constructivist assumptions. While some widely used inductive approaches (e.g., Glaser & Strauss, 1967; Miles and Huberman, 1994) are based on a postpositivist perspective, the model I have presented is designed specifically to accommodate constructivist assumptions. Further, I believe it is possible to adapt my inductive model for work undertaken within critical/feminist and poststructuralist paradigms. Even though the nature of the data, the elements of domains, and the themes that emerge will be different, the basic structure of the model does not preclude its use by researchers across the paradigmatic continuum.

This inductive model will not work with every kind of study. It is well suited for studies that emphasize the discovery of cultural meaning from large data sets that include observational data—for example, ethnographies, microethnographies, participant observation, grounded theory, symbolic interaction, and naturalistic inquiry studies. It works less well for studies that focus on answering narrowly defined questions or that rely on interview data almost exclusively—for example, many focus group and interview studies. In addition, some studies that emphasize interpretation (as opposed to description and analysis) (see Wolcott, 1994) will find interpretive analysis procedures described next to be a better fit than the inductive model—for example, many narrative studies, educational criticisms, and phenomenological studies.

The strength of inductive analysis is its power to get meaning from complex data that have been gathered with a broad focus in mind. It provides a systematic approach to processing large amounts of data in ways that allow researchers to feel confident that what they report is indeed representative of the social situations they are examining and/or the perspectives of participants they are studying. It provides a way to analyze data that can be adapted for use in a wide variety of studies within any of the research paradigms. In some ways, it is basic. All qualitative researchers need to have a working knowledge of inductive analysis. Even if they never apply the model directly, it is hard to imagine that they can participate in the qualitative research community without a solid understanding of what inductive analysis is all about.

INTERPRETIVE ANALYSIS

Again, what to call this framework is troublesome. Interpretation is a defining element of all qualitative research. At all stages of the research process in any of the approaches discussed in this book, interpretation permeates everything that is done. Qualitative researchers are quick to acknowledge that as they design studies, consider theoretical bases, collect data, do analyses, and write up findings, they are constantly making interpretive judgments (e.g., Atkinson, 1992; Geertz, 1973; Schwartz & Schwartz, 1955). As Denzin (1994) so aptly summarizes, "In the social sciences, there is only interpretation" (p. 500). In fact, some researchers (including Denzin) would like to drop the term *qualitative research*, arguing that *interpretive research* better represents what goes on in this kind of work (e.g., Denzin, 1989b; Erickson, 1986; Graue & Walsh, 1998).

I like the term qualitative. It is well established and connotes a certain relationship to the traditional positivist paradigm that I find useful (see Eisner, 1991). While I fully agree that interpretation is included all along the research process, my decision to call this kind of analysis "interpretive" is based on Wolcott's (1994) notion that individual qualitative researchers transform data in different ways, emphasizing either description, analysis, or interpretation. He says that all studies have elements of each of these three ingredients, but the balance among them is different. Depending on the purposes of individual studies, one of these elements comes to the fore. The interpretive analysis model described here details a way to transform data that emphasizes interpretation.

Interpretation is about giving meaning to data. It's about making sense of social situations by generating explanations for what's going on within them. It's about making inferences, developing insights, attaching significance, refining understandings, drawing conclusions, and extrapolating lessons (see Denzin, 1989b, 1994; LeCompte & Schensul, 1999; Patton, 1990). Interpretation situates the researcher as an active player in the research process. Interpretation is undertaken with the understanding that it is a "productive process that sets forth the multiple meanings of an event, object, experience, or text" (Denzin, 1994, p. 504). Interpretations are constructed by researchers. The model proposed here provides tools for linking interpretations to data; but finally, they are the researchers' best efforts to produce meaning that makes sense of the social phenomena they are studying.

I acknowledge up front that describing a model, indeed *an analytic model*, for doing interpretation is tricky business. Interpretation is rightly seen as the artistic, creative side of qualitative work (e.g., Denzin, 1994; Wolcott, 1995). To try to formalize strategies for interpreting will seem incongruent (oxymoronic?) to some, confining to others, and heretical to still others. My objective is not to take away the creative intensity necessary for making sense of social phenomena in context or to turn the complex, artistic processes of interpretation into mechanical activity. I want to give folks inexperienced in doing this kind of work a framework for exercising their creative and artistic powers in productive ways. The interpretive analysis model provides a process for constructing meaning from data that goes beyond the analytic emphasis of the models described so far. A framework from which inexperienced researchers can apply the processes directly, modify them to suit different preferences, or adjust them to suit individual studies should provide new qualitative researchers with a "way to go" that is not provided elsewhere.

Steps in the interpretive analysis model are listed in figure 4.4. In this section, I will discuss each of these steps as if the researcher decided at the outset that he or she was going to use interpretive analysis and began with step one from the model. In reality, it will often be the case that researchers will have done a typological or inductive analysis at some level, then move to the next level in order to add an interpretive dimension to their earlier analytic work. I actually prefer this mode of operation. I think interpretations

FIGURE 4.4
Steps in Interpretive Analysis

1. Read the data for a sense of the whole

2. Review impressions previously recorded in research journals and/or bracketed in protocols and record these in memos

3. Read the data, identify impressions, and record impressions in memos

4. Study memos for salient interpretations

5. Reread data, coding places where interpretations are supported or challenged

6. Write a draft summary

7. Review interpretations with participants

8. Write a revised summary and identify excerpts that support interpretations

will be better grounded in the data if researchers have spent time transforming data in descriptive and analytic ways (see Patton, 1990). So while it will be possible to begin data analysis at step one of the interpretive model described here, most studies will be richer and findings more convincing when interpretive analytic processes are used along with or in addition to typological or inductive analyses.

Read the Data for a Sense of the Whole. The integrity of each analytic model depends on the researcher's ability of situate whatever insights are drawn out in relation to the context represented in the data set as a whole. The logic of the interpretive model parallels that of the inductive model in that pieces are put together in meaningful relation in order to construct explanations that help readers make sense of what's being examined. Researchers must start by being immersed in the data to the extent that whatever impressions are formed throughout the analytic process are considered within the context of the overall data set. Reading through that data set over and over is the only way to be immersed at the level required. I recommend starting interpretive analysis with a careful reading just to get an initial sense of what's included and not included in the data. I would resist the temptation to jump in and start recording impressions until the entire data set as it exists to that point has been carefully read.

Review Impressions Previously Recorded in Research Journals and/or Bracketed in Protocols, and Record These in Memos. This step assumes that researchers have followed the advice given in the data collection section of this book and kept a research journal recording impressions as research processes unfolded (see example of research journal entry in appendix C). These records, as well as impressions that should have been bracketed as part of data collection and protocol creation, will provide rich starting places for developing interpretations. The whole idea of making a record of impressions during the process of gathering and processing data is to capture potentially fruitful explanations that can be systematically examined later. Later begins now.

The object of your review is to get a handle on which impressions might lead to more careful examination and which ones may be left for another day. If you have chosen to do an interpretive analysis, you should have a good idea based on your data and research questions of what phenomena you will be trying to illuminate. If you are like me and have recorded impressions on a wide variety of topics, it is likely that many of your research journal entries and bracketed impressions will be easily set aside at this point. They may be important or interesting, but they don't fit the project at hand. I recommend that potentially salient impressions be noted in some way in the research protocols and/or in the research journals. This can be done with highlighter or some other distinguishing marking by hand or by using the file-making capacities of computer programs, if one is being used to assist in the analysis. The idea is to take a careful look at the impressions that came to you as you collected data and generated research protocols and to identify those impressions that you think will be useful as you prepare to undertake some systematic interpretation. If you are unsure if certain impressions will be useful or not, it is better to include them in the set you intend to study later. It's easier to drop them if they don't pan out than to try to retrieve them if you see later on that they will be important to the interpretive analysis.

The process of reviewing these impressions will almost always lead to the identification of relationships among impressions and the formation of new impressions. In this and the next step, I like the idea of writing special kinds of memos to capture the dimensions of your impressions and force you to begin to articulate the interpretations you are making when these impressions are played out. These memos are like those described by researchers such as Denzin (1994), Emerson, Fretz, and Shaw (1995), and Graue and Walsh (1998). Such memos "elaborate the researcher's understanding . . . by making connections and positing hunches about what is going on. Put more simply, memos are written notes to yourself about the thoughts you have about the data and your understanding of them" (Graue & Walsh, 1998, p. 166). Denzin (1994) discusses memo writing as a tool for "sense making" that leads to decisions concerning "what will be written about, what will be included, how it will be represented, and so on" (p. 503).

Memos can take many forms, but at this point they should be written in tentative, hypothetical language. I recommend complete sentences and paragraphs. The thought processes required to write sentences and organize paragraphs puts structure on your thinking and makes you make sense in ways that can be communicated to others. Memos may be written as possible explanations for behavior recorded in the data. They may describe potential insights that seem to be emerging. They may posit conclusions that can be drawn from studying particular settings. Or they may discuss the potential significance of observed events. Topic sentences that might organize some of the forms memos may take are offered as examples below:

1. Students may be acting defiantly in class as a way to express solidarity with their peers.

2. Could it be that the teachers avoid discussing pedagogical matters in the teachers' lounge because they are afraid others will judge them negatively?

3. It looks possible that all of the bus drivers interviewed feel they are underappreciated by school staff.

4. College faculty members seem to have withdrawn into their own teaching and research since the reorganization plan was vetoed by central administration.

The remainder of each paragraph would be an explanation of what the topic sentence means and why the researcher thinks it may be so.

Not every highlighted impression will lead to the writing of a memo. Some will be impressions that the researcher has a strong sense will be important to answering the research questions at the base of the study. Others will connect with other impressions and merit a memo that describes that connection. Some will be set aside. Remember, at this stage, we are only looking at impressions formed during data collection and processing. The next step involves systematically examining the complete data set in a search for impressions. The memos written at this stage will no doubt influence the search to follow, but the more comprehensive sense making begins with the next step.

Read the Data, Identify Impressions, and Record Impressions in Memos. The bracketed notes and research journal entries were made spontaneously as data were recorded and processed. In their original form, they may or may not look like the memos just described. In this step, you will be much more deliberate in your attempts to make sense of what is going on in your data. Your goal is to read through your data with a mind to systematically making and recording your interpretations of what is happening within the social contexts captured in your data.

The memos written as part of the previous step will influence the way you read the data. It is natural to be aware of the tentative interpretations you have just recorded in memos as you read the data in search of other impressions. Eventually, you will be making judgments about whether or not all of your interpretations are supported by the data, and every reading of the data will be done with an awareness of the potential explanations hypothesized to that point. But your major focus in this step should be on discovering new impressions that may develop into interpretations that bring meaning to your data.

The general questions that drive this reading of the data will likely be framed in terms related to understanding, meaning, and explanation—for example, What is going on here for the participants? What sense can be made of these events? How can these behaviors be explained? What meaning do these activities have for the players in the social setting? Why did that happen? This broad focus on attaching meaning to behaviors and events will be shaped by the design of the study, so the research questions, contexts, and data of the study will circumscribe this search for impressions. For example, the "What is going on here for the participants" question will translate into something like, What is going on in this elementary physical education class for the children with disabilities? The idea is to start with a manageable list of such questions, then let these questions guide the reading of the data in a search for impressions.

I recommend making notes to yourself as the search for impressions goes forth. These notes are not memos per se, but they are, in effect, data from which formal memos like those described in the previous step will be constructed. These notes can be kept on separate sheets, they can be written in margins or on sticky notes that get attached to the research protocols, or they can be inserts that are placed in the original data stored in electronic data or word processing programs. It should go without saying that, whether working with paper or electronic protocols, this level of processing should be done on copies rather than on original documents.

Once the data have been carefully read and impressions noted (and this might mean going through the data several times), you should next study the impressions noted and write memos in the same form as described above. Again, you will likely find some strong impressions that seem to be supported by many events in the data, some that seem important but not especially evident, and some that just don't pan out. Wolcott (1994) says that interpretation ought to be linked to research purposes. It is time to write up impressions that seem to hold promise for getting at the purposes of the research in the form of memos that express your working hypotheses. To this point the process has been decidedly inductive. You have been looking at particulars in the data and forming impressions of what those particulars might mean within the overall context under investigation.

The products of this and the previous step will be sets of memos that form the raw material on which more formal interpretations can be based. In order for these memos to be useful for analysis in a research project, they must be generated based on a careful reading of the data. We are dealing with impressions, but these impressions were not constructed willy-nilly from thin air. Interpretation is subjective, creative, and individual, but the interpretive work I am describing is rooted in a data-based conception of the research enterprise (see Gubrium & Holstein, 1997). In order for researchers' interpretations to be useful, they must be firmly grounded in the contexts being studied, and those contexts must be fairly represented in project data. Denzin (1989b, p. 31) identifies "contextualization" as one of the criteria of interpretation, and Eisner (1991) offers a definition that places context at the core of interpretation: "To interpret is to place in context, to explain, to unwrap, to explicate" (p. 97). Geertz's (1973) famous quote highlights the importance of grounding interpretations in careful descriptions of context:

> If anthropological interpretation is constructing a reading of what happens, then to divorce it from what happens—from what, in this time or that place, specific people say, what they do, what is done to them, from the whole vast business of the world—is to divorce it from its applications and render it vacant. (P. 60)

Good data are a record of "what happens," and interpretations that are not based in that data are indeed vacant. The procedures described here are intended to lead researchers through a process of interpretation solidly rooted in data.

Study Memos for Salient Interpretations. Coming out of the previous step, you should have a collection of memos—one set based your spontaneous impressions made during data collection and protocol making and one based on a systematic reading of the data. This step is essentially a data reduction process in which you study the collection of memos and decide which memos express interpretations that are salient to the research at hand. I have said that the memos should be written in tentative, hypothetical terms. At this stage, you begin the process of deciding if the insights within them are worthy of becoming part of your final report.

I recommend reading through the entire set of memos for a start. Doing so will give you a sense of the whole and suggest connections among memos that may not have occurred to you as they were written. Next, I would organize memos according to how they relate to one another and how they connect to the issues you want to address in your research. It may be, for example, that several of your memos offer explanations for why parents at the school you are studying do not trust school personnel or that you have a number of memos that reveal reasons why dress code policies are seldom enforced. The idea is to begin to get a sense of the big picture you will be drawing for your reader. Some memos will fit with others and become automatic "keep-ers." Some will stand alone as so powerful or so important that they cannot be discarded. And some will not fit or appear not to be sufficiently salient to the present study and will be put aside for another analysis on another day.

The outcome of this step will be an organized collection of memos that address the concerns of the research project at hand. For some, it will be log-ical and easy to put these into a formal outline. Others will prefer to keep the organization less structured. I would try to resist that need to get to premature closure and keep the interpretations in the memos at the level of "working hypotheses." The balance you seek is between developing such a tight orga-nization that the structure limits further exploration and having such a loose organization that everything is still up in the air.

| Reread Data, Coding Places Where Interpretations Are Supported or Challenged. |

Now that you have narrowed and refined the interpretations that may be reported, you should go back to the data in a systematic search for places that relate directly to the interpretations in your memos. This is a deductive activ-ity. You are asking, Where are all the places in the data where my interpreta-tions are addressed? Once located, these should be coded so that they tie to the organization created above. If you have constructed an outline, then cod-ing will look a lot like that suggested in the inductive analysis model above. You will have identified elements in your outline in terms of letters and num-bers that can be marked on protocols, and data collection dates and page numbers can be recorded on your working outline. If you have organized your memos in some other form, you will need to create a coding system that will allow you to easily identify all the places in the data related to the salient memos identified.

This process will, in effect, produce data on which you will decide if your tentative interpretations are supported by the data. The integrity of your findings hinges on your being able to look your committee, your critics, and your readers in the eye and say, "My interpretations are grounded in the data of the study." As with typological and inductive analyses, decisions about suf-ficiency are based on evidence of support and on lack of counterevidence. Taking the considerable time necessary to find and code all the places where your interpretations are addressed gives you the data necessary to make good decisions about whether interpretations ought to be reported or not. It will always be a judgment call, but at the least, a convincing argument should be made in your own mind (and later in your final report) that how you explain what's happening is supported by your record of that context and that evi-dence to the contrary can be explained to the extent that you are confident in your interpretations. Anything less may be interesting, even intriguing, but will it be research-based? As Wolcott (1994) summarizes,

Qualitative researchers are welcome to their opinions, but focused inquiry is not a soapbox from which researchers may make any pronouncement they wish. Plainly put, studies purported to be research-based must be just that. When the claim is made that an interpretation derives from qualitative/descriptive inquiry, the link should be relevant and clear. (P. 37)

Write a Draft Summary. Now is the time to bring the pieces together into a meaningful whole. You have written memos that represent salient interpretations that are supported by your data and organized these into a form that makes sense. The next step is to write a draft summary that communicates your interpretations at a level that others who are not familiar with your context can understand. This summary is not intended to be written as the findings chapter of your dissertation or the findings section of your report. It will not include an extensive data display or context description but will be focused on communicating the explanations, insights, conclusions, lessons, or understandings you have drawn from your analysis. While parts of this draft will likely find their way into your final report, the intent is not to write this summary as a findings chapter.

The idea behind writing the summary is to force you put the interpretations in your memos into a "story" that others can understand. The act of writing for an audience places constraints on how ideas are put together and communicated. Making yourself write the story of your interpretations will provide a test for the logical consistency of your thinking and expose any gaps in your argument that might exist. Interpretive researchers are storytellers who construct narrative tales with beginnings, middles, and ends (Denzin, 1994; Van Maanen, 1988). Writing this summary helps determine if you have a story to tell.

Wolcott (1995) recommends that qualitative researchers begin writing early in the research process, drafting "expanded pieces" (p. 100) as data collection proceeds in order to start to get a sense of what ought to be written up and what form it might take. Denzin (1994) argues that "[f]ieldworkers can neither make sense of nor understand what has been learned until they sit down and write the interpretive text, telling the story first to themselves" (p. 502). While I have done little draft writing during early stages of my research projects, I see the power of the case Denzin and Wolcott make for writing as a way to move sometimes disconnected or incomplete interpretive thinking to the level that it can be communicated sensibly to others. The writing of summaries that I am suggesting will give new researchers a way to find the stories in their interpretive analyses and see if they hold up when organized in narrative form.

The summaries that result from this step are drafts. It is assumed that they will become richer and more elaborate in future iterations, but they should include enough substance to account for the interpretations included in the memos identified as salient to the research project and enough detail that sense can be made of the stories they tell. While they are written for yourself in the sense that the writing will tell you if you have something to say, summaries should be written for an audience in the sense that someone who does not know the particulars of your study could still understand what is happening in your narrative. In other words, don't write the summary in shorthand based on your own special knowledge of the setting, but put together an account that could be comprehended by someone not familiar with your research.

Review Interpretations with Participants. For those approaching interpretive analysis from a constructivist perspective, it will be important to include a "member check" (Lincoln & Guba, 1985, p. 236) as the next step in the analysis. Constructivists are interested in the coconstruction of meaning in partnership with their participants. While it is presumed that constructivist researchers will have provided many opportunities for collaboration throughout the research process, inviting participants to give feedback on interpretations is a vital step in coconstruction.

Member checking at this point will look different for different studies, depending on the nature of relationships between researchers and participants and the kinds of interpretations that have been made. At the least, participants should have the chance to consider and give their reactions to the interpretations included in the summary just written. This minimal level member checking might be used when participants are distant from the researcher or scattered in many places. On the other extreme, researchers may present participants with their written summaries along with copies of their memos and even their research protocols, then invite participants to a working session during which they revisit the process of turning data into memos and memos into summaries. Again, how member checking gets done will depend on the history of what has gone before. In some projects, participants will have been involved in the data collection and the previous analysis steps, so their involvement at this stage will continue to be significant. In others, collaboration will have been minimal so member checking will be more formal and less intense.

Not all studies that use interpretive data analysis as described here will be designed and implemented based on constructivist assumptions. That does not mean that they will never ask their participants to review their interpretations. For example, postpositivist researchers may want participants to review interpretations as a way to argue for the "validity" of their findings. The logic of the research will dictate whether member checking in relation to reviewing interpretations is essential or not.

Write a Revised Summary and Identify Excerpts That Support Interpretations. As feedback is gathered from whatever member-checking activities are applied, summaries should be revised to take that feedback into account. This will move you closer to the full-blown findings section (or perhaps, a separate interpretations section) of your final report. With each iteration of your draft summaries, you should be refining and clarifying interpretations so that they communicate the understandings you have constructed, clarify what they mean in the contexts of your study, and represent what is captured in your data.

In preparation for writing a final draft and as a way to continue to ground interpretations in your data, this is the time to search your data for excerpts that might be used in a final report to support the interpretations you intend to write up. If you have followed the procedures described above, you will have marked places in the data protocols where your interpretations are supported. Going back through these looking for potential quotes to include in your final version should not be difficult. The idea is not to find *the* quote or other piece of evidence that will go with each segment of your case but to identify a collection of possible quotes that will help convince your readers that your interpretations are well founded. Linking potential excerpts to places in your summary where they may eventually fit at this point will save time later in the writing process.

Additionally, as with the analyses models described above, this search for relevant excerpts can serve as another check to be sure your interpretations are indeed supported by the data. On occasion, I have come to this step and discovered that I can identify no data excerpts that are good examples of the case I am trying to make. This calls for a careful reexamination of proposed interpretations. As we will see in the reporting qualitative research chapter to follow, analysis continues through the creation of the final written version of your report. If you cannot support your interpretations with examples from your data, it is likely that something is not right. If you decide your interpretations are on target but have no direct evidence, you will need to explain to yourself and your readers how that can be the case.

Interpretive analysis fits most comfortably within the assumptions of the constructivist paradigm. Interpretations are usually framed as one set of explanations for what is happening in the setting. It is understood that the researcher *constructs* those explanations and that other interpretations are possible. Often, participants are active coconstructors of the understandings that emanate from interpretive analysis, and it is possible to engage participant involvement all along the analysis process.

Denzin (1989b) characterizes the act of interpreting an event or process as a "construction" (p. 31), but in other writing, he discusses how interpretation has a place in postpositivist, critical, poststructural, and constructivist work (Denzin, 1994). I agree and have designed the political and polyvocal models to follow as specialized kinds of analyses that depend on interpretation within specialized worldviews. Still, the interpretive analysis model described here can be adapted to studies done within paradigmatic frameworks other than constructivism.

I mentioned above that my preference is for new researchers to build interpretation on previous data transformation that emphasized description and analysis (see Wolcott, 1994). This can be done by combining inductive and interpretive models so that the steps comingle, or the process may be more stepwise, adding steps in the interpretive model after inductive analysis is complete. Each of these approaches seems like a logical way to add an interpretive dimension to postpositivist work. Wolcott (1994) also notes that new researchers are often reluctant to and sometimes discouraged from including a lot of interpretation in their work. He suggests, and I agree, that framing early efforts as "alternative plausible interpretations" (p. 259) is one way to include an interpretive dimension without adding too much risk. Still, when students have interpretations that are powerfully supported by their data, I tell them to go for it!

Critical/feminist and poststructuralist researchers who opt not to use the political or polyvocal models may adapt the interpretive model to their analyses. This can be accomplished by self-consciously framing their impressions, memos, interpretations, and summaries within their paradigmatic assumptions. Students who are new to research are sometimes reluctant to call their work "critical," "feminist," or "poststructural" but have been influenced by the power of these perspectives to explain social phenomena discovered in their analyses. Some of these students do a more traditional inductive or interpretive analysis, then add a section that addresses their findings from a critical, feminist, or poststructuralist perspective. These new researchers are likely not to feel comfortable with the political and polyvocal models but can modify the interpretive analysis model so that their political and philosophical sensibilities can be included in their reports.

Interpretive analysis can be used with virtually any kind of data, but the quality of interpretation will be in direct proportion to the richness of the data. It will be difficult to support significant interpretive leaps based on standardized interviews because data will be narrowly focused on specific questions. It will be far more likely that meaningful explanations will be possible from analysis of complex data sets that include rich interview and/or observational data. Specialized methods for interpreting archival and historical data are not addressed here (see Hill, 1993; Scott, 1990), but the general inductive model can be used when unobtrusive data are included in the overall data set.

Some kinds of research, especially those rooted in constructivist assumptions, depend on interpretation and are a natural fit with the interpretive

*POLITICAL
ANALYSIS*

analysis model. Most of the research done under the names of *narrat[ive], [edu]cational criticism,* and *hermeneutic phenomenology* is included in this categoʃy. But any kind of study that goes beyond description and analysis ought to be guided by some kind of systematic method for generating interpretations and grounding them in data. The intent of the interpretive analysis model is to provide such a method.

POLITICAL ANALYSIS

Again, deciding on an identifier for this model was a problem. I call this kind of analysis "political" to signal its distinctiveness from the other models I am describing. As with the inductive and interpretive models presented above, the name chosen identifies what is emphasized within the model.

Just as all qualitative research involves inductive thinking and interpretation, so is all qualitative research political. I used to argue with my critical and feminist friends that I could tell them what their findings would be without seeing their data because their political agendas framed their research in such ways that they could only find what they were looking for. Their counter was that it is impossible to do research that is not political (including my own), and they were just being up-front about their own political positionings (while I was not). I have since learned a great deal more about critical and feminist approaches and have come to accept the basic premise behind their counter: all research is political (see Carr, 1995).

I believe that the framework presented can be adapted so that it might be useful to researchers operating within any of the paradigms that organize this book, but researchers who conceptualize their work within the assumptions of the critical/feminist paradigm will see immediate connections between the steps in this model and the application of their worldviews in the research process. The overall intent is to provide a framework that builds in analytic integrity so that findings are grounded in data while acknowledging the political nature of the real world and the research act. A more specific goal is to give critical/feminist researchers tools for doing data analysis that fit within the assumptions that characterize their perspective.

I have long since moved away from my naive view that there is inherent conflict between data-based and politically framed research, but I agree with Denzin (1994) that the discussion of methodological issues associated with how to do politicized qualitative research has been left unclear. If you buy into my notion that qualitative research of any type relies on systematic, rigorous data gathering and analysis techniques, then you will understand the attempt here to build on the data collection strategies described in the previous chapter by providing steps for ensuring that findings from politically driven studies are solidly grounded.

Deserved or not, much critical and feminist research is dismissed by mainstream science because it is seen as biased and/or not empirical. Findings are often read as political position statements rather than reports of research. The issues associated with bias reflect a lack of understanding or acceptance of the critical/feminist paradigm as a legitimate research perspective. Given Kuhn's (1970) dictum that the logic of each paradigm only makes sense to those standing within it, it may be foolish to try to convince those not inside the circle of the legitimacy of the ontological and epistemological assumptions of critical/feminist work. However, if the work is empirical, in the sense that it is based on a "recording of real world phenomena" (LeCompte & Preissle, 1993, p. 31), I believe researchers can and should do a better job of explicating how their data are gathered and how their analyses are done. The steps described below (see figure 4.5) offer a framework for doing rigorous data analysis within a political perspective.

Read the Data for a Sense of the Whole and Review Entries Previously Recorded in Research Journals and/or Bracketed in Protocols. In order for any analytic model to claim to be grounded in the data, the researcher must start with a solid notion of what is included across the data set. As with the models above, this means reading through the data with the express purpose of getting a sense of

FIGURE 4.5
Steps in Political Analysis

1. Read the data for a sense of the whole, and review entries previously recorded in research journals and/or bracketed in protocols

2. Write a self-reflexive statement explicating your ideological positionings and identifying ideological issues you see in the context under investigation

3. Read the data, marking places where issues related to your ideological concerns are evident

4. Study marked places in the data, then write generalizations that represent potential relationships between your ideological concerns and the data

5. Reread the entire data set, and code the data based on your generalizations

6. Decide if your generalizations are supported by the data, and write a draft summary

7. Negotiate meanings with participants, addressing issues of consciousness raising, emancipation, and resistance

8. Write a revised summary and identify excerpts that support generalizations

the whole. It will be natural for you to begin the mindwork associated with any form of analysis as you read through your protocols, but I recommend that you resist stopping to make notes or to mark up your protocols at this stage. Now is also the time to review the bracketing you have already done in your protocols and/or to read through all the entries you have recorded in your research journal. By review and read through, I mean see what's there. Again, you are trying to get a sense of everything you have as data to that point. Stopping to critique or classify or synthesize will change the nature of the whole at the same time you are trying to construct a picture of it. You will have plenty of opportunity to analyze the details later on. The object of this reading is to see the forest—the trees will not go away.

Write a Self-Reflexive Statement Explicating Your Ideological Positionings and Identifying Ideological Issues You See in the Context under Investigation. As part of a panel presentation at a research conference, a group of colleagues and I decided to open the session with the kind of self-disclosing introductory statements that characterize meetings of Alcoholics Anonymous. I was talking about ethical issues associated with observing young children, so I said something like: "My name is Amos, and I'm a voyeur." Of course we were trying to be provocative (and cute) to get the audience's attention, but the idea of giving your audience a sense of who you are and what you believe is important in all qualitative work, and vital in work that is framed within feminist or critical assumptions.

It is likely that your statement of "true confessions" (Schwarz & Jacobs, 1979, p. 58) will find its way into your final report in some form, but the purpose at this point is to give you a chance to spell out what you believe and where you stand on issues related to your study. It's important to do this in writing and to do it honestly and carefully. The act of writing forces you to organize your beliefs in a different way than thinking or even talking about them. If you have chosen this paradigm, you should have no problem being honest. In fact, if you have problems being direct about your ideological positionings, you may need to go back to the examination of your metaphysical, ontological, and epistemological assumptions suggested in chapter 1. Being careful about your descriptions means thinking through what you are saying and saying it clearly enough so that others could understand, even if they disagree.

What do you say? I would start with a broad statement framed like my self-disclosure above: My name is _____ , and I am a _____ (feminist, critical, other) qualitative researcher. Then it gets hard. There are many kinds of feminist researchers (see Harding, 1987; Olesen, 1994; Reinharz, 1992), many kinds of critical researchers (see Denzin, 1994; Morrow & Brown, 1994), and many other kinds of researchers who count their work as political in nature (see Denzin, 1994; Stanfield, 1994). Your job is to locate yourself in enough detail that you and your potential audience will have an idea of what your positioning means for how you think about and see the world. It will be necessary to justify your selection of the critical/feminist paradigm as the framework for your research. But especially detailed explanations will be needed because of differences in the approaches possible within the parameters of the paradigm. A straightforward example is the distinction between feminist research that starts with the assumption that women's perspectives are particular and privileged (e.g., Belenky et al., 1987) and feminist research that rejects the notion that there are special ways of knowing that are particular to women (see Hawkesworth, 1989). The point is that proclaiming that you are a critical theorist, feminist, or whatever is not enough. Knowing where you stand within many possible positions will take study and introspection. It's worth the time to stop and do this in some depth. If you are not prepared to locate yourself politically at this point, how can you start your politically framed analysis?

A second phase of this step is to write out your best guesses about the ideological issues that are salient to the context you are studying. This goes beyond self-disclosure to an exposition of what you suspect is going on in the settings you are studying based on your ideological predispositions. For example, if you are a critical theorist who believes that, at some level, schools are in place to reproduce a social order that keeps powerful people in power and keeps others in their place, your suspicions will likely be that the ways students are selected for programs for the gifted or placed in programs for the developmentally disabled will follow certain patterns related to race, class, and gender. It's important to get these ideological issues and your position related to them out on the table before systematic analysis begins. Your goal is not to admit some hidden bias that has to be somehow held in check. Here, you are making explicit your overtly political positioning in relation to the issues you are studying. Your belief system will guide how you proceed and shape what you will look for. Within the assumptions of this paradigm, that is not a problem to be managed; it is a reality to be understood and utilized.

Both statements should be written as narratives in paragraph form. If you have difficulty writing in the self-reflexive manner discussed here, it may be helpful to try some of the "writing experiments" suggested by Goodall (2000, pp. 142–46), which are designed to help you write about who you are and what makes you tick. After the narratives are written, you should make a list of the issues you identified in the second phase. These will be useful in the next step of this analysis. Writing these statements will help you articulate what you believe and where you stand. Without them, your analysis will likely wander, and your findings will seem fragmented. If you have followed the advice in earlier chapters, this step will be a logical extension of what you have done so far and provide a strong starting place for developing the rest of your political analysis.

Read the Data, Marking Places Where Issues Related to Your Ideological Concerns Are Evident. Now is the time to go back to the data with the list of ideological issues you projected in the last step. You will be reading the entire data set, asking: Where are all the places in the data that include information related to the ideological issues I have identified? This is like the second step in typological analysis in that you are reading the data just to locate excerpts that seem related to issues (categories in typological analysis) you have identified ahead of time. If you have five issues, it's easy to number them and mark your protocols with the appropriate number (or create separate computer files) as data tied to particular issues are identified. As with typological analysis, in this step, I recommend that beginners take one issue at a time and read the data searching for information tied to that issue, then do the same for the others. More experienced researchers may be able to read excerpts and then pull back and ask if and how they are related to their issues. Of course, it's a matter of experience, comfort, and personal style. What counts is that at the end of this step, you will be able to pull together all of the data related to each of your issues. Remember that many excerpts will fit into more than one issue and that whatever your sorting mechanism (hand marking or computer filing), the whole must be preserved. This means marking on copies of protocols (not originals) and copying (not cutting and pasting) computer files.

While this search involves deductive thinking—finding examples that fit your issues, it is possible that in your reading of the data, you will discover other issues that you did not foresee as you prepared your ideological statements. When this happens, you think inductively, establish a new issue, add it to your list, and do a systematic search for evidence related to it. It also makes sense that issues will be clarified and sometimes altered during this process. It is a good idea to keep this step as deductive as possible, but to ignore insights that emerge from the data, even during this sorting phase, would be a serious error. You will be analyzing data within issues later, but keeping track of ways your conceptualizations of issues might be changed as data are identified for inclusion is essential. If it is clear that issues need to be recast, split, joined, or significantly altered, stop and do that before continuing with this search. If it's more a matter of refining the ways the issues are stated, make notes and come back to it after you complete this step. The bottom line here is to not let your predetermined issues keep you from making sense of what the data are telling you.

Study Places Marked in the Data, Then Write Generalizations That Represent Potential Relationships between Your Ideological Concerns and the Data. This step again parallels procedures used in typological analysis in that you will be pulling together all of the excerpts you have just identified as related to one of your issues and examining these data separately. If you have used a computer program that sorts protocols based on your coding, then you will start by printing out all of the data excerpts coded as fitting with your first issue. If you have copied and pasted with a standard word processing program, you will begin with a printout of what you have pasted into the first file created around an issue. If you have hand marked your protocols, you will be reading those places identified with your first issue, or you may physically cut out copies of the excerpts that belong together and paste them on file cards (as I was trained to do in my doctoral program). As noted above, you will have some data that may fit within two or more issues. That means they will be copied as many times as necessary and treated independently within each issue.

As all the data related to a political issue are studied, the goal will be to search for relationships between the ideological issues you identified in your self-reflexive statements and what's happening in the social scene being examined, as represented in your data. The basic question for this kind of analysis is: What evidence exists in my data to support, alter, refine, or refute my beliefs about what is going on in this setting? If you have anticipated that parents of children of color would be treated differently than white parents in a study of the implementation of a school voucher program, you will have pulled together all of the data related to that issue and will now read the data asking if parent groups are treated differently and, if so, how.

This analysis is an important step toward ensuring that your findings are supported by your data. That means that you must be disciplined as you process the data. You will need to search carefully for evidence that supports your beliefs and read just as closely to identify data that run counter to what you expected or suggest alternative explanations for what appears to be going on. The final products of this step will be sets of generalizations related to each of your issues. These generalizations are still tentative at this point. In later steps, you will go back to the whole data set for a closer check on whether or not they hold up as written, but they must be based on the data at hand. When evidence is found that runs counter to what you believed you would find, you must construct generalizations that account for what is actually in the data. This will likely add to the complexity of your generalizations, but dealing with the real complexity of the real world is one of the hallmarks of qualitative work, and your study will be much stronger for it.

So this step is about pulling all the data related to each of your issues into separate sets, studying each set in an effort to discover the connections between what you thought you might find and what is there, then developing written generalizations that express the relationships discovered within each issue. You should be open to the likelihood that this kind of close reading and careful processing will reveal new insights that may lead you to create new issue categories and force you to go back to refining the previous steps. Yes, you can make yourself crazy trying to keep up with all that is going on when you do this or any kind of serious qualitative analysis, but forcing yourself to be disciplined and systematic will pay big dividends in the end. If you are not made a little crazy by the process, you are probably not doing it right.

Reread the Entire Data Set and Code the Data Based on Your Generalizations. Coming to this step, you should have a set of issues and lists of generalizations within each issue. For me, this is easily represented as an outline. It's easy to assign Roman numerals to each issue and capital letters to each generalization. You can use your own system, but some kind of straightforward code will be needed prior to implementing this step.

The code will be needed because this step involves another reading of the entire data set. If you have studied the analysis strategies above, you will see that going back to the "whole" is essential in all qualitative analysis. When pieces of the data are pulled out, as they must be for close examination, the potential exists to lose sight of the whole while looking at the parts. In addition, as the close reading within parts proceeds, elements are revealed that may have important connections to data that were not included in the segments as they were originally parsed. So moving back and forth between pieces and the whole is important.

I recommend going back to copies of the original complete data set when doing this step. You will have your outline in hand and read your protocols asking: Where are all the places in my data related to this generalization? You will mark, copy and paste, or use your data analysis program to code the evidence that in any way touches each generalization. It will be tempting to skip the places where you have spent considerable time in the previous step, but force yourself to consider each data piece anew, even if you can do it quickly.

Decide if Your Generalizations Are Supported by the Data and Write a Draft Summary. This step builds on the last as the source for your claims that your findings are based on a rigorously executed, data-based analysis. I have reviewed or read many studies undertaken from within the critical/feminist paradigm that have left me with the sense that the authors were probably right about the oppressive practices they described but that I had little confidence from what was presented that their descriptions were supported by careful data collection and analysis. I don't dispute the value of position papers to raise awareness and move people to action, but if it's presented as *research that takes a position*, then the elements that make it research need to be evident. These steps help ensure that your findings count as research that takes a position.

In this step, you are deciding if your generalizations hold up against all the data you have so far. Once coding is complete, it's a matter of reading through all of the data coded as being related to your generalizations and asking one by one, Is this generalization supported by my data? Some initial generalizations will stand, some will fall, and some will be changed. As with the strategies above, it's a good idea to mark especially salient data excerpts so that these can easily be located when it's time to select data for display in the write-up of your findings.

The final product of this step will be a draft summary that reports the final versions of your generalizations organized as a narrative. You will be taking this back to the participants in your study, so your summary should be written with them as a primary audience. As with interpretive analysis, the involvement of participants in political analysis is vital. While it is assumed that critical/feminist researchers will involve their participants throughout the research process (see Lincoln, 1995; Thomas, 1993), taking a draft of potential findings back to participants as part of data analysis is an important way to facilitate the kind of dialogue that can lead to the transformations expected from scholarship of this type. Producing a draft summary that is useful for generating dialogue will mean different things for different groups of participants. No matter what the form, the draft needs to be true to the potential findings summarized in the generalizations.

Negotiate Meanings with Participants, Addressing Issues of Consciousness Raising, Emancipation, and Resistance. In the interpretive analysis model, meanings are negotiated with participants in an effort to involve them as coconstructors of research findings. Here, the intent is somewhat different because researchers operating within a critical/feminist perspective believe that helping participants understand and resist the oppressive forces that keep them down is an important element of the research process. While supporting participants in an effort to help transform their lives is essential throughout the research process (see, e.g., Denzin, 1997; Stewart, 1994), I have built it into this step of the analysis process to emphasize the importance of addressing transformative efforts directly.

As with the interpretive model, taking the draft summary back to participants is an important part of this step. But the nature of these summaries will be quite different from those generated by interpretive researchers. These summaries will be designed to expose the dimensions of oppression experienced by the individuals being studied. Obviously, this can be very sensitive territory. For some participants, reading about the conditions that limit their life chances will be self-affirming and generate or reinforce motivation for social action. For others, such revelations will be threatening and may cause denial and/or withdrawal. For still others, cultural values and expectations may make the kinds of resistance encouraged by researchers seem outside the realm of possibility (see Hoffman, 1999). Much of how this is handled will depend on the relationships formed from the outset of the research process. If participants agreed to join in research efforts with an understanding that personal and social transformations were part and parcel of the research, and researchers have established trusting, reciprocal relationships with them throughout, then the nature and substance of the summaries presented at this point should not be a surprise. In any case, how summaries are presented and what you want to happen because of them should be carefully thought out.

Some of the issues that will likely need addressing as participants process summaries with researchers are consciousness raising, emancipation, and resistance. I count each of these as subelements of the larger construct of transformation. This kind of research is transformative in that it has as an express purpose "to provoke transformations and changes in the public and private spheres of everyday live—transformations that speak to conditions of oppression" (Denzin, 1997, p. 275). Researchers may be more comfortable trying to influence change in the public domain than addressing the immediate concerns of individuals' day-to-day lives, but most critical/feminist research will be based on close personal relationships with participants (Creswell, 1998; Lincoln, 1995; Reinharz, 1992; Smulyan, 2000b) that build in a moral imperative to work with them to raise consciousness, seek emancipation, and sometimes stage acts of resistance.

In a society that blames its victims for their depressed state, it is not surprising that many victims internalize social scapegoating and come to believe that they deserve the oppressive conditions they are forced to endure (deLone, 1979; Ryan, 1976). Others are so overwhelmed with the material realities of their oppression that they are more interested in survival than resistance (Polakow, 1993). A first step in helping individuals transform their lives is to help raise their consciousness about what is going on around them, who benefits, and why (Carr & Kemmis, 1986; Lather, 1991b; Orr, 1991). The substance of your summary ought to address these issues head on, and again, your narrative should describe the conditions in the participants' settings in enough detail and clarity to provide a compelling place for starting or continuing a dialogue about oppression.

Emancipation and resistance build on consciousness raising. Once individuals recognize the oppressive social conditions in which they live, what do they do about it? In this model, it is not enough to facilitate others' deconstruction of false consciousness. Critical, feminist, or other politically positioned researchers have an obligation to help their participants find ways to free themselves of the oppressive forces that confine them, and this sometimes means actively resisting (Denzin, 1994; Lather, 1991b; Roman, 1992). How consciousness raising, emancipation, and resistance will play out will be different in each research situation. But individuals committed to operating within this research paradigm obligate themselves to the kinds of ongoing involvement that will bring about significant, meaningful change in the lives of those they study. This step in the analysis process is not the only place to enact those obligations, but it is essential that the transformative nature of the research be evident as summaries are brought back to participants.

Write a Revised Summary and Identify Excerpts That Support Generalizations. The forms of knowledge produced using politicized research methods are value-mediated critiques that challenge existing power structures and promote resistance (see chapter 1). In preparation for writing such critiques for a wider audience than your participants, you should revise your summary to include what you learned from the negotiations in the previous step. It will likely be the case that the processes you experienced in that step will add insight that will help you frame your summary for that wider audience, so a record of your work to encourage change will become important information that may shape this version of your research findings.

I have stressed throughout this model the importance of using data to support the assertions that naturally come from political critiques. Because you have generated an analysis based on the model, the arguments generated in your final report will not be merely rhetoric or polemics; they will be reports of research. You will be standing on different intellectual ground when you support your assertions with data that have been systematically gathered and analyzed. That does not mean that everyone will agree with your findings or methods, but it does mean that can point to empirical evidence for your arguments.

As with all of the models described, displaying data to support your findings will be an important element of your final written report. Returning to your data after you construct your revised summary to search for data excerpts that support your case will set you up for writing your findings. An easy way to do this is to make an outline of your revised summary and use the elements of your outline as a code for marking your data when potential quotes are found related to each element. Be sure to write on your outline the pages on which potential excerpts have been found. Having marked salient places in the data throughout the analysis process will facilitate this search, but given the expectation that your summary will change in the process of reviewing your work with participants, going through the entire data set is important. Doing it now while the data are fresh in your mind, rather than waiting until you are in the middle of writing your final draft, will save time and reduce the necessity of having to review notes that will likely have grown cold.

It should be clear that political analysis would not be the model of choice for researchers operating within the postpositivist or constructivist paradigms. It is designed to accommodate critical/feminist epistemological assumptions that all knowledge is subjective and political and that researcher values frame the inquiry. As I mentioned in discussions of the other models, it may be possible to add a political dimension onto typological, inductive, or interpretive models. But using the basic processes of the political model to frame work in postpositivist or constructivist studies does not make sense.

The political analysis model can be adapted to fit the many kinds of studies that can be framed within the critical/feminist perspective. It is possible to design ethnographies, focus group studies, historiographies, narrative studies, case studies, action research projects, and collaborative studies using critical/feminist principles. The strength of the political model is that it can be modified for analyzing virtually any type of observation, interview, or unobtrusive data collected in these kinds of studies. Some researchers who call themselves critical or feminist poststructuralists use data analysis techniques that parallel those described in this section. That certainly works for the political side of their work. As discussed above, dealing with the conflicting assumptions of critical/feminist and poststructuralist paradigms is another issue. For those who see no conflict, modifying the political model for data-based poststructuralist studies will make excellent sense. For others, who see themselves as poststructuralists but want to do data-based work that is not necessarily framed in political terms, I developed the polyvocal data analysis model presented next.

POLYVOCAL ANALYSIS

One of the lessons I have learned from studying postmodern thought is to embrace paradox (see Hatch, 2000). The note at the top of the outline I am looking at as I start writing this section says, "How can I structure a poststructuralist analysis?" I have gone round and round trying to decide if I should stay with the same pattern and suggest steps for such an analysis, if I should try to write a section that describes analysis as an activity that needs its own postmodern form, or if I should abandon the effort altogether because the poststructuralist paradigm is just too different from the other worldviews. My final decision is made based on the same thinking that motivated me to try to describe systematic analysis procedures for all of the models above: New researchers and others new to qualitative research need a place to start. As with the other models presented, I don't see the steps for what I am calling "polyvocal analysis" as anything more than a place to start to do a particular kind of postmodern analysis.

Polyvocal analysis is framed as one kind of analysis that fits within the assumptions of the poststructuralist paradigm. It is not meant to prescribe, but

FIGURE 4.6
Steps in Polyvocal Analysis

1. Read the data for a sense of the whole

2. Identify all of the voices contributing to the data, including your own

3. Read the data, marking places where particular voices are heard

4. Study the data related to each voice, decide which voices will be included in your report, and write a narrative telling the story of each selected voice

5. Read the entire data set, searching for data that refine or alter your stories

6. Wherever possible, take the stories back to those who contributed them so that they can clarify, refine, or change their stories

7. Write revised stories that represent each voice to be included

to suggest what needs to be considered to complete such an analysis. It should be undertaken with the full awareness that it involves taking a structured journey toward a poststructuralist destination. If you want to do this kind of scholarship and cannot embrace paradox, you had better be prepared to at least live with it.

In my description of poststructuralism in chapter 1, I noted that three kinds of inquiry are associated with this paradigm: deconstructions ala Derrida (1981), genealogy as described by Foucault (1977), and what I called "data-based studies." Obviously, this book has emphasized data-based inquiry. Polyvocal analysis is one data-based approach that fits within the assumptions of poststructuralist thinking, especially the notion that multiple truths exist and that these are always partial, local, and historical (Richardson, 1994). Polyvocal texts speak with multiple voices, telling multiple stories (see Doherty, Graham, & Malek, 1992; Lather, 1991b). Constructing such texts means finding ways to listen to many voices in our data and exploring ways to tell many stories in our findings. Polyvocal analysis is a tool for working with data so that polyvocal texts can be written. As with the other models in this chapter, it is possible to adapt the steps of polyvocal analysis to studies done within the assumptions of other paradigms, but in the description below, I will focus on its use as a poststructuralist approach.

Read the Data for a Sense of the Whole. Even though it is assumed that data will be gathered with the explicit intent of capturing multiple perspectives on particular social phenomena or circumstances, it remains important to have a sense of the entire data set as analysis begins. As with all of the models, I recommend that this step be undertaken as a reading activity just to get an overall feel for what's there. If analysis is undertaken before data collection is complete—for example, as new perspectives are added to a growing data set—then the new whole data set should be read before analytic steps proceed. Even though polyvocality is the goal, that does not mean that the multiple voices represented have no relationship to each other. Missing those relationships means missing a big part of the point.

Identify All of the Voices Contributing to the Data, Including Your Own. In all likelihood, you will have structured your data collection around your objective to capture particular voices. Your interviews, observations, and other kinds of data collection will have been organized around that objective, and identifying voices you want to include in your final report will be straightforward and direct. The notion of voices here is meant to include those of individuals and of identifiable groups. For example, Bloom and Munro (1995) created a kind of polyvocal text that represented the life stories of each of four female administrators. In contrast, Tobin, Wu, and Davidson's (1989) polyvocal text presents the perspectives of Japanese, Chinese, and American preschool teachers, administrators, parents, children, child-development experts, and the authors.

If individual voices are to be captured, identifying them should be fairly easy. If group voices are to be analyzed, care in selecting them may have been taken early in the design of the study. However, if, in the process of collecting data or reading through the data, you discover unanticipated voices, these need to be added to your list. The objective of this step is to identify all possible voices. Later, you will decide whether or not to actually include all the voices in your final report. Finally, it is essential that you count your own voice. It is important that you be reflexive about your own place in the telling of others' stories. In a real sense, all of the voices you hope will be heard in your findings will be interpreted through your own voice (see Bruner, 1984; Hatch & Wisniewski, 1995). You will decide who to talk to, what to ask, what will be recorded, what will be analyzed, and what will be included. You will construct the text that frames what your participants have to say. Your place in representing the voices you present must be reflexively acknowledged.

Read the Data, Marking Places Where Particular Voices Are Heard. This is a fairly low-level sorting activity. You have identified individual or group voices. Now you will assign some sort of identifier to each voice, read the data, making decisions about whose voice is represented in each data excerpt and then mark the data (or create separate computer files) based on those decisions. The question that guides this step is, Whose voice (or voices) is (are) represented here? The outcome of this step will be separate sets of data divided by voices. It is important to be aware that multiple voices may be included in single excerpts and of the possibility that important new voices may be discovered in the data. Such an awareness will make your analysis much more complex and increase your confidence that your data analysis has an inductive dimension.

Study the Data Related to Each Voice, Decide Which Voices Will Be Included in Your Report, and Write a Narrative Telling the Story of Each Selected Voice. Once data have been organized by the voices represented, you can study each set to decide which voices will be telling stories in your final report. I recommend that you start by reading each set of data separately while asking, What does this individual/group have to say about the focus of the study? You will have designed your study with particular issues, contexts, or social phenomena in mind, and now you are asking the data to tell you what each voice you have identified has to say about your research focus. Now is the time to pay special attention to your margin notes, bracketed places in your data, and your research journal. Entries related to particular voices should be processed along with the hard data at this time. I would keep running notes of important elements you find as you read each set of data.

Based on your reading, notes, and bracketed information, you will need to make a decision about whether or not each voice will be included in your report. Again, if you have designed the study to capture the stories of selected individuals or easily identifiable groups, then this phase may be simple. But, be careful not to ignore other unanticipated voices that may be present in your data, and be sure that decisions about their inclusion or exclusion are founded on more than convenience. The most important criterion for inclusion is the contribution of each voice's story to revealing different perspectives on the topic of study. You are operating within a paradigmatic framework that assumes that multiple understandings of events, activities, and phenomena are not just possible, but inevitable. You are not searching for the Truth in any one story, but trying to bring out as many truths as are salient to your examination. If stories are to be included, they must have something to say about what you are studying.

Further, there must be sufficient support in your data to construct a story for each voice you select. If the data set you are reading is full of rich detail, lots of exemplary quotes, and plenty of contextual complexity, this may make it more difficult to write up as a story, but it will be clear that a story must be written. If there is sparse detail, few quotes, and not much context, you must proceed carefully, even if you are sure there's an important story to be told. If this is data-based research, the stories that make up your findings must be supported by your data. Here is another place where doing analysis as part of data collection will allow you to go back to your participants to collect more information when you discover an important potential story that you need more data to support.

The final phase of this step is to draft an initial version of the story you plan to tell for each voice. The language of voice and story goes well with the notion of polyvocality, but I take a broad view of what form the "stories" we're talking about here may take. Certainly, they will be narratives, but they may be structured like findings from traditional qualitative reports or organized in ways that have roots in literary, journalistic, theatrical, or other traditions (see Ellis & Bochner, 1996; Polkinghorne, 1995; Richardson, 1994; Tierney, 1993b; Zeller, 1995). One example of how to construct stories from data is Polkinghorne's (1995) notion of narrative analysis. The stories Polkinghorne describes are special kinds of discourse productions in which "events and actions are drawn together into an organized whole by means of a plot. A plot is a type of conceptual scheme by which a contextual meaning of individual events can be displayed" (p. 7). Narrative analysis is a strategy for constructing stories (emplotted narratives) from data. The basic analytic activity involves developing or discovering a plot that links the data together. Polkinghorne characterizes the strategy as a synthesizing process that configures the data into a coherent whole, and he details ways to connect plot development to data and proposes guidelines for story development. Narrative analysis is one way to use data to construct a particular kind of story. The point here is that data-based stories of whatever type need to be drafted. Drafts should be complete in the sense that that they include all the elements that make up a complete story. They need not be complete in the sense of being a polished, final draft.

Read the Entire Data ASet, Searching for Data That Refine or Alter Your Stories. In order to improve the quality of the stories you have drafted and to ensure that they represent the entire data set, as opposed to only the data that were pulled out for particular voices, you need to go back to the whole. Here you are searching the data for information that confirms, extends, or calls into question the findings expressed in your stories. What you are asking during this step is, What other data do I have that can clarify the stories I have written? Because your goal is to capture multiple perspectives in multiple stories, finding discontinuities among stories should not be a surprise. Poststructuralists would not expect everything to fit together in a tidy package. The complexity, incongruity, and paradoxical nature of real life ought to be explored across your stories. The objective of this step is to be sure your story drafts adequately represent the broad data set on which they are based.

Whenever Possible, Take the Stories Back to Those Who Contributed Them so That They Can Clarify, Refine, or Change Their Stories. This step builds on ethical and methodological concerns about appropriating the stories of others. Efforts to "give voice" to participants can work to reproduce the power relationships we are trying to reduce, actually underscoring perceptions that those with whom we do our research are incapable of speaking for themselves (see Smulyan in Hatch & Wisniewski, 1995). Inviting participants to read and comment on their stories as presented by the researcher improves the balance of power in the construction and ownership of stories. This step also makes it possible to improve the quality of the stories that have been drafted. Depending on the research bargain established at the time they signed onto the project, participants are given the opportunity to edit, clarify, add to, or sometimes veto the publication of their stories.

Depending on the situation, I recommend that when individual stories are told, participants be given the opportunity to read the story drafts, then make written comments directly on the drafts and/or discuss their concerns and share further insights with the researcher. When group stories are presented, it makes sense that as many individuals as possible are given the chance to read and respond. Obviously, tensions are possible when participants want to edit or remove material that researchers see as vital. I know of cases where researchers have regretted making research bargains that allowed participants to refuse to have their stories published. For me, it comes down to asking, Whose story is it? You need to decide the answer to that question *before* you make bargains with participants about how much power they will have over the final disposition of the stories you hope to tell (see Goodall, 2000).

Write Revised Stories That Represent Each Voice to Be Included. In preparation for writing the stories as findings, you should now revise your drafts, taking into account the comments and concerns of your participants. If written or verbal comments are extensive, or if stories are to be changed dramatically, this may mean going back to earlier steps in this model. As part of your formalized findings, you will likely have to make sense of the relationships among the multiple stories you will be telling. In one sense, you will be telling your story of the stories you have collected. You will no doubt see relationships among stories all along the data collection and analysis process. It's a good idea to keep track of your ideas for connecting stories—your story of stories—in your research journal, but I would resist making such connections a part of the stories you are telling and revising at this point. The spirit of polyvocal analysis is to give voice to a variety of perspectives. Your job at this stage is to tell the stories from the perspectives of your participants. The final product will be a set of stories that capture the voices of the individuals or groups you have studied.

Polyvocal analysis was created to give data-based poststructuralist researchers a way to systematically generate findings from their work. The specific intent is to provide a framework for allowing many voices to express many truths, as opposed to an authorial voice to pronounce *the Truth*. I have described polyvocal data analysis in terms of voices and stories. This makes it easy to see connections between poststructuralist aims and narrative and life history work (see Hatch & Wisniewski, 1995). Connections to other kinds of research are possible but should be made with care. For example, I can picture multiple case studies that are organized in ways that generate cases representing a variety of perspectives or a polyvocal ethnography that presents many truths through the lenses of different participants. Given that the data are rich, include multiple perspectives, and are narrative in nature, the polyvocal analysis model presented here could be adapted to fit such studies and others like them when the production of multivoiced texts is the objective.

COMPUTER-ASSISTED ANALYSIS

As I have indicated throughout the descriptions of the models above, using computer programs to assist in the sorting and organization of data is an efficient alternative to doing the same work by hand. It is not and never can be a satisfactory alternative to doing the mindwork associated with analyzing and interpreting data. Several of my students have used computer programs designed to help qualitative researchers do data analysis, and they have found them helpful. I have colleagues who would not think of trying to analyze large data sets without the support of their favorite data analysis software. In my own work, I use word processing programs to help me copy and paste material once I have coded it by hand, but, so far, I have been reluctant to rely on special data-handling software programs as I do my analyses. For me, it has to do with being comfortable with familiar strategies and uncomfortable placing an extra layer of technology between the data and myself. But I have learned from my students and friends that using the technological assistance available does not necessarily mean giving up the rigorous mental processing required of this kind of work. My concern for new researchers is that they might see the elaborate possibilities available with new programs as substitutes for the careful reading and complex thinking necessary for making sense of qualitative data. I agree with Glesne and Peshkin (1992) who summarize, "The products of computer-assisted analysis are only as good as the data, the thinking, and the level of care that went into them" (p. 145).

In order to help new researchers decide whether or not to use computer-assisted data analysis in their work, I have synthesized lists of advantages and disadvantages, drawing on my observations and a number of sources (Creswell, 1998; Glesne & Peshkin, 1992; Graue & Walsh, 1998; LeCompte & Schensul, 1999). Readers are encouraged to consult these and other sources, including overviews and reviews of available programs such as those published by Fielding and Lee (1998), Fisher (1997), Kelle (1995), Tesch (1990), and Weitzman and Miles (1995). In addition, appendix A includes annotated descriptions of internet sites devoted to qualitative research, including several related directly to computer-assisted data analysis.

Advantages of computer-assisted analysis include

- Programs provide file systems that assist researchers in storing and organizing large amounts of textual data.

- Computers can save time and reduce drudgery, especially in the areas of coding, retrieving, displaying, counting, and sorting.

- Computers force researchers to be organized and to plan well, thus encouraging systematic approaches to analysis.

- Most analysis programs force researchers to study data line by line, ensuring a more careful reading of the data.

- Computers make writing, editing, and rewriting easier.

- Some programs can create graphic displays from analyses that would take much longer and/or require special expertise.

Some *disadvantages of computer-assisted analysis* are

- Most programs are complex, and their manuals not very helpful, meaning it takes nonproductive time to learn to use them to their full advantage.

- Researchers may make analytic decisions based on what the computer can do rather than what should be done.

- Computer use may encourage researchers to lose sight of the contexts of the study and the data set as a whole.

- As categories are set within computer programs, researchers may be reluctant to rethink or change them.

- Computer programs vary in their features and applicability to certain research approaches, meaning that inappropriate programs may be selected for certain projects.

- Data and completed analyses can potentially be lost through technical failures and human errors.

Learning about computer-assisted analysis is important, but I recommend that final decisions should not be made without some practice actually using such programs to work with real data. Deciding to use a certain program, then learning how to do it as dissertation data are analyzed could lead to a disaster. It would be much wiser to learn how to use a program, practice it on preliminary data, and then decide if and how it will be useful in a full-blown study. Qualitative methods courses and courses on specific software programs often give students this kind of opportunity.

CRITERIA FOR ASSESSING DATA ANALYSIS ADEQUACY

As in the preceding chapters, the questions below will serve to summarize the data analysis approaches described in this chapter and provide a framework for assessing the adequacy of data analysis procedures for individual studies. As with the chapter on data collection, the criteria for data analysis assessment will be presented in two sets—one general set of criteria that apply to all qualitative data analyses, and one set that addresses issues that arise within each of the particular models described. As with all of the suggestions in this book, readers are invited to study and adapt the criteria presented to fit their particular circumstances and needs. The models were created to provide frameworks, and the criteria for adequacy will need to be adjusted as models are modified for actual studies. You will note that I have included "Are the findings supported by the data?" in the general criteria and, in some form, in each of the specific question sets. This reflects my emphasis throughout this book on encouraging data-based approaches to qualitative inquiry.

General Questions for Assessing Data Analysis Adequacy

1. Is it clear how and when data were analyzed?
2. If utilized, is the role of computer programs designed to support data analysis spelled out?
3. Do data analysis procedures make sense given the research paradigm, the kind of research being done, the data collected, and the research questions to be answered?
4. Are analysis procedures systematic and rigorous?
   A. Are procedures clearly articulated?
   B. Can the analysis be explained and justified?
   C. Are all deviant cases and disconfirming data accounted for?
   D. Can the analysis be organized into coherent research findings?
   E. Are the findings supported by the data?

Questions for Assessing Typological Analyses

1. Do typological analysis procedures fit with the types of data collected for the study?
2. Are initial typologies tied to project aims and research questions?
3. Did analysis include a search for patterns, relationships, and themes within and across typological categories?
4. Are all salient data accounted for in the findings?
5. Are the findings supported by the data?

Questions for Assessing Inductive Analyses

1. Do inductive analysis procedures fit with research assumptions, purposes, and questions?
2. Was a thorough, inductive domain analysis completed?
3. Was a systematic search for relationships and themes completed within and across domains?
4. Was a master outline created that organizes the findings into a coherent whole?
5. Are all salient data accounted for in the findings?
6. Are all findings supported by the data?

Questions for Assessing Interpretive Analyses

1. Do interpretive analysis procedures fit with the assumptions, purposes, and questions that drive the research?
2. Were impressions and tentative interpretations recorded as memos?
3. Are interpretations supported by the data?
4. Were data-based interpretations summarized in writing?
5. Were interpretations shared with participants and summaries revised based on participant feedback?

Questions for Assessing Political Analyses

1. Were ideological positionings explicated and political issues related to the study identified in a self-reflexive statement?
2. Were generalizations written that represent relationships between ideological expectations and the data?
3. Are generalizations supported by the data?
4. Were data-based generalizations written as a draft summary?
5. Was the summary used as a tool for addressing issues of consciousness raising, emancipation, and/or resistance with participants?
6. Was the summary revised to include insights shared by participants?

Questions for Assessing Polyvocal Analyses

1. Were the multiple voices to be included in the analysis identified?
2. Were narratives written to represent the stories of each voice to be included?
3. Are the stories supported by the data?
6. Were the stories taken back to participants for clarification, alteration, or refinement?
7. Were stories revised based on feedback from participants?

CHAPTER FIVE

Reporting Qualitative Research

How do I write up my findings? What form should my dissertation take? How can I publish my research results? This chapter provides guidelines for turning the hard-earned products of design, data collection, and analysis into findings that communicate what has been learned. More than a few new scholars have gone through all of the steps described so far in this book and hit the wall when it comes to writing up their final results. The narrative style associated with qualitative reports requires the art and skill of a writer, and not all good researchers see themselves as good writers. I cannot teach you how to write in these pages, but I hope to give you some ways to think about the writing process, some ways to conceptualize a dissertation, and some ways to report findings that will help you keep going when you feel like stopping.

Understanding that all writing is personal and idiosyncratic, I try to provide some insights into the general writing process drawing from my own experiences as a writer, editor, and mentor to novice writers and from what other writers and qualitative researchers have to say about writing. I discuss issues that confront most students facing down the dissertation process, address the process of converting data analyses into findings sections for dissertations and other reports, provide some tips for publishing qualitative reports, and conclude with criteria for assessing the adequacy of final reports.

WRITING PROCESSES

Writing about writing is awkward. Writing is as much a part of doing qualitative research as design, data collection, and analysis. As Wolcott (1990) notes, "Writing is integral to qualitative inquiry, not an adjunct" (p. 48). Judging by how doctoral students talk about the horrors of writing dissertations and by how much writing doesn't get done or gets delayed as long as possible, some discussion of general writing processes seems important. Others have written more comprehensively about the place of writing in qualitative research (e.g., Becker, 1986; Emerson, Fretz, & Shaw, 1995; Golden-Biddle & Locke, 1997; Goodall, 2000; Van Maanen, 1988; Wolcott, 1990; Woods, 1999). I have borrowed from these and other sources and recommend that new researchers, especially those who see themselves as new writers, read all they can about writing.

I organize this discussion as a set of tips for getting words on paper. I start with the assumptions that writing involves a special kind of thinking, that writing takes discipline, and that writing is difficult work. I'm sure that somewhere lives a writer for whom words flow onto the page as freely as water runs downhill, a writer who gives up other activities because he or she cannot wait to sit down at the keyboard, a writer who is mystified by others' reticence because he or she sees writing as an easy and natural act. But I have yet to meet this person. Further, graduate schools do a generally poor job of teaching or even talking about the writing process. I agree with Golden-Biddle and Locke (1997, p. x) that "this is ironic given that [writing] is a practice that consumes so much of our professional lives." The tips that follow may not apply to every new writer, but I hope they will be of help to those who think writing is hard work that requires special thought processes and serious self-discipline.

Just Write. It will never be just right, so just write. This silly sounding advice that I have given to both first graders and colleagues with doctorates is actually central to the act of constructing meaning on paper. Some of my friends from graduate school have never written or have written only enough to get tenured where they work. Some did not finish their doctoral programs because they did not write a dissertation. One of the reasons they claimed they could not write was because they were sure they could not get it just right. They were sure they had nothing new to say and that their way of saying it would express more about what they didn't know than what they did. They seemed to think about writing as an act of uncovering the perfect paragraph or sentence or word as if there is one best way for each piece of text to be written. Only a genius is up to measuring the worth of his or her writing by that standard. In contrast, Richardson (2001, p. 35) characterizes writing as a "method of discovery," explaining, "I write because I want to find something out. I write in order to learn something that I did not know before I wrote it." This approach fits my experience and removes the daunting expectation that there is a perfect text to be uncovered. I love the explanation I heard a noted children's author give for the difference between her successful career and that of those who dream of being writers. "I have learned to embrace imperfection," was all she said. For ordinary mortals, there is no perfect text, no just right. There are only our texts, our stabs at sharing meaning with others in print. This cannot happen unless we are willing to write, to move the pen across the page or the cursor across the screen. So just write. Start by expecting yourself to write and making yourself write. As we will see below, your first efforts may not turn out words that make it to your final draft, but you have no chance of getting to even the roughest draft unless you just write.

Accept Anxiety. It makes me feel better to know that writers I admire experience lots of anxiety when they are trying to write. Peshkin characterizes writing as "primarily a matter of dealing with demons" (Glesne & Peshkin, 1992, p. 155), and Woods details the travails of accomplished writers from many genres, summarizing, "Pain is an indispensable accompaniment of the [writing] process" (1999, p. 11). I hate to say it, but I think both are right. When I am in the middle of a writing project, I experience a running battle between demons telling me I'm guilty of not working hard enough whenever I am not writing and those that make my stomach hurt whenever I force myself to sit down to write. I am afraid to write. My nervous system does the same stuff when I climb the stairs to the spare bedroom where I write as it does when I'm getting ready to make a presentation before a large group. But I always get myself to the top of the stairs, just as I always make my speeches because I refuse not to face my fears. For me, writing is painful. Knowing that others experience the same pain does not really make it less painful, but it does make me feel less alone and less crazy. The advice here is to accept anxiety as an inevitable, even indispensable, part of the creative process. If you expect to overcome your anxiety *before* you write, you will probably never be a writer. Writing itself is likely to be the only way to deal with demons that accompany it.

Avoid Avoiding. It makes sense to avoid pain, so I understand why so many graduate students and new professors find wonderful excuses to avoid writing. Any excuse will do. Some of the most interesting have to do with substituting something unsavory but not quite as painful for writing. So folks catch up on their ironing or stain the deck when they should be writing. They wouldn't think of going to the golf course or renting a movie, but it's OK not to write if the substitute activity is bad enough. Another pattern is rationalized around not being ready to write. This means that more time needs to be spent searching the data bases, reading the related literature, polishing the analysis, conceptualizing the findings, or organizing the outline. Individuals stuck in this mode sometimes never get ready to write. There is always one more source to be checked, one more pass at the data to be made, one more outline to be drafted. My own excuses are no more sophisticated. "I need a large block of uninterrupted time" is my personal favorite. When I started this book, I sometimes took weeks away from writing because my schedule was too hectic to fit in regular sustained writing periods. I was avoiding. Another excuse I have used with some success is that I just don't have the energy to write. Writing takes a great deal of concentrated effort, and even when I have the time, I can't be productive if I am exhausted from doing the other work that professors at an institution like mine have to do. Pretty good avoidance tactic, huh? In the next section, I will describe how I have developed writing rituals to deal with these avoidance strategies. The key is to recognize your excuses as devices for avoiding the anxiety of writing and realize that the anxiety can only go away when you avoid avoiding and get on with writing.

Create a Writing Ritual. At least 80% of this book has been written between 6:00 and 10:00 A.M. I started the book trying to fit writing into my usual pattern of working at my university office. On my calendar, I marked a morning here and an afternoon there and tried to hold them for working on this book. Even though this pattern had been fine for writing articles and producing edited books, it was not working for this book. It was too easy to drag out my avoidance excuses—not enough sustained time and not enough energy when I needed it. It happened that my older son started college and moved his computer out of a spare bedroom at the same time I decided I needed a different writing routine. I bought a computer to match what I have at the university, dragged all my books and library materials home, and set up a writing space in the spare bedroom. More important, I created a ritual that has moved me from writing a couple of hours per week (when I could find the time and energy) to working 12 to 15 hours per week (at times when my energy is concentrated on writing). My ritual is to get up at 5:30, walk the dog to wake myself up and get some exercise, eat a quick bowl of cereal while I read the front section of the paper, pour the first of two cups of coffee, tell my wife I am "Off to the mines," then climb the stairs and start writing. I make myself write at least four mornings per week. I have been able to keep my teaching in the afternoons and evenings during fall and summer terms but have morning teaching in the spring, meaning that I write on many Saturdays and virtually all Sundays during that semester. Of course, this is only an example of a ritual that works for me. It helps me to not have to decide if I have enough time or energy to write. I just get up and do it. The point is that it may be useful (essential?) for you to develop your own writing ritual (see Becker, 1986; Goodall, 2000; Wolcott, 1990). A good starting place might be to examine the excuses you use to avoid writing, then set up a ritual that reduces the chances of allowing those excuses to get in your way.

Set Production Goals. I like writing down goals and marking them off when they're completed. I keep a folder with career goals, 5-year goals, annual goals, and semester goals. I make a to do list every day and mark off what is completed. It keeps me going to know that something is getting done. I had a chapter outline on my office bulletin board for this book with a timeline showing when I expected chapters to be completed. It gives me satisfaction to check off when chapter drafts are finished, and it gives me a shot of guilt when I see I'm behind schedule. Other social scientists set production goals that specify how many pages or sections they expect to write in a given period (e.g., Goodall, 2000; Woods, 1999). My approach is to make myself put in the hours. Some mornings are spent processing information and organizing, so few words make it to the page. I still count this as writing time (being careful not to create another avoidance strategy). I figure that for every hour of writing time, I will produce about one page of text, and my own regimen for this project calls for at least 12 hours per week. When I set up the timeline in my office, I did so by estimating how many hours each chapter might take. I know lists, goals, and timelines are not for everyone. You will have to decide what works for you, but be honest with yourself. I'll go out on a limb here and suggest that the more you dislike the idea of production schedules, the more you probably need them. Sustained writing projects, such as dissertations, require large amounts of time and a great deal of self-discipline. Giving yourself a production goal in terms of pages, chapters, or hours can be a helpful motivator for managing your time and engaging your discipline.

Get Organized. Just as you will develop rituals that get you into your writing each day, so will you create rituals that frame how you go about putting ideas on paper. The next several tips are suggestions for organizing yourself to get going and keep your momentum once started. The physical space I am writing in is surrounded by reference materials. At my right on the floor are the books and articles related to the section I am working on. Along the wall on my left are stacks of books and a box of article copies that I have brought from my office and checked out of the university library. If I were writing up a study, my data would be in an organized pile in the room. Whenever I see a citation for some material that I need, I make a note and add it to my "stacks" at the next opportunity. Before I start a new chapter, I go through all of the materials I have on hand and make note of ideas that may find their way into the text. I keep separate sheets of paper for each source and write down enough information (usually just a phrase or a few key words) so that I can remember the idea, and I record the pages where the ideas are located. I next put together an outline that includes at least the section headings and subheadings of the chapter. Then I go back through my summary sheets and put the ideas I might use in the appropriate sections. As I start each section, I refer back to the materials identified for each section. My outlines change as I write, but I can't imagine starting without some way to organize where I think I'm headed (see Glesne & Peshkin, 1992; Wolcott, 1990). As I mentioned, I made a broad outline of the chapters I anticipated as I planned this book, but I created a more detailed outline as I started each chapter. Specific organizers for dissertations and other research reports will be addressed in the next section. The point here is that for any writing project, you need to have a way to organize the resource materials you need and to develop some form of outline to lay out a general roadmap for your writing journey. I make it a habit to share that roadmap with readers in the introduction so that they can easily follow my thinking through each chapter.

Get Details Right the First Time. If you have the impression I'm compulsive from the descriptions above, you will likely see me as anal-retentive based on this tip. I keep up with my references as I go, I check every citation and quote as I use them, and I write everything using a prescribed professional style. This qualifies me as the kind of writer Wolcott calls "that bleeder type who wants everything correct from the outset" (1990, p. 41). At the end of each writing session, I add that day's new citations to my references. This provides a nice way to wrap up a session, and it keeps me from losing track of where I am in the referencing process. I almost always check sources and double check quotes as I write—that's one reason I keep my sources within arms' reach. When I have to go to sources not immediately at hand, I make a note to myself and take care of it as soon as possible. I make decisions about the professional style I will use before I start to write, and I stick with it throughout. It seems foolish to me to go into a dissertation or even to write up an article without checking to see what your university or the journal you are writing for expects in terms of style. Others will find their creative juices blocked by such close attention to the details of writing, but the details are vital to the quality of the final product. For me, taking a large amount of time to go back to a cold text to fill in all the details is much harder than giving them a small amount of careful attention when they are first encountered.

Edit Every Time You Reread. Woods (1999) suggests that writing is 10% creating and 90% editing. While this estimate seems a bit over the top to me, it does indicate how important revising, rewriting, rewording, reorganizing, and restructuring are to the writing process. Some writers work best by letting the words flow while paying little attention to conventions such as grammar, usage, punctuation, and the like. They typically get their ideas down in some rough form, then go back later to clean up their texts. Others work more deliberately, paying closer attention to conventions as they compose. No matter where you fit on the continuum, you will spend time editing and revising your work. I recommend that you be prepared to edit every time you read your work. It is a good strategy to read over the previous day's work as a way to get you into each day's writing (see Wolcott, 1990). I like to do this, especially of I have not been able to write for a few days. But when I read my work at this or other times, I am always editing and revising. Again, my compulsivity may not make sense for everyone, but anytime I read my texts, I am looking for ways to improve the quality of the writing. I edit as I go and build time into my overall plan to edit carefully at the end of the project. If you are new to writing or want to improve your ability to communicate clearly, several sources provide helpful advice for directing your editing efforts. Some of the most helpful are Glesne and Peshkin (1992), Sherman (1993), Strunk and White (1972), Wolcott (1990), and Woods (1999).

Quit at a Good Place. I always try to think ahead to my next writing day whenever I anticipate ending a writing session. I want to be able to pick up where I left off without taking a great deal of time. On days when new chapters or sections are begun, more start-up time will be necessary, but my goal is to leave an easy place to resume as I decide where to stop. One trick I use is to have my outline typed into the manuscript. When I see I am going to finish one section but not be able to get into the next, I write the topic sentence for the first paragraph of the next section before I quit, or I type in a few key words to reorient myself the next morning. I like to wrap up the section I am working on before I quit whenever possible (c.f., Wolcott, 1990) but give myself a clear way to go when I return to the manuscript.

Work through the Blockages, and Go with the Runs. I love to play golf. I am not a good player, but if I can get out two or three times a month, golf makes my life better. My experience as a golfer is that sometimes I cannot hit the ball well no matter what I do (this happens more times than not), and sometimes I seem to be on automatic (everything falls into place for a round or two). The way I handle these ups and downs on the golf course is the same way I handle the ebbs and flows of writing. When I'm struggling on the links, I make myself "keep swinging." I figure the only way to get my game back is play through my problems. It doesn't help much to read about golf or contemplate golf or curse golf, although I've tried all of these. The only way out of playing badly is to play. When I am driving the ball off the tee, striking the ball on the fairway, and rolling the ball on the green, I just try to maintain my rhythm and ride my good fortune as long as I can. When I get to places in my writing where I feel like I am blocked, I make myself "keep writing." It may be effective for some to pull back and take a break, but for me this would be avoiding the confrontation I eventually have to make with myself. I have to write my way out of writing blockages. Writing when I feel like I can't write another word is slow and painful and discouraging, but it's the only way I know to get my confidence back. And when I get into that rare state that might be called a writing "zone," I ride it as hard as I can, giving my writing all the time and energy I can muster because I know it will not last. It may be helpful to know that other writers, even accomplished writers, experience blockages (see Woods, 1999), but it's still up to you to face down your own demons and keep writing.

Read like a Writer, and Write like a Reader. There is much to be learned about writing by examining the products of other writers. Of course, being conversant with what is being written in your discipline is essential to working in most academic environments, and making appropriate connections with the scholarship of others requires thoughtful and careful reading (see Coffey & Atkinson, 1996; Glaser & Strauss, 1967). It is also instructive to read widely in your field as a way to become familiar with a variety of writing styles and approaches, see what's possible, and determine what you might want to emulate or avoid (Golden-Biddle & Locke, 1997). Further, researchers such as Woods (1999) recommend reading outside the usual social science fare so that you can be inspired by and learn from authors of poetry, novels, and drama. I encourage children learning to make meaning in text and graduate students learning to write up qualitative research to "read like writers." By that, I mean that they should be aware of the place of the writer in whatever they are reading and do a kind of ongoing metacognitive analysis of why the author chose to make certain structural and rhetorical moves throughout the text. Learning to read like a writer can make invaluable contributions to writing improvement. Turning the phrase on its head, learning to "write like a reader" (to place one self in the mind of the reader as text is composed) will bring direction and clarity to anyone's writing. I try to have an imaginary reader in my mind as I write anything from memos to poetry, and I am constantly asking myself what that reader will make of what I have to say. The reader's job is to make meaning from text. When I write like a reader, I try to make that job as interesting and, for expository texts, as easy as possible.

Solicit Feedback. It's hard to get better at writing unless you get feedback on how you are doing. With most dissertation writing, chairs and, sometimes, other committee members will provide lots of this. This kind of feedback is vital to the dissertation process and helpful to the development of a particular kind of scholarly writing because these readers represent a primary audience for such work. I recommend that you solicit feedback from other readers to accomplish other ends. Most of my students do what I did in graduate school; they find others they trust and agree to work together to improve their research and writing skills. Sometimes this is done with another individual, and sometimes it happens in a group. Sometimes the groups are informal, and sometimes they hold regular meetings. The idea is to solicit feedback, but it's a good idea to be specific about the kind of feedback you want.

In graduate student support groups, it may seem more important to encourage than to critique, but without some level of honest criticism, getting better will be difficult. Depending on where they are in their programs, some students will want feedback on their research rather than their ability to communicate. I have heard stories of students who did not welcome feedback about their writing when they were really looking for help with their analysis schemes. The trick is to get everyone on the same page about what kind of help the author wants. My advice is to seek critical feedback about your writing, be clear about what kind of feedback you want, invite your readers to be honest, then expect to learn from a critical reading.

Expect to Revise. Wolcott is right when he says that "as long as we invite critique, we will get it: The process never ends" (1990, p. 44). Unless you plan to publish your own books and articles in your basement, you will have to face the fact that reviewers and editors will be asking you to revise your work. When you submit a manuscript to an editor, you invite critique, and you will get it. When you submit your dissertation to your committee, you invite critique, and you will get it. I understand the frustration of doctoral candidates who feel "whipsawed" between the conflicting expectations of different members of their dissertation committees, but I am always amazed when they are surprised that their committees want another revision. The nature of writing for publication is that the critical readings built into the process virtually guarantee that revisions will be required. I tell my students that the object is to make the manuscript as strong as possible. Learning to expect, rather than resent, the need to revise will help you make your writing as strong as possible.

Enjoy Having Written. I made a big deal above of how much I fear the act of writing. Writing is painful to me, but I love the idea of being a writer. I can't find the original source, but I believe in the old standard that says that you are not a novelist until you have published a novel. I was not an educational researcher until I published some educational research. When I did, I enjoyed that special status. I don't count myself as a great writer, but I enjoy having written. I get a kick out of seeing my words in print. I get a little chill when I see my work cited in the writing of others. I like the idea that something I wrote might actually influence the thinking of someone else. I enjoy having written enough to make myself write, even when it hurts. Goodall got it right when he summarized: "Nobody is born a writer. It is an identity we invent for ourselves and then try very hard to live with, and within" (2000, p. 24). You may not identify yourself as a writer. You may see writing as a necessary evil that must be endured to get your doctoral ticket punched. Still, even if you never write another word after your doctoral program, I hope you will at least experience the satisfaction of having written a dissertation. What follows are two sections focused on that specific writing task.

DISSERTATION ISSUES

Dissertations are odd birds in the literary aviary. They are written for academic purposes that severely limit their usefulness to other than highly specialized audiences. They are intended to make sure that graduates can do all the things that researchers are supposed to be able to do, but they are enacted in ways that guarantee that many graduates will never do research again. For many students, they are as much a rite of passage as an act of scholarship. For some, writing a dissertation seems more like obedience training than knowledge creation, and the products feel more like collections of true lies than reports of research. While many colleges in many universities are experimenting with alternative forms by which advanced graduate students can demonstrate their research competence, the overwhelming majority still require a dissertation that looks pretty much like what has been done for longer than anyone can remember.

I wish I could say that such criticism is meant exclusively for quantitative dissertations done in the positivist tradition, but I cannot. I do think that students drawn to the qualitative paradigms are more likely to be creative in their resistance to traditional dissertation expectations and that there is generally more flexibility among those likely to be directing qualitative dissertations, but the institutional constraints are firmly in place for almost everyone. What follows are some suggestions for dealing with issues associated with writing up a qualitative dissertation. While my recommendations are meant to be applicable in any setting, they are designed specifically to help students make accommodations in places where the traditional model prevails. I will save a discussion of ways to write up findings from qualitative data analysis for the section to follow.

Three issues that come up often in my interactions with doctoral candidates on my campus and students I've talked with from around the world are format, audience, and voice. Format is the most pervasive concern, and the most complex. I will briefly discuss issues of audience and voice, then turn to format. I'll conclude this section with some suggestions designed specifically for dissertation writing.

Who is the audience for my dissertation? The pat answer is, "Your committee," but that's a little too pat for me. It's true enough that you will have to satisfy your committee (or external examiners, if you are doing a doctoral thesis in Australia or many European countries), but I think most committees have the expectation that you will write for a broader audience. Even in the face of traditional expectations, advisors and committees hope that the good work in the study will have a life beyond the dissertation stacks in the university library.

I know some students are told to write dissertations for experts in the field. I encourage my students to conceptualize an audience of "scholarly peers"—folks like them who know something of the scholarship in which the work is grounded but who have not yet reached the exalted status of "expert." It seems pretentious for students to act like experts and write for other experts. Yes, they know a lot about what they are studying, and they will have plenty to say to others about what they have learned, but writing for an audience of smart people who want to learn what they have discovered seems much wiser than pretending to expertise that is not earned.

The dissertation will look different if "scholarly peers" are the audience as opposed to "experts" or "your committee." Scholarly peers will need a more careful explanation of your rationale and research questions, clearer connections between your review of the literature and your study, a more thorough explication of your data collection and analysis procedures, more comprehensively written findings, and more thoughtfully constructed conclusions and reflections. Assuming expertise in your readers or writing to the idiosyncratic backgrounds of your committee will narrow your report in different ways, neither of which will make the finished product something that will be accessible or useful to others. Selecting an audience of people who are a lot like you will help you as you write and as you work postdissertation to publish your work.

The tradition of the positivist dissertation is to pretend the researcher is a disembodied reporter who hides his or her voice in a passive, third-person, "objective" account. Qualitative work is different in character and requires different kinds of connections between researcher and text. To start with, virtually all qualitative reports place the writer as an important player in the unfolding of the research and its description. There is no pretence that the stories of the research represent some verifiable objective reality, and the settings under examination are taken to be complex, dynamic places. It just makes no sense to try to write qualitative dissertations in the voice of the detached, objective researcher. Virtually everyone writing about writing up qualitative work insists that accounts be written in first-person, active voice (e.g., Glesne & Peshkin, 1992; Wolcott, 1990), and this should include qualitative dissertations as well.

I like the idea of writing up research as a way to contribute to the conversation about what's important in my field (see Golden-Biddle & Locke, 1997; Goodall, 2000; Murray, 1986). When I encourage students to find their voices as emerging scholars, contributing to the conversation is the frame of reference I use. The object of qualitative research is not to find the Truth and make pronouncements on it. It makes much more sense in a dissertation (and all academic writing) to construct contributions to "a continuous professional conversation" than to try to "deliver the Truth—Moses like" (Murray, 1986, p. 147). When I prompt students informally and in dissertation defenses to justify their work, I always ask what their research contributes to the current conversation about what's important in their field. Writing a dissertation with that question in mind gives new researchers permission to take on a voice that has something to say without the pressure of pretending to have all the answers.

Do I have to organize my dissertation into the five chapters listed in the graduate school handbook? I hope not. My experience is that most universities have changed their requirements or become more flexible in interpreting outdated guidelines. Alternative formats may not be the mode, but at most places, it no longer takes an act of divine intervention to break the five-chapter rule. Of course, you might be working with a committee that only knows one way to organize a dissertation or studying in a college where some associate dean has made it his or her mission to make sure all dissertations look the same.

Meloy (1994) studied the qualitative dissertation process, collecting the reflections of graduate students going through the experience. She noted that for some students, dissertation formats emerged as research processes unfolded, while others felt constrained by the influence of traditional expectations. Students adjusted to the real and perceived expectations around them. That makes perfect sense to me. Every study, every context, and every researcher will be different. I believe there are ways to adjust, even in settings where traditional dissertation reporting formats are required. These range from letting your study tell you what format will be best to using the traditional format while creatively subverting it from within.

In the best of all worlds, the form of your dissertation will follow naturally from your study. You will want to give your readers a clear understanding of where you stand, what you did, why you did it, what you found out, how what you found out fits with what else is known about the subject, and what it all means. The internal logic of research I have stressed throughout this book should be evident in your final report, no matter what the form. If you have followed the logic suggested, all of the parts of your story, including paradigmatic assumptions, research questions, design, data collection, analysis, and findings, need to be described. But your story need not be a serial recounting of these parts. For ideas, look at the organization of high-quality, book-length reports of research done within your paradigm. For grounding, work closely with your committee. If you plan an alternative format, let them see your outlines and hear your rationale before you go too far.

On the other end of the continuum, if you are forced to have chapters that follow the traditional dissertation format (something like Introduction/Problem, Review of Research, Methods, Findings, Conclusions), it may be possible to retain those labels but be creative enough within the chapters to give readers a flavor for the richness and complexity of your work. For example, the traditional chapter 1 includes a statement of the problem. Identifying "a problem" often baffles qualitative researchers whose purpose is to describe a particular social setting or understand the enactment of a social phenomenon in a particular context. My advice is to structure the problem as a lack of knowledge or understanding that the study can help resolve. I argued in the design chapter of this book that grounding the study in relevant theory and research is vital, but having a serial litany of disconnected research summaries is not the only way to write a research review. Most dissertation chapter 2s are boring to read and write. They can be interesting position papers or critiques *and* reviews of research. Methods chapters can retain that label and still be interestingly written stories of how the research happened, and conclusions can retain that heading and still include your reflections about the research process and its outcomes. The point is to not let the necessity of using the required labels keep you from being creative about what gets included in the chapters. Again, if you plan to subvert the system, make your committee coconspirators early in the process.

Other alternative formats that fall between making up a structure to using what is required include moves such as combining chapters 1 and 2 into a backgrounds chapter, organizing findings into multiple chapters, and adding a reflections chapter at the end. Such adjustments should follow the logic of the study and the desire to make the dissertation as interesting and informative as possible. The paradigmatic assumptions of the researcher and the kinds of studies done will lead to different decisions about adjusting traditional formats. I have served on committees for a constructivist narrative study that reported findings in two chapters organized around narrative analysis and analyis of narratives, a postpositivist historiography that imbedded the research review in the findings, and a critical interview study that concluded with a discussion chapter comprised largely of the author's neo-Marxist critique of much of the work previously done in his area. More on these issues as they relate to organizing findings is included below.

I want to conclude this section on dissertation writing with some further suggestions. Based on my experience reading dissertations and theses, these suggestions are meant to supplement the general writing tips above, but have special relevance for dissertation writing. These suggestions are based on some of my frustrations and might be called "ways to avoid making your dissertation chair crazy."

Tell the Reader What the Study Is about in the First Few Pages of the Dissertation. Nothing is more annoying than to have to read 50 or 60 pages before you know what you are reading about.

Write an Introduction and Conclusion for Each Chapter and Most Sections. Help readers keep up with your thinking by providing a roadmap through the ideas in each chapter. Let them know when you are finished with a section and how what has come before fits with what is to follow.

Have Something to Say about the Significance and Usefulness of Your Study. This is often blown off in the last few paragraphs of a dissertation when the author is apparently exhausted and desperate to be finished. Tell the reader why it's important to take the study seriously and suggest what should be done as a result.

Limit Appendices to Necessary Materials. Some appendices are longer than findings chapters. I see no need to include raw data in appendices except as possible examples. Keep what is included to only that which is necessary to understand how the study was done and what the findings mean.

Compromise with Your Committee but Do Not Capitulate. Listen to your committee and take their recommendations seriously. Do whatever it takes to make your dissertation as strong as possible, including making compromises. But do not give up the integrity of your research. Some students come away with the sense that they gave their dissertations away in the process of getting them approved. I believe most of these situations must have been failures to communicate. If you have compelling reasons not to compromise, fight to keep it *your* research by focusing on those reasons. You will lose if the conflict turns into a power play, but you can win by arguing from the position that you too want to make the dissertation as strong as possible.

WRITING UP FINDINGS FROM DATA ANALYSIS

In chapter 4, I argued that data analysis continues as findings are written up. It is also true that the products of data analysis models like I described in that chapter naturally lead to certain kinds of findings and certain forms of writing. The bulk of this section will address how to convert data analyses into findings, using the data analysis models presented in this book as examples. Prior to that discussion, general considerations for writing up qualitative findings are presented.

Findings sections of *quantitative* dissertations, books, and articles look like the easiest parts of such reports to write. They are almost always straightforward accountings of the outcomes of statistical analyses; the object is clarity and precision; and the style is literal as opposed to literary. In contrast, while the findings of *qualitative* studies report the outcomes of analyses, they are seldom straightforward; the object is to bring understanding to complex social phenomena that cannot be reduced to precise, statistical relationships; and they are written in a style that uses literary sensibilities to take readers inside the issues and settings under investigation.

I think qualitative findings are the hardest sections to write up. Unless systematic data analysis procedures have been followed, it's hard to imagine where a qualitative researcher would begin. But if they have, the products of those analyses, at the least, provide a starting point for writing up findings. As we have seen throughout this book, different assumptions lead to different questions and different approaches, which lead to different data and different analysis models. These different analytic models generate different findings that will take different written forms. Again, the models detailed in chapter 4 are only examples of what's possible. I will use these models below to demonstrate what's possible in terms of generating findings sections of qualitative research reports. I hope these will be useful, but expect researchers to adapt the ideas presented to their own special circumstances. But first, here are some general considerations for writing up qualitative findings.

General Considerations

The process of writing up findings from virtually any kind of qualitative study is more than reporting out the results of analyses that are already complete. As mentioned earlier, writing involves a special kind of thinking that is hard to do except during the act of constructing meaning in text. As writing proceeds, you will likely see relationships, patterns, and themes in new or different ways. When this happens, it will mean a return to the data to be sure that what's new or different is supported there. You should expect that findings will be shaped by the writing process. This is a good thing, even though it means going back to data analysis steps that seemed more or less complete. It helps to expect your writing to generate new analyses and to remember that, in the end, your analysis is "not finished, only over" (Van Maanen, 1988, p. 120).

An issue that doctoral students often face as they write up dissertation findings is how much data to include. Some want to let their data tell the story, while others see less need to display raw data in the text. Of course, balance is what you want, and the balance will be different for each study. My rule of thumb is that sufficient examples should be included to give the reader confidence that the researcher's assertions about the topic at hand are supported by his or her data. This means to me that whenever generalizations are presented, patterns are described, impressions are painted, or critiques are generated, researchers should provide excerpts from their data to give the reader a real sense of how what was learned played out in the actual settings examined. This does not mean making a statement, then stringing together a set of data excerpts without explanation. It does not mean including every incident in the data that is related to the phenomenon under close examination. It means selecting the right data excerpts in the right places and helping the reader see why they are the right examples to strengthen their understandings.

As part of each analysis model described in the previous chapter, I included a step for identifying representative data excerpts to support the results of analysis. As findings are written up, the selected excerpts should be reviewed, and especially prescient examples should be selected for use in the text. One or two excerpts are usually sufficient to support major points. Excerpts are meant to *represent* what the overall data set has to say, so it is not necessary to pack the findings with endless data displays. It is also important to explain how the data excerpts support what you have to say. Do not assume that the connections you see will be picked up by the reader. I agree with Atkinson (1990) that the persuasive force of qualitative reports comes from the "interplay of concrete exemplification and discursive commentary" (p. 103). It's your job to develop a persuasive argument by discursively explaining how you have used your concrete examples to make a strong case.

As excerpts are written into findings, new researchers often wonder if they should edit those excerpts or include them exactly as they appear in the data. I think they should be edited, but carefully. On a basic level, it is usually not necessary to include every "um," "uh," and "you know" that appears in ordinary speech (see Glesne & Peshkin, 1992). The exception would be when these verbal space fillers provide insight into what is going on in the interchange, as in when individuals appear nervous or unsure. At a more complex level, editing transcript excerpts ought to be based on criteria that insure the integrity of the participants' words while keeping excerpts manageable and on target. Emerson, Fretz, and Shaw (1995, p. 187) recommend the following general criteria to guide excerpt editing: *length* (you don't want excerpts to ramble endlessly), *relevance* (you want to include the qualities that connect the example to your case), *readability* (you want the excerpt to make syntactic sense), *comprehensibility* (you want the reader to be able to understand what participants meant), and *anonymity* (you don't want to reveal informants' identities by including certain kinds of sensitive information). As a general rule, I recommend editing with a light touch. The driving question to keep in mind as excerpts are edited is Am I being true to what my participants had to say? No editing is justified if it deletes, changes, or distorts the meanings intended by informants.

Being true to those who have trusted you enough to participate in your studies goes beyond safeguarding their anonymity. My mentor taught me to picture my informants looking over my shoulder as I write up my findings. The idea is to not write anything that I would not want my informants to read in my presence. Many of my early studies involved the social interactions of young children, and for each study, I placed pictures of the children I was writing about in my workspace to help me remember to be true to them as I constructed their stories. I acknowledge that, like all writers, I have taken some literary license in an effort to construct rhetorically persuasive stories (see Goodall, 2000), but I hope I have never violated the trust of my participants by using their words in ways that distort their intent. Another dimension to be balanced is the place of theorizing in the presentation of findings. As always, this balance will be different with different types of studies, but the issue needs to be addressed directly as decisions are made about how findings are to be presented. Although some will want to leave extensive connections to extant theory and research to implications or discussion sections of later chapters, I think most qualitative findings sections will be improved with appropriate ties to the literature as the findings unfold. For me, this can be a natural part of the "discursive commentary" mentioned above. Your goal is to help your readers understand what is going on in the settings you have studied, and linking the local meanings discovered in your data, through your analysis, to related theory and research can improve that understanding (see Emerson, Fretz, & Shaw, 1995; Golden-Biddle & Locke, 1997). This does not mean interrupting your argument with a long review of theory or research. You should have already included such a review in earlier chapters, and you will probably provide an extended discussion of the relationship of your work to what has been been done previously in your final chapter. At this point, simply signaling your reader of the relationships you see between what is being explained and pertinent research and/or theory is sufficient. Such signals help you make your points and let the reader know you know where your findings fit within the larger picture.

How to use visual representations in findings is another issue that needs to be addressed. Coffey and Atkinson (1996) identify two kinds of visual materials that can be used in qualitative reports: (a) data and analysis displays organized into graphs, charts, tables, matrices, and diagrams; and (b) materials such as photographs or reproductions of artifacts. Miles and Huberman (1994) detail the possibilities for data displays that go beyond the inclusion of quoted materials from research protocols. Some research projects lend themselves to the inclusion of more visual representation than others, and my experience is that some researchers are more inclined than others to include a lot of visual representations in their findings. For me, it's a question of clarity. If data displays summarized in matrices (or graphs, taxonomies, or whatever) help clarify the complexity in the data, then I am for them. If, as sometimes happens, they hide rather than clarify the complexity, I am against their inclusion. The same criterion applies to the use of photographs and other visual material. Just because you have them doesn't mean they should be included in your findings. They should be there because they help clarify the case you are trying to make.

Another important consideration as findings sections are planned and written is the level of generality that will be used to frame the presentation. Coffey and Atkinson (1996, p. 112) discuss this issue in terms of identifying "units of narrative" when making decisions related to this consideration. They relate the concept of units of narrative to the notion of units of analysis. When decisions are made with regard to units of analysis, researchers are decided if they are studying individual social actors, small groups that share a particular setting, larger groups that share similar characteristics, all stakeholders in a particular social event, or all members of a subcultural group. Decisions about the unit of analysis will have powerful implications for what the researcher looks for and where. Units of narrative are Coffey and Atkinson's construct for deciding the level of generality that will frame what is written about in final reports. Again, researchers will ask themselves what actors, groups, or social contexts are the focus of their research, then frame the narratives that make up their findings based on their answers. If you have followed the research logic that I have described throughout this book, deciding on a level of generality should be a no-brainer—the unit of analysis should have been identified at the design stage, and data collection and analysis should have led to findings that are framed in a way that now needs only to be described. However, if your level of generality is not self-evident, a careful reexamination of your research design needs to be done, starting with a look at the relationship between your research questions and your data analysis.

This leads to a final, and essential, general consideration: What narrative form should my findings take? As we will see below, different kinds of data analyses lead to different options with regard to how findings will be organized and presented. Several of those options have been described in the qualitative research literature, and I will review two of the most widely cited descriptions to provide a framework for deciding on narrative form. Hammersley and Atkinson (1983) present several models for organizing ethnographic texts that can be adapted for writing findings for other types of qualitative work. These include: "the natural history" (the report of research is ordered in a linear fashion that parallels the natural unfolding of the research itself); "the chronology" (the passage of time organizes the text, but rather than follow the implementation of the study, the chronology details some "developmental cycle," "moral career," or "timetable" of the settings or actors being studied); "narrowing and expanding the focus" (the presentation moves through different levels of generality in the way a zoom lens moves the focus from general to specific and back); "separating narration and analysis" (the story is presented as a whole, while the author's discussion of themes and issues is saved for later; and "thematic organizations" (texts are organized based on the themes, categories, and patterns found in the analysis) (Hammersley & Atkinson, 1983, pp. 215–27).

Van Maanen's (1988) widely known description of alternative formats divides narrative models into the following: "realist tales" (the author writes third-person accounts based on "scientific" analyses that document the details of everyday life from the perspectives of those being studied); "confessional tales" (first-person accounts are constructed that acknowledge the researcher's presence throughout the research process and report the researcher's interpretations of what's important in the setting); "impressionist tales" (literary devices are used to produce evocative stories that take the reader inside what happened, while readers are generally left to form their own interpretations of what it means); "critical tales" (authors often use a Marxist framework to describe the effects of social structures on the diminished life chances of disadvantaged groups); "formal tales" (formalists are specialists within the qualitative field such as ethnomethodologists and sociolinguists whose principle aim is to document the application of particular theoretical perspectives to the analysis of specific events); "literary tales" (such accounts rely directly on nonfiction writing techniques and combine a journalistic concern for what is noteworthy with the drama associated with good novels); and "jointly told tales" (both researcher and participant voices are represented in a dialogic or polyphonic format designed to bridge gaps between meaning systems) (pp. 45–138).

While Van Maanen devotes whole chapters to the first three tales and only a few paragraphs to each of the others, all of the possibilities described in his work should be live options for new researchers. Similarly, although there is overlap with some of Van Maanen's tales, suggestions by Hammersley and Atkinson can be helpful to new researchers as well. As writing up findings generated from the various data analysis models of this book is discussed below, connections back to the writing forms presented by Hammersley and Atkinson and Van Maanen will be made. The discussion to follow assumes familiarity with the analysis models presented in chapter 4, so a review of the analytic steps described there will be helpful in understanding writing suggestions for each model. It is also important to remember that it is more likely that you will adapt bits and pieces of the models discussed below rather than find a single model as the answer to your "how do I organize the findings" question.

Findings from Typological Analyses

The outcomes of a well-executed typological analysis will be a set of one-sentence generalizations that capture the patterns, relationships, and themes discovered in the data and a collection of data excerpts that support the generalizations identified. Remember typological analysis is best suited to interview data that have been collected using fairly structured interview schedules with informants or focus group participants who represent selected points of view. Typological analysis involves searching for and verifying generalizations that characterize the informant perspectives captured in the data. So the broad organizer for typological findings will be the presentation of participant perspectives as captured in interview or focus group data. This is a more restricted stance than the exposition of a social phenomenon that may have been studied through more direct means. For example, if teachers have been questioned about working with difficult-to-manage children, the findings will be reported specifically as teachers' understandings related to teaching this special population, not as an examination of the general issue of difficult to manage children. This model aligns closely with Hammersley and Atkinson's (1983) description of thematic organization and shares characteristics with Van Maanen's (1988) realist tales.

A basic, but effective, way to report typological findings is to organize the writing around your generalizations. If you have identified themes from your analysis and stated these as generalizations, themes can become your major headings. If you have patterns and relationships expressed in the form of generalizations that fit under your themes, these can become your subheadings. If you want to follow this format, and your generalizations are not organized this way, another level of analysis to discover relationships among your generalizations will be needed. The key is to create an organization that makes the relationships among all the parts make sense in terms of the whole. Once this organization is clear to you, the writing is a matter of helping the reader see your organization, then presenting, explaining, and making the case for your generalizations.

Findings sections reporting typological analyses in the way I'm describing should start with an overview of how the overall findings fit together. This introductory material need not begin to argue for the efficacy of the generalizations but should provide readers with a sense of what is to follow and how it is organized. This can be accomplished in a few paragraphs.

Major sections to follow should be introduced by stating the thematic generalizations that characterize those sections and identifying the patterns and relationships that will be explored as the dimensions of the theme are explicated. The goal is to give the reader an advance organizer for processing the information you will be sharing. Once your organization is clear, your general writing mode will be deductive. You will present each generalization in turn, then explain in detail what your generalization is all about. Here is where you make the case that your generalizations are supported by the data, so this is the place where data excerpts that you have selected as part of your analysis (or that you find as you write) are presented to the reader. General issues associated with using data excerpts described above apply here. Your objective is to provide evidence for the efficacy of your generalizations by displaying data *and* explaining how the data support your case. Neither the data displays nor the explanations are sufficient by themselves; both are essential to helping readers see the perspectives you are trying to illuminate.

As major themes are described and patterns and relationships are reported and supported, it is appropriate to weave references to relevant literature into your discussion. While some researchers prefer to save connections to research and theory for later sections (see Hammersley & Atkinson, 1983 on separating narrative and analysis), my view is that when such connections will help readers make sense of findings as they are being presented, this is the time to bring them in. For readers who know the literature or have paid close attention to your review of research, it will seem dumb not to make the ties explicit. For more casual readers, connecting to the relevant research and theory will enrich their understandings of what your findings mean and where they fit. As will be suggested for all the models, findings sections should conclude with summaries that remind readers of what has gone before, without necessarily repeating it in detail.

Of course, findings based on typological analyses can be presented in other, more imaginative and complex ways. It is key, whatever organization and format you chose, to focus on the generalizations that were generated in your analysis. They represent what you found out, and your goal ought to be to share what you found out in an effective and interesting way. My experience is that most doctoral candidates who chose to do typological work find the straightforward model described to be effective at getting them through the difficult process of writing up their findings and interesting enough that they are proud of their efforts.

Findings from Inductive Analyses

The inductive data analysis model is best suited for studies that have generated complex data sets based on postpositivist or constructivist research perspectives. The primary outcome of an inductive analysis will be a master outline that captures the domains discovered in the data and the relationships of those domains to each other and to the whole. Another product will be data excerpts selected to support the elements on your outline. As I argued when describing this model, not only does the master outline provide a way to bring the parts of the study into meaningful relation, but it is also a ready-made organizer for writing up findings. When such a master outline is used to frame findings, the organization will definitely be thematic in Hammersley and Atkinson's (1983) terms. But the kind of tale (Van Maanen, 1988) that is generated from the master outline will be different depending on the assumptions that framed the study. There is a natural fit for inductive work based in postpositivist principles that generates realist or formal tales. But if the study adopted a constructivist perspective, a confessional tale could be the outcome, and critical tales could result from reporting inductive analyses of data collected using critical/feminist perspectives. Whatever your paradigmatic point of departure, if you have come out of inductive analysis with a master outline and excerpts to support it, you should have a terrific starting place for writing up your findings.

If your master outline helps you make sense of the social setting or phenomenon you have studied, then sharing that outline and following its logic ought to help your readers make sense of what you have to say. It is possible that your master outline, or an edited version of it, could become the headings and subheadings that comprise the table of contents for your findings chapter—this was the case for my dissertation (see appendix E). If your outline is too complex to become a sensible table of contents section, it should at least be included as an appendix and referred to in the text. If you are going to write from your outline, sharing it with your reader is a good advance organizer.

Making the participants and contexts of the study "real" to your readers will help your findings come to life. In dissertations, participants and contexts will often be described in detail in methods chapters, but in any report based on inductive analysis models, careful descriptions of the players and the contexts in which they act are vital to making findings ring true. As with any qualitative work, data will be used to support the domains presented, and writing a section that gives their readers a rich image of participants and settings will improve the readers' understandings of your data displays and the analytic points you are trying to make.

The domains discovered in your inductive analysis carry the cultural meanings you want to share in your final report. Describing those domains will be the stuff of your findings. If yours is a formal or realist tale, the exposition of your domains can be efficiently organized into sections in which you present the dimensions of your domain, use your data to demonstrate how the cultural knowledge that made up those domains played out in the settings you studied, and theorize the place of your domains in relation to the immediate understandings of your participants and the larger social contexts involved. Golden-Biddle and Locke (1997, p. 59) describe a "sandwich structure" in which authors explain how a theoretical point will be evidenced in the data, present the data, and then tell what the data showed. No matter what the order (and using a combination probably makes sense), having all of these elements is a good idea for formal or realist reports.

Confessional tales, by definition, locate the researcher as an important part of any study. Constructivist researchers who adopt a confessional mode will be writing up the meanings that they and their participants have coconstructed through the research process. That does not automatically preclude the generation of a master outline that can be used to organize findings, but it does mean that the voices of the researcher and his or her participants will be heard more directly in the text. Similarly, critical/feminist researchers may use inductive analyses that generate useful master outlines, but the findings will be critical tales, reported in a decidedly political tone. Having a master outline provides a great place to start. But after you have experienced converting a complex outline into a findings section or chapter, you will understand that declarations such as, "Once I had my outline, the findings basically wrote themselves" are mostly meaningless. As has been mentioned several times, the act of writing will cause you to see the dimensions of your domains and relations among domains in new ways. The act of explaining the connections between your data and the points you are trying to make will cause you to read your excerpts new ways. The act of tying your work to a larger body of theory and research will make you think about how it all fits together in new ways. Although it will make you crazy, having such realizations is all good. Your work and your development as a scholar will be enriched in new ways.

Findings from Interpretive Analyses

If you have completed an interpretive analysis based on the suggestions in the previous chapter, you will come to the findings stage of your study with a "revised summary" that has been developed through a process of writing interpretive memos, searching data for evidence that supports interpretations, drafting preliminary summaries, and reviewing these with participants. The revised summary and data excerpts produced as a result of applying interpretive analysis procedures should provide a useful framework for writing up your findings. The idea was to produce stories in enough detail that you were confident you had something to say and identify data excerpts that would give readers confidence that what you had to say was supported by your data. It should be expected that your stories will become more elaborate and your explanations more detailed as you write up your final results, but, done well, the interpretive data analysis process should give you a leg up on writing your findings section.

The processes required to convert revised summaries into the final versions that appear as findings will be different depending on the analysis you have done and the ways you want to organize and present the stories that communicate your results. Interpretive analysis is closely aligned with constructivist principles, and findings will usually take shape as stories with beginnings, middles, and ends. This means that organizational schemes like those described by Hammersley and Atkinson (1983) as chronologies, narrowing and expanding the focus, and separating narrative and analysis can be useful in making decisions about the form findings will take.

In chronologies, the passage of time organizes the stories in the text. If yours is a study of the development of classroom social relations over a year's

time or a record of the implementation of a new dress-code policy, a chrono-
logical organization may make perfect sense. Other social phenomena may be
better captured by taking readers inside the experiences of participants using
an alternating focus on specific details and broader generalities. An example
might be a study that looks at the immediate experience of pregnant girls in
high school while pulling back to examine the general contexts of school and
community in relation female students. In both of these organizations, analysis is integrated within the telling of the stories. But narration and analysis
can be separated. In this organization, the story is presented as a whole before
being theorized by the author. An example might be a study of a special magnet school program emphasizing technology, in which the story of the program is told without interruption, then an analysis and ties to the literature
are presented in a later section. Any of these modes of writing offer useful
guides for organizing the detailed stories that grow from interpretive findings.

Van Maanen's (1988) description of confessional and impressionistic
tales offers another perspective on writing up interpretive findings. Confessional tales highlight the researcher's place in the study and report his or her
interpretations of what happened. Impressionist tales emphasize the importance of literary devices to tell an evocative story, leaving much of the interpretation to the reader. Confessional tales take readers inside the research
settings, reveal understandings jointly constructed with participants, and
clarify connections between what was found and what has been previously
reported. They fit nicely with the products of interpretive analysis, and I see
no inherent conflict between a confessional stance and the organizational
options from Hammersley and Atkinson reviewed above. But, for new
researchers who are interested in constructing impressionist tales of the type
described by Van Maanen, I recommend an adaptation of the strategy from
Hammersley and Atkinson that separates narration from analysis but does
not leave out the analysis altogether. I know there are graduate students who
are brilliant writers (with understanding committees) who can pull off doing
a dissertation as a purely impressionistic tale, but most of us are journeyman
or good writers (with ordinary committees) who should explicate the connections among our stories, our data, and the related literature.

Those whose sensibilities attract them to seek realist explanations
expressed in thematic organizations will likely have no clue when it comes to
writing up interpretive findings. But, those choosing the path that leads to
interpretive analysis should not be put off by the challenges of writing up
findings as stories. Again, certain kinds of assumptions lead to asking certain
kinds of questions that can be answered with certain kinds of data collection
and analytic methods. If you have done a study based on constructivist
assumptions and asked questions that led you to coconstruct meanings with
your participants and conducted an interpretive analysis with feedback from

those participants, you should be at a place where developing the final versions of your research stories will follow logically from what you have done. Converting such analyses to a thematically organized, realist tale is not an option at this late date. Going back to the original data and applying inductive analytic strategies might work, but the point is to avoid surprises by knowing your paradigmatic assumptions from the outset, then following them where they lead.

Findings from Political Analyses

The paradigmatic assumptions that would lead to writing up findings from a political analysis are obviously tied to the critical/feminist research perspective. While it is possible to adapt political analysis procedures so that a political dimension can be added to other kinds of analyses, the steps of the political model described in chapter 4 lead logically to writing up findings framed within the critical/feminist paradigm. The products of a political analysis will be summaries that have been revised based on feedback from participants and excerpts supporting the generalizations that make up the stuff of the summaries. These summaries will be different in nature than those described as the outcomes of interpretive analysis in that they will explicitly be built around an analysis of the political dimensions of the research. The summaries from political analysis will likely include generalizations that draw out relationships between participant experiences and the oppressive conditions in which they live. The summaries will be in narrative form, but they may lack the elements of story that usually characterize interpretive findings. This makes sense given the critical/feminist ontological view that material structures have real impacts on individual lives. However, even though they are different in form, the revised summaries that result from political analyses serve similar functions for the writing of final results as those generated from interpretive analyses.

Most summaries from political analyses apply a critical or feminist framework that critiques the social conditions in which participants operate. As with interpretive summaries, the outcomes of political analyses need to be expanded and theorized in formal findings sections. The final versions of political findings will be written in a form that fits Van Maanen's construct of critical tales. While Van Maanen's (1988) brief description is organized around Marxist political critique, he acknowledges that other researchers who share "a crusading spirit" (1988, p. 129) will be writing up findings in the form of critical tales as well. Such critical tales use data excerpts to take the reader inside the experiences of oppressed individuals or groups while making the case that the social, political, and economic conditions in which those experiences play out are stacked against those being oppressed. Critical tales are critiques of particular circumstances that reflect the unequal nature of the broader social world. Findings from political analyses detail the particular circumstances and theorize their connections to the broader social, political, and economic contexts.

In my description of political analysis, I discussed the emancipatory purposes at the base of critical/feminist qualitative research. As an early step in the political analysis model, I built in the process of self-reflexively examining political positionings and identifying ideological issues related to the research. These purposes and positionings must be revealed to the reader. If these have not been made clear in introductory or methodological sections, they must be included in findings. Further, when efforts have been undertaken to transform the oppressive conditions being examined through raising consciousness, seeking emancipation, or encouraging resistance, these need to be a part of the final report as well. Again, if they are not explained elsewhere in your report, descriptions of efforts to help participants transform their social circumstances must be a part of findings.

If there is a developmental dimension to the study because of interactions between researchers and participants around transformative efforts, Hammersley and Atkinson's (1983) natural history or chronology models may be useful guides for organizing findings. You could organize your final report around how the entire study unfolded or how the transformative dimensions of the study influenced the development of findings. By doing so, you will have a way to include a discussion of your interactions with participants around emancipatory issues while imbedding them in the contexts of the study as they played out over time.

It is also possible to modify Hammersley and Atkinson's (1983) thematic organization if your revised summaries are in the form of generalizations that can be stated in terms of themes or patterns. It is possible, for example, that you have done a systematic analysis of ways self-identified gay and lesbian students are treated as less than normal in a high school setting. The revised summary and excerpts from your political analysis will be a set of generalizations describing and documenting each of the ways identified. Writing up your findings as an exploration of how these patterned examples of oppression played out could take form in a thematic organization. If this kind of organization makes sense, it will probably be necessary to develop separate sections in which self-reflexive statements and explanations of transformative efforts are spelled out.

No matter what the form, the character of findings based on political analysis processes will be different from findings generated from other analytic models. More traditional researchers, even some qualitative researchers, may not see your work as "empirical" because of its openly political nature. My experience is that you will probably not be able to change their minds.

But if you have been clear throughout about your critical/feminist paradigmatic stance and have been consistent as you have gone about design, data collection, and analysis, no one should be surprised that you frame your findings in transformative terms. As with all of the models described in this book, I recommend a generous exposition of data as findings are reported. Even though you are arguing from a political stance, this is qualitative *research*. Using data to provide empirical support for your political critique makes your findings much more powerful and compelling than armchair analyses of the same important issues.

Findings from Polyvocal Analyses

Polyvocal analysis procedures were described as one way to process data gathered using poststructuralist principles. This section is about how to write up findings from that particular kind of poststructuralist, data-based approach. Others (e.g., Ellis & Bochner, 1996; Tierney & Lincoln, 1997; Richardson, 1994) have described alternative writing modes for poststructuralist work that may be useful to new researchers, but they will not be directly addressed here. As with those discussed above, findings following from polyvocal analysis will only make sense within the logic that frames the study from its beginnings.

Polyvocal analysis naturally leads to the production of polyvocal texts, which are similar in form to what Van Maanen (1988) calls "jointly told tales." The object of such texts is to present the reader with multiple "truths" by letting multiple voices, including those of researchers and participants, tell their own stories. The products of polyvocal analysis will be drafts of stories created through a process of studying data, identifying voices, drafting narratives, going back to the data and participants, and refining the narratives into individual or group stories.

Depending on the quality of the work done during analysis, writing up findings will be a matter of putting the stories into their final form and providing readers with enough information to make sense of the narratives being presented. As I mentioned in my description of polyvocal analysis, the narratives generated may take a number of forms, including any of those identified by Hammersley and Atkinson (1983). But whatever the form, if they are to fit within the assumptions of the poststructuralist paradigm, they must present a dialogic or polyphonic account of what is being examined. It is appropriate to include the researcher's voice among the accounts, but that voice should not be privileged in relation to the other voices presented. In this kind of work, the idea is to let each voice tell its own story in an effort to allow the reader to see a small part of the complex and sometimes paradoxical nature of the real life situations being examined.

In my description in chapter 4, I used Polkinghorne's (1995) narrative analysis construct as an example of how certain kinds of stories, emplotted narratives, could be generated through polyvocal analysis. To continue the example, if you come out of a polyvocal analysis with revised drafts of stories in which events and actions are organized around a plot, your job will be to further refine these stories and design a way to present them to your readers so that they will be able to understand why the stories are included and how they relate to one another. This may be as simple as explaining what you are doing to the reader, then presenting the stories in series. Or it may be as complex as imbedding the stories you wish to tell within your own "story of stories," creating an overarching narrative that organizes the narratives within it in a way that it tells the story of the research from a variety of perspectives.

It should go without saying that if you plan to present your findings as a set of stories, this should not be a surprise to your doctoral committee, funding agency, or editor. Even if emplotted narratives are not the products of your polyvocal analysis, allowing participant voices to speak for themselves will seem unusual to individuals who do not share your paradigmatic point of view. That you are working within different research assumptions and that that will lead you to different kinds of findings should be made clear all along the way. In this and any kind of research, it is vital that you remain true to your paradigmatic principles and that you communicate those principles to those who have responsibility for approving your work.

TIPS FOR PUBLISHING QUALITATIVE RESEARCH

As someone who has worked as editor of a qualitative research journal, served on editorial boards for journals that publish some qualitative work, and published qualitative findings in a variety of places, I am often asked to talk about what it takes to publish qualitative research. In an effort to guide new qualitative researchers who are often new professors starting their publishing careers, I have summarized some of my thoughts on publishing qualitative research in the tips presented below. While some of my well-published colleagues may see these tips as simplistic or perfunctory, I hope new scholars will be able to use them to make a start on getting their work into print.

Think of Publishing as a Game That Requires Skill, Strategy, and Some Luck. I see a clear distinction between what might be called "writing intelligence" and "publishing intelligence." The former has to do with the ability to communicate ideas in text, while the latter is about finding ways to put that text into print. It may be necessary to have writing intelligence in order to publish (though that is not for sure), but it's entirely possible for someone with advanced writing abilities, but no publishing savvy, to never be published. The tips that follow are examples of the kinds of skills and strategic thinking that are part of the publishing intelligence idea I am playing around with. If you are fortunate, your graduate school experience will include mentoring by individuals who know and are willing to share the secrets of the publishing game. And I tell my students it is a game. It has a competitive element (others are competing for the same journal pages and tradebook lists), a strategic dimension (using publishing intelligence), and an element of luck (even really good stuff sometimes gets ignored, while junk gets published). Assuming that publishing is a completely rational enterprise in which quality always gets rewarded makes the inevitable rejections just too hard to take. Better to understand the vicissitudes of publishing as a game that can be played well, but with no guarantee of winning every time.

Get Something Out There. You cannot drag the pot unless you ante up. You cannot win at poker or any game unless you join the action by investing something. You cannot publish unless you submit something for review. I talked earlier in this chapter about colleagues who would not submit their papers to editors because they never felt their work was ready. The answer is still that it will never be ready, but you have to get it out there before anything can happen. Demystify the game by playing it. Let the reviewers and editors tell you what your manuscript needs to be ready. Enjoy the satisfaction from being taken seriously. Learn how to make your work publishable by paying attention to what happens when it gets rejected. Send in your best efforts, but don't wait for the perfect manuscript, or you'll never get in the game.

Have Something to Say. I like Stake's (1994, p. 241) assertion about the place of novelty in case study research: "A new case without commonality cannot be understood. Yet a new case without distinction will not be noticed." If publishing is about joining the intellectual conversation (Goodall, 2000), then deciding what you have to contribute to the conversation and where it fits are important considerations (see also Richardson, 2000). Extending the wisdom in the Stake quote, all qualitative researchers need to have something to say that makes their ideas stand out, while framing the ideas in a way that helps readers (represented by editors) see how they connect with what has already been said. I have reviewed papers in which the substance of the research is so esoteric that it's hard to imagine who the audience might be, and I've seen many more manuscripts that seem so mundane it's hard to imagine who might be interested. When you think about your research findings in terms of publishing, ask yourself what you have learned that might be interesting and important to a certain audience. Get clear in your own mind what you want to say, then say it in a way that emphasizes its distinctiveness while acknowledging its commonality.

Rework Your Dissertation as a Book. In 1990, Wolcott warned of the slim chances associated with finding publishers for book-length versions of qualitative studies. My take is that it's still a long shot, especially for new scholars, but some of my colleagues have made it happen. You should know that the odds are virtually impossible for having your dissertation published *as is.* Publishers will sometimes read dissertations and express interest or not in seeing ideas for turning them into books. But many will not even consider such projects without complete plans for how dissertations will be reworked, along with one or two sample chapters that have been written for the purpose of inclusion in the proposed book. An advantage of working with book publishers is that you can put together a prospectus and sample chapters and circulate them among several different publishers at once. Journal manuscripts can only be submitted to one journal at a time. If you believe your study is best suited as a book-length report, and you are willing to rework the manuscript to make it attractive to a book publisher, I recommend that you take a look at what houses are publishing qualitative studies as books, examine how those books are organized and written, find out who is responsible for deciding if such manuscripts get published (usually acquisitions editors), and contact those persons for advice on how to proceed.

Break Out Pieces of Your Dissertation as Articles. This is the strategy I used to publish my dissertation findings and what I usually suggest to my dissertation advisees. The advantages of this approach include that you may have multiple publishable pieces on which most of the work has been done and that refereed journal articles are highly weighted when you are looking for work and when your papers are being reviewed for promotion and tenure. I tell my students to look beyond their findings and consider all of the parts of their dissertations as potential journal-length manuscripts. Well-written literature reviews can be adapted (usually condensed) and submitted to journals that publish reviews of research. Sometimes sections in which researchers reflect on research processes can be modified for journals that include discussions of research methods and issues. And findings sections can be organized into manuscripts that report all or parts of research outcomes. Again, it would be very unusual for new Ph.D.s to be able to simply lift sections from their dissertations and submit them as manuscripts without considerable editing, reorganizing, and rewriting. You should expect to have to do more work. Some students are reluctant to break up the findings because they are sure that the whole gets distorted when pieces are carved out. My response is that they are right; but in the process of reshaping their previous work, new wholes will be created that have merit in their own right. As I discussed in the general section above, writing is about communicating with an audience. You have busted your butt to write a dissertation, and you may never have a richer source of publishable ideas. Find a way to share what you have learned with a wider audience than the few folks who read dissertations.

Write with Particular Journals in Mind. Reframing dissertation sections as journal articles or writing up new studies as journal manuscripts should be done with specific audiences and particular journals in mind. A major part of success in the publishing game is tied to being smart about who will be interested in your work and figuring out ways to make your manuscripts attractive to editors and reviewers who represent those interested groups. Some new scholars start with the assumption that their audience is other researchers, so they should be publishing in the research journals of their field. This is, of course, a legitimate audience, and publishing in such journals is highly valued because competition is stiff, and standards of review are rigorous. But for some work, the audience for your research might be other professionals in the field who can utilize your findings to make better decisions about real world issues of policy and practice. Topical journals that publish articles for a professional audience will typically want manuscripts that report research with an emphasis on substance rather than method. This means framing your findings in a way that will make sense to and have meaning for the readers of particular journals. So, look at what you have to say to a variety of audiences. Study the journals published for your potential audiences, and select a particular journal for each manuscript you write. Examine the particulars of length, style, and format in the journal's call for manuscripts, and analyze articles included in recent volumes to see what editors have chosen for publication. As you write the introduction to your manuscript, be clear about why your paper ought to be of interest to the audience of the journal, then make sure the rest of the article is.

Start at the Top. When I am deciding on what journals to write for, my question for myself is Where is the best place I could get this published? Anyone who has spent serious time in an academic library knows that not all journals are created equal. Some are prestigious and apparently impossible to publish in unless you are part of some not so invisible circle, and some are less highly regarded and appear to publish whatever comes in. Most are somewhere between, publishing articles based on fairly rigorous peer reviews. I like to start at the top of my list of possible journals. I try to make a reasonable judgment about which journals make the possible list, pick the best of those, and go for it. My experience is that the "better" journals generally do a better job of reviewing and giving constructive feedback once your paper gets into the review process. I take it as a success to have editors decide my work is worthy of review, and even rejections from excellent journals help me rework my manuscripts for the next journal on my list. Plus, by taking the extra risk, I give myself the chance to land an important publication in a high-profile journal. Finally, I almost never give up on a manuscript. I will work my way down the list or reframe an article for journals on another list before I will give up. Don't let rejection stop you from playing the game. Learn from it and play smarter.

Take Reviewers' Comments Seriously but Not Personally. I hate rejection. In the rest of my life, I hate rejection so much I usually don't ask for anything unless I am pretty sure I will get the answers I want to hear. If I took that approach to publishing, I would still be waiting to submit my first manuscript. Rejection is built in, and it still hurts, but you can't let it keep you from going forward. Most refereed journals send along some indication of why articles are rejected when they are. Sometimes the editor summarizes reviewer critiques, and sometimes reviewer comments are excerpted. When I was editing *Qualitative Studies in Education*, our policy was to send the reviewers' exact words to all authors. Reviewers knew this was the case and were encouraged to be specific in their critique and to offer suggestions for improvement. On rare occasions, comments were edited because my judgment was that they would not help authors, but overwhelmingly, *QSE* reviewers wrote constructive critiques that I had no problem sending along. I have been burned in review processes, and I have been hurt by shallow or unfair reviews, but I have also been helped. Suggestions made by reviewers of rejected papers have shaped revisions and improved chances for success in other journals. I always take reviewers' comments seriously, even when I think they are wrongheaded. I try not to take them personally, even when I think they are meanspirited.

Always Revise and Resubmit. I think Goodall's (2000) assessment of the review process is right on target: "By a kind of secret consensus among the tribal elders, nobody's first draft is *ever* good enough. The best we can hope for is an encouraging letter from an editor that asks us to 'revise and resubmit'" (p. 26, emphasis in original). Folks who have not played the publishing game may think that winning is an acceptance letter, so they are disappointed with anything less. My advice is, like Goodall's, to shoot for revise and resubmit letters. It means that work has to be done and, perhaps, compromises have to be made, but it is almost always good strategy to take advantage of an editor's invitation to continue the review process with his or her journal. While it's not binding, you are entering a kind of implied contract with the editor that your revision will get special consideration. As an editor, I felt great reluctance to reject work that had been revised based on reviewer recommendations. When this occurred, it was because authors did not meet the intent of the requested revisions. So, treat revise and resubmit letters as victories, and do your best to address the concerns raised in the reviews.

Respect Your Editors, but Be True to Yourself. If you play the publishing game for long, you will experience a revise and resubmit or even an accept with revision letter that asks you to make changes that you cannot, in good conscience, make. Such changes may violate the integrity of the perspective that frames your research (as in when you are asked to calculate interrater reliability or do a t-test), or they may distort the essence of your findings (as when you are asked to complete another analysis based on data that are not there). My strategy in situations like this is not to tell the editor to take it or leave it, but to do everything I can to meet other expectations that will undoubtedly accompany such requests. I then write a cover letter for my revision that tells the editor all the things I have done at his or her request, acknowledging how helpful those suggestions were for making the article better. I then explain what I did not change and why. Here, I don't blame the reviewers or the editor for being ill-informed, small-minded, or out-of-touch. Like Prawat (2000, p. 310), I just "carefully explain to the editor why [I] have chosen to be less than responsive to the reviewers' concerns." I respect editors and assume we both want the best manuscript possible, so that's the angle I use to bring us closer together. I never attack, even when I disagree. I figure the worst I'll get is a polite rejection, and that's where I was when I realized I could not compromise the integrity of the study.

Avoid Alienating Your Editors. Editing is a mostly thankless task that grinds on the time, energy, and emotions of already busy people. Most journals have rejection rates of between 60% and 90%, so most of an editor's contact with authors is to deliver bad news. Editors race from deadline to deadline on a cycle that doesn't end until the journal moves to another editor. Editors are folks just like you trying to do the best job they can. You don't owe them any special treatment beyond what you would expect for yourself, but I recommend that you try not to alienate editors who in some ways serve as gatekeepers between you and your potential audience. I have made a list of things that bugged me as an editor and converted them into suggestions that I recommend as ways to avoid alienating editors. First some things to do:

- know who the current editor of the journal is and address all correspondence to him or her
- know and follow the submission guidelines of the journal, including page limits and referencing style
- know the audience for the journal, and write for that specific audience
- know the discourse style of the journal and use it
- know the journal well enough to make a reasonable decision about your manuscript's chances of being published.

Some things not to do:

- do not write cover letters that go on and on about you, your funding agency, or your paper
- do not submit papers you know are not ready, hoping to get lucky or receive free feedback on how to proceed
- do not submit papers without page numbers
- do not submit manuscripts that have not been carefully proofread by someone competent in the mechanics of expository writing
- do not harass editors about delays in the review or publication process
- do not yell at editors about referees' comments
- do not challenge editors' final decisions.

Do Good Work. This suggestion is bigger than "Have something to say." It is possible to write something in an interesting way or address an issue of importance but do a lousy job of designing or implementing a study. Yes, there is a gamelike dimension to publishing, but unless the research is well conceived and executed, no amount of publishing intelligence will make the work good. "Do good work" ought to be the standard that drives everyone's scholarly life. It's even more important for qualitative researchers to meet this standard because many editors and reviewers remain skeptical about the status of qualitative work as real research. One of the reasons I have written this book is because I have read so many manuscripts as an editor and editorial board member that do not qualify as good work. I am a sympathetic reader who wants qualitative studies to be published in the journals I read for, but I see far too few manuscripts that I can recommend for publication. This book is designed to provide a framework for doing good qualitative work. As with preceding chapters, I will conclude with criteria for assessing adequacy. The criteria below are meant to synthesize the criteria from other chapters and provide overall benchmarks for judging what constitutes quality from a qualitative research perspective. Meeting the criteria do not guarantee that your work will be publishable, but it will give you a place from which to argue that you have done good work.

CRITERIA FOR ASSESSING THE ADEQUACY OF QUALITATIVE REPORTS

If you buy into the logic of this book and have taken the arguments seriously, the questions below will make good sense as tools for evaluating the quality of your work. Other writers and researchers have discussed issues of standards in qualitative work (e.g., Creswell, 1998; Denzin, 1989b; Leedy, 1997; Lincoln, 1995), and readers are encouraged to seek these out for other perspectives and further guidance. What I hope the criteria below provide that is not found elsewhere is a framework for assessing qualitative research adequacy that is based on direct, answerable questions. The answers will look different for studies done within the assumptions of different paradigms, but I believe having a defensible answer for each question is essential if quality is to be assured. Criteria are organized according to the structure of this book and, except for those that come from this chapter on writing up findings, are synthesized from questions presented in much greater detail at the conclusion of previous chapters. Understanding the criteria, at some level, presumes familiarity with the logical development of this book. If criteria are unclear, referring back to appropriate chapters may be necessary.

1. Has the researcher located himself or herself in relation to particular qualitative paradigms?

2. Has the researcher selected appropriate qualitative research approaches, given his or her paradigm choices?

3. Has the researcher described his or her methodological and substantive theory bases?

4. Has the researcher articulated a set of research questions that make sense given his or her methodological and substantive theories?

5. Has the researcher described the research context and provided a rationale for why the context was selected?

6. Has the researcher described how access and entry were negotiated?

7. Has the researcher described procedures for selecting participants and establishing working relationships with them?

8. Has the researcher described and justified participants' level of involvement in the various phases of the study?

9. Has the researcher described all of the data collected as part of the study?

10. Has the researcher made it clear how and when the data were collected?

11. Has the researcher made the case that the data are sufficient to answer research questions and appropriate given the paradigmatic framework and methodological orientation of the study?

12. Has the researcher explained and justified data analysis procedures used in the study, making it clear how and when data were analyzed?

13. Has the researcher applied data analysis procedures that are systematic and rigorous?

14. If utilized, has the researcher spelled out the role of computer programs in supporting his or her data analysis?

15. Has the researcher argued convincingly that his or her data analysis makes sense given the paradigm, methods, data, and research questions of the study?

16. Has the researcher made clear connections between his or her findings and relevant theory and previous research?

17. Has the researcher demonstrated how his or her findings are supported by the data of the study?

18. Has the researcher written his or her report using a narrative form that communicates findings clearly?

19. Has the researcher presented findings that flow logically from his or her paradigmatic assumptions, methodological orientation, research questions, data, and analysis?

Selected Internet Resources

General Resources:

International Institute for Qualitative Methodology
http://www.ualberta.ca/~iiqm/
> Founded in 1998, the International Institute for Qualitative Methodology is a multidisciplinary institute at the University of Alberta. The site contains links to journals, conferences, workshops, and ongoing research at the Institute.

Qualitative Research: University of Colorado at Denver
http://carbon.cudenver.edu/~mryder/itc_data/pract_res.html
> This index offers updated links to information on qualitative educational research, design methodologies, and emerging practices surrounding information learning technologies.

QualPage: Resource for Qualitative Research
http://www.ualberta.ca/~jmorris/qual.html
> This page provides links to organizations, interest groups, and resources related to practicing and teaching qualitative research.

Kerlins.net: Qualitative Research
http://kerlins.net/bobbi/research/qualresearch/
> This includes a comprehensive list of resources related to all aspects of qualitative research. Makes it possible for those interested to explore Kerlin's "Getting Started with Nudist" or join the Qualitative Research Web Ring.

Qualitative Research in Information Systems
http://www2.auckland.ac.nz/msis/isworld/
> This Web site provides an overview of different philosophical perspectives related to qualitative research, modes of analysis, and data collection.

MERlin
http://www.merlin.ubc.ca/
> Created in 1991, MERlin is the Multimedia Ethnographic Laboratory in the Faculty of Education at the University of British Columbia. Researchers at MERlin develop theories and tools for conducting ethnographic inquiry using digital video technologies.

Qualitative Research Resources on the Internet
http://www.nova.edu/ssss/QR/qualres.html
> This site includes papers and other textual resources, syllabi from instructors responsible for teaching qualitative methods courses, and The Qualitative Report electronic journal (see below). It also provides links to other qualitative web pages and journals.

Sites Related to Grounded Theory:

The Grounded Theory Institute: The Grounded Methodology of Barney G. Glaser, Ph.D.
http://www.groundedtheory.com/
> This contains information about Dr. Glaser's work as well as links to grounded theory resources on the Internet.

Grounded Theory: A Thumbnail Sketch
http://www.scu.edu.au/schools/gcm/ar/arp/grounded.html
> From Resource Papers in Action Research, this link provides an overview of the process of grounded theory.

Online Publications:

Action Research International
http://www.scu.edu.au/schools/gcm/ar/ari/arihome.html
> Visitors to this site may submit papers to the refereed online journal and join in an electronic discussion related to issues in action research.

FQS Forum: Qualitative Social Research
http://www.qualitative-research.net/
> A peer-reviewed, interdisciplinary journal for qualitative research, FQS promotes discussion and cooperation between qualitative researchers from different social science disciplines in different countries.

Sociological Research Online
http://www.socresonline.org.uk/
> Sociological Research Online publishes applied sociology, focusing on theory and methods as they relate to current political, cultural, and intellectual topics.

Social Research Update
http://www.soc.surrey.ac.uk/sru/
> Published quarterly by the University of Surrey, the purpose of this site is to help social researchers stay abreast of the latest developments in social research and data analysis.

The Qualitative Report
http://www.nova.edu/ssss/QR/
> The Qualitative Report is a peer-reviewed, on-line journal devoted to writing and discussion of and about qualitative, critical, action, and collaborative inquiry.

Associations and Professional Organizations:

Qualitative Interest Group
http://www.coe.uga.edu/quig/
> From the Department of Education at the University of Georgia, QUIG sponsors the Annual Conference on Interdisciplinary Studies. Site makes it possible to review past conference proceedings or join the QUIG listserv.

Association for Qualitative Research
http://www.latrobe.edu.au/www/aqr/index.html
> Founded in 1997, AQR is an international organization for people interested in qualitative research. Readers can learn more about their annual conference and qualitative research journal by visiting this site.

Society for the Study of Symbolic Interactionism
http://sun.soci.niu.edu/~sssi/
> SSSI is a social science professional organization of scholars interested in qualitative, especially interactionist, research. The site provides information on annual conferences and current issues in the field.

Software Links:

QSR International
http://www.qsr-software.com/
> QSR International's site provides information about their qualitative analysis software, including NUD*IST and Nvivo—software packages designed to help researchers interpret and manage rich data.

Qualis Research Associates, The Ethnograph v. 5.0
http://www.qualisresearch.com/
> Home site for the Ethnograph, a software program designed to make the analysis of qualitative data easier and more efficient. The Ethnograph handles data in the form of interview transcripts, open-ended survey responses, field notes, or other text-based documents.

ATLAS.ti—The Knowledge Workbench
http://www.atlasti.de/
> Website for ATLAS.ti, software for the qualitative analysis of large bodies of information. Using "Visualization, Integration, Serendipity and Exploration (VISE)," ATLAS.ti helps researchers uncover complex themes in textual, graphic, audio, and video data.

APPENDIX B

Protocol Excerpt

October 10—"Schedule Description Protocol"

8:45 Enter Classroom. Talked with teacher about staying for the whole morning and not just during the one-hour taping. She said it was all right. I made a copy of the "daily schedule" (attached).

I helped Rick finish setting up camera and helped with hanging microphones, then testing them with camera/recorder.

9:05 Teacher is making a late start today. She says: "Oh my golly, all my friends and so many things from their house to share with us." [She may be making an excuse for me because she is already off the schedule which she gave me to copy.] Teacher: "We're gonna see how many friends came to this school today. When I call your name, can you think of a color?" She goes through the roll, and the following is the order of color words that were given by the children. The only child who did not respond was Norm: pink, yellow, purple, blue, red, black, orange, red, pink, green, blue, blue, red, pink, red, green, purple, silver (teacher praises Stan for naming an unusual color), silver [Mel appears to copy Stan but doesn't get the same reaction] purple, blue, purple, blue.

9:09 Teacher assigns classroom helpers using helpers chart behind her chair. She asks the kids to read the names. Sharon calls out (in a loud voice) all the names to be read [not giving other children a chance to respond].

The children sing "Today Is Friday."

[I see Norm sitting off to himself at the edge of the rug. He seems to be absorbed within himself. When the children do a horse movement activity—that is, they crawl around the block shelves in a long line—he is the only one who does not participate].

9:15   The teacher describes the activities planned for the day: "In our classroom today. . . ." The water table is open with red water, which will be turned into purple water by adding blue. The teacher also announces that children can write stories down at the block area. She says: "I will add something new to the block area." She puts paper and markers and a little writing tray and says that they can write down what they are making or have an adult write down what they are doing. She calls it "Sign Writing." At the art table, she reminds the children that they will be doing "Scriggly things and pasting them on a piece of paper." [The teacher manages to get each child involved in each of these activities by keeping a list of who has done what]. She mentions that the woodworking bench will be open and tells the children that there are spiders at the science center. She mentions that one spider has been killed because someone was "looking with his hands and not his eyes."

Teacher invites the parents and university helpers to get up and move to their preassigned positions. And she says: "While teachers are getting up, let's do our poem about new leaves." The children do movements and recitation while the teacher points to the words on a handmade chart.

9:20   The children are sent to their centers [based on who is quietest and sitting most erect?]. Taping starts at the block area.

I talked to the teacher about two children who started but are longer in the group. The one child is Candace, the child of the organizer of the parent group. The other (Janet) is the only black child. Teacher assured me that their movement to other days with the afternoon group was not related to participation in the study. Janet was moved for "financial" reasons. [Parents couldn't afford fees or had to work afternoons?] And apparently Candace was moved because teacher needed more parent assistance in the afternoon.

9:22   Tape is on as I get to block center, and Norm is working alone in the corner. He is in the corner of the rug next to the wall nearest the bookshelves. [Norm reminds me of Lester from "outsiders" study—it would be interesting to focus on him and his interactions with peers.]

Kenny comes to the rug on the opposite side (near the puzzle/manipulative table), and Kenny sits down and works on a puzzle.

Susan comes to the rug and takes a position close to Norm. I did not see any exchange. There were no words passed. [I will check the tape to see if I missed something]. She is sitting two feet from him with her back turned to him.

Gina comes into the block area. She looks at Susan's structure and kneels down [as if to join]. Susan [sensing her reluctance?] says: "Remember, you know me. Susan, you know me." No response from Gina.

Susan (after 20 seconds): "Wanna play with me?" Gina: "Yea." Susan: "Look what I made." They begin playing together.

When Susan finishes her structure, she says: "There" [invitation for Gina to look]. Gina looks but makes no response. Susan repeats: "There." Gina: "My ladder keeps falling down." Gina is putting two blocks together next to a boxlike structure, and she calls the two blocks a ladder, and indeed they keep falling. Susan waits and watches Gina working with her ladder. Then says: "Look." Gina does not stop, and Susan again says: "There." Gina seems to give up on her ladder, and Susan says: "Look." This time, Gina looks and smiles. Susan says: "Want me to do that for you?" Gina puts up her hand and signals that she does not.

Susan (referring to her structure): "Look what I made all by myself." Gina, says: "Oh, oh." And giggles. Susan says: "It is tall. Wanna make one like me?" Gina: "I'll make something like this. I'll make a little tiny ladder."

Susan knocks her structure down accidentally and says: "Oh!" and both girls giggle.

9:28   Kenny has entered the part at the block area occupied by Norm. Kenny is between Norm and the girls. He turns his attention away from Norm and joins the girls, rolling a cylindrical block down Susan's ramp. Susan protests: "I don't want these. I don't want these (blocks)."

Gina [playing off Kenny to tease Susan?] starts flipping blocks onto and into Susan's structure. Susan: "You don't mess up my thing!" Gina: "Here." And she puts more pieces into the original structure giggling [to recover?]. Susan responds: "Thanks, we need that." Both girls laugh. They repeat this four times. Gina continues to lay the blocks on, and Susan says: "Thanks, we need that." [There is an undercurrent of conflict in this interaction, covered with giggles]. Gina puts pieces down into Susan's structure. Susan moves them away, and Gina giggles.

Finally, Susan says: "Don't knock this down." Gina continues doing it. Susan turns her back and says: "You can't see me." Gina comes around to face her, and Susan closes up like a ball [strategy to keep Gina from putting more blocks into her structure?]

9:31   Gina leaves. Susan puts the little blocks away in their box.

9:33   Susan leaves.

Norm is still on his own in his corner.

[This is the first day that Jeffrey has not been in the block area during the block taping period. I wonder why.]

Norm has constructed a very elaborate structure. We exchange eye contact briefly, and he goes back to work. [Norm looks unhappy. I see him talking to himself while he is playing. He seems to wear "higher" fashion clothing (designer labels) than most kids. He has blond hair. Ordinary size and features. Clean and neat. He has a "detached" look in his eyes that troubles me.] Norm, piece by piece, systematically knocks down his structure. When it is down, he seems to be looking in the block shelves for something that he doesn't find. Norm leaves.

9:36   Gina and Susan come back again. Gina is still giggling. They are on the corner of the block area, and Susan points to a doll in the playhouse area and says: "Looka that baby." They both head for the playhouse.

9:39   Norm, having circled the block shelves, returns to the block area. Sees a clear plastic purse which he takes down from the table where the children leave things that they have brought from home to share. He takes out a chap stick from the clear purse, removes the cap, and then hides the cap and the chap stick behind the blocks on a lower shelf. [Interesting that he knows I am watching, but that doesn't deter him].

9:41   Norm leaves the block area.

9:42   The camera is off and moving to the playhouse.

Daily Schedule

9:00–9:15   Attendance
                   Discussion of the new day
                   Sharing Time—listening to friends

9:15–10:25	Free Choice Activities Directed Free Play including Discovery Table, Woodworking Bench, Easel Painting, Sand/Water Play, Reading Center, Housekeeping Area, Manipulative Activities, Block Area, Writing Center, Art Area
10:25–10:30	Cleanup Time (Transition)
10:30–10:40	Story
10:40–10:55	Snack (served "family style")
10:55–11:25	Large Muscle Time Gymnasium or Outdoor Activity – Weather Permitting
11:25–11:30	Preparation for departure

APPENDIX C

Research Journal Entry

December 13

Second meeting with the teacher. Met at the school to explain the study further and to get informed consent signed by her and give her the forms to be sent home to parents.

I made it clear that I would not record teacher behavior except as a way to provide context for the children's peer interactions. I would not interact with the kids but move around the room taking notes. We agreed that I should not move too much during the first few observations to let the kids get used to my presence. She says she will say something to the kids like: "A man is coming. He wants to find out what we do in kindergarten, will write down what we do."

She seems comfortable with my coming on a flexible schedule. I told her I would let her know at least a week ahead when I would be coming and for how long. She seems very confident about what she does and how she does it. She believes in interaction and play. She has refused to use workbooks. Says, "I'm a kindergarten teacher—will not think of myself as part of the faculty." (She means 1–5 faculty.) "I have established myself (she's taught K for 20 years) and have never used a workbook and never will. I'll teach the skills my way." The assistant superintendent who suggested her thinks she has widespread community support for doing it her way.

She is interested in teaching the whole child and seems like a strong opponent of academic kindergarten. Says, "Who cares if a child can read on a third-grade level if he doesn't know how to fasten his zipper," and she'd rather have "people who are able to talk with others than smart people who don't." She says she'll quit if the state goes to all-day kindergarten.

She gave me her schedule, the special programs schedule, and a map of the school. She volunteered to ask the specials teachers (library, P.E., art, and music) if I can follow the kids to their classes. I need to think about this and what it means for human subjects.

We set up meeting for both of us to meet with the principal on January 2nd and set the first two observation days for Tuesday the 8th and Thursday the 10th.

Meeting went very well. She seems to know what the study is about and is willing to share her classroom. I don't think she will change a thing because I am there. Looks like the morning group is a good choice. She notes that some kids have "some (peer relations) problems we've not worked out." I have a good feeling about the teacher and the setting. I'll need to be careful not to let my admiration for the teacher's strong personality and my attraction to her philosophy of teaching K get in the way of studying how the children's peer interactions actually unfold in her classroom.

Teacher Interview Transcript

Teacher #63

May 27

I: Why don't you start off by talking a little bit about how you became a kindergarten teacher and why you chose to do that kind of work. Sort of work history and education history.

T: OK. I started out going to school for a two-year degree in nursery school education. Went out and worked in a few nursery schools and had a lot of student teaching experience, and, over a period of like a year, I decided I wanted to go back and get a four-year degree and teach in public schools. So I returned, I went to _____ State. I got my four-year degree in early childhood education.

I: And the two-year degree. Where did you go to school?

T: _____ Community College. After getting the . . . my degree, I was hired immediately that fall after I graduated here at _____ Elementary for the kindergarten position. Eight years ago, and that is where I have been since—in the kindergarten position.

I: Did you take time off to have a child? [We had talked about this before the tape started.]

T: Yes. Just one year. I left in March. Finished out that school year in sick time, and I came back. Stayed home a full year on maternity leave; this is my first year back.

I: Have you thought about changing grade levels? Do you like kindergarten?

T: I love kindergarten. I like the little ones. I think you can do a lot with them. I have thought about trying first grade. I did student teaching in first grade and did some extra volunteer time in first grade. I like that, too. It is a little more involved, work wise. I like having the different groups of kids, too. In kindergarten you have the morning and afternoon. You have different groups.

I: And that is an advantage?

T: I like it. It is a lot of kids to work with and a lot of kids to remember. But I do like having a different class come in during the day.

I: That leads me to ask about going to a full day where you would have just one group. Do you have strong feelings about going to a full-day program?

T: I have mixed feelings about it. I see so much of the time where there are large groups of children that I think could not handle a full day because they have a hard enough time . . . it is maybe like half year before they can handle just making it through the whole day of school. In this situation, there are so many children now who are going to nursery school two years before they even come here so they . . . already have been in school so much they are comfortable with it. And there are quite a few kids who could handle a full day easily. But I think if I had my choice, I would have the first half of the year be a half day and the second half stretched to a full day. Except that scheduling that many children would really be hard.

I: But if you were just making the decision for kids, what is best for kids, that might be a good alternative?

T: Uh-huh. I think so. When they get to first grade after being in a half a day kindergarten, they have a lot of trouble stretching it and waiting all day long. It takes at least a month before the kids can wait till lunch and can wait till the end of the day.

I: Could you just take me through what a typical morning looks like in your classroom? What kind of activities go on? Maybe if you just did that chronologically through the day.

T: We start out . . . they come in from the bus, and they have what is called free time. Where they have centers that are set up in the room, and they have their choice of working at any one of the centers, the block area, the playhouse. It is more like a free time for them to choose what they want and have time to explore the different activities. Some days there are more specific things set out at the tables. Other days it is just free for them to choose. And that lasts about 15 to 20 minutes.

I: I'll let you come back to that. How do you decide what is going to be at these individual stations or centers?

T: They usually change in emphasis every so often. Like, the block area is always there. The easel is always there. The painting. The science center is always there. I have one table that I will change the emphasis at either weekly or biweekly. This week it happens to be all rhyming games, so they were working on different kinds of rhyming games. Last two weeks it was on simple addition. With all kind of games and different things there for them to do, in worksheets if they would rather do paper work or whatever. Sometimes I would just rather, instead of playing with the block area or large muscles things, I set things out at the tables like peg-boards and clay and those kinds of things that they can choose to sit at and do. They still have the choice out of all that what they want to do, but they have unlimited table activities.

I: OK. I'm sorry. Back to the day.

T: After free time is over, we clean up. We meet together as a whole group. That is when we do the attendance and we do some music, and songs.

I: Do that on the rug?

T: Yes. Up front at the rug. And a lot of records because I'm not good at singing. So we do a lot of record activity songs. I usually have a story at that time. And that is where we more or less teach the lesson of the day. Like if it is going to be a big science lesson, I'll do that then. Or a math lesson, we'll do that then. And then I explain what the jobs are for the day. Today, we had two worksheets and an art project. And each day—some days it is more involved in art and some days it is heavier on the worksheets. It depends on what the theme is because I organize my class by weekly theme. And, I go through each job, and I always have two jobs. They write their name each day and do a weather calendar, which they have to cut out and paste onto a calendar, which they have made and written out themselves. So those are usually done right away. The jobs are usually done in order, and they do those right away. Also, they have the choice of doing those on their free time, on their own time. So they can just get into their jobs right away at work time.

I: And some students choose to do that?

T: Yes. Quite a few of them do. It doesn't . . . the jobs don't take very long, so they can do them, and they can get them done with, and they don't have to worry about it at work time. They have sometimes five or six jobs. I have the jobs written on the board, written out. We go over each one, what it is. I explain, I show it. If it is an art project, I demonstrate it.

Unless it is something I want them to get following directions, I will just demonstrate it, and they will go back and do it, or else I just explain the directions. I explain all the jobs in order that they are supposed to do and then we ask any questions. We usually go have music, moving around the room a little bit, come back up front, and then sit down. So they have gotten two full times, complete going through them. Directions. And then the children all go back to their assigned tables, and they move about at their own speed. Usually it is about an hour, sometimes an hour and 15 minutes, to complete all of the work time. They get their own jobs from the back shelf where they are located. They go to their own table and do their own work at their own speed. Most of the time it is in order on what I have listed on the board, cause I list them in order of priority. While they are working at their seats, that is when I begin to call the reading groups up which I have grouped. I work on . . .

I: How many groups do you have?

T: Right now I have three in one class and two in the other. It's changed over the course of the year. Sometimes I've combined them, sometimes, I've changed them. One group that I had which was going to first grade, for a while got to the point where they couldn't continue on. So now we bring them back to kindergarten. So I had to make time for them in my groups, too. Which was just for oral reading now. So I do my calling up for reading groups. So in addition to their jobs, they are coming back, and they also have reading groups which they also have a workbook page or two to do. Then they go back on their own and do it.

I: So they come to reading groups, and there might be some sort of lesson there?

T: Right. It is usually a big book lesson, or this one group that we're reading with now, they read out of the oral reading and that kind of thing. And then . . .

I: And then you might give them some sort of reading activity to go with the lesson?

T: Right. Workbook page or an activity. That's when I have mother helpers come in. I will have those mothers work on a fishing game or we have these little plastic objects where there is a sorting game where they will take certain kids out of that group like two or three kids at time and work in another area with them on these same skills that we have been doing in the big book. So that there is reinforcement right away. And work time continues on until usually 10 or 15 minutes till the end of class. And sometimes I finish the day with a story. Sometimes it might be a science lesson, or sometimes it might be the math big book if we used that for the lessons. Something that brings it back up front and ties it all up. Then we get ready to go home for the bus. That takes 15 minutes right there, getting ready to go home. And that is pretty much a normal day.

I: Nicely done.

T: Oh, thank you.

I: You described it well! When you are making decisions about what to do, you talk about these different parts of the day, when you are deciding what is going to happen, when and what particular activities are going to be done with the reading groups, say, how do those decisions come about? How do you decide what you are going to do?

T: You mean the jobs at work time?

I: Yea.

T: OK. Well I divide my time into weekly units that I usually stress. Like one week will be on transportation. And all the activities and resources I have gathered over the years on transportation, all the books to read or whatever stories, I will plug them into those weeks for transportation.

I: How do you decide to teach transportation at all? Where does that come from?

T: From the curriculum. There are certain topics and subjects that have to be covered in science or social studies, like learning about other cultures. We learned about children of other cultures, which is in our curriculum guide. And so to stress that more, we spent a week on Japan. Bringing in the difference between children in America and children in Japan. The differences and similarities. We use the curriculum guide. When we finish certain goals of math, we pass that point, and we go on to the next. Now we are on simple addition. And those children who have gone that far will be introduced to the simple addition and will work on that. They will be doing those projects. There will be just a handful that maybe can't do that. Because of the individualized approach at the school, they are provided with other things they have to do. Extra work with the moms in small groups.

I: Tell me more about that. I think the district supervisor called that a continuous progress approach.

T: Right.

I: Describe that. How does that work in your classroom?

T: In the beginning of the year, when the children come in, that is what I spent a couple of weeks doing, assessing the children. How much their knowledge is of letters, say. How many they can recognize, how many they know, capital, lower case, what the difference is, and then grouping the children according to that. And those children who have a knowledge of letters will begin the big book right away and go at a little bit faster pace. Whereas those who weren't sure of their letters, didn't know their letters will start, will do a lot of preliminary activities learning the difference between a letter and number, whatever. And then begin the big book when they are ready to start actual learning of the letter name. The math . . . that group goes on a little bit slower making sure that they absorb it. Get all the . . . before they go on. Individual progress meaning that if I have a student who comes in already knowing how to add and subtract, then that child is provided with a first-grade math program or where they fit into and given activities and extra help by maybe moms coming in and working with them.

I: When you described your day, you talked a little bit about having [a] unit in mind. But as I read the curriculum guide, I don't remember reading about units. So how do you connect the objectives in the guide with your notion of units?

T: OK. How to explain that? I think the best way is there are a lot of topics in kindergarten that are covered and that are fun units to do with the kids and fit into . . . take those units like you are doing seasons and nature . . . and you find ways to fit the math program into that by doing the counting of seeds or writing skills where you or sequencing skills where you talk about how a seed grows. You fit all those things into the other categories. Like you can say this is a math skill, but it fits into seasons and nature.

I: Do you start with the skill, or do you start with the theme?

T: I start with the theme because I've got my class so organized that throughout the year there are different ways different themes go, and certain topics are just good to cover. A lot of it goes with a lot of social studies and science units. I used transportation as an example or seasons and nature. Then you kind of fit into that . . . right now being the end of the year, we've worked so much on beginning sounds and all that that we're trying to work on rhyming. Ending sounds and rhyming. So we have used this whole week just for rhyming words. We do a lot of the rhyming sounds and everything like that. But I also am reinforcing what we did last week, which is the math skills and simple addition. And they also are working on projects like that. So I start with the theme and then I try to plug in all the activities that will cover math, science, reading in the same way, handwriting skills, and that sort of thing.

I: How do you make sure that you have covered all the objectives? Or is that one of your goals to cover the objectives?.

T: I don't know. I know what the objectives are. I've helped write a lot of them for one thing. I guess I just know what they are and know what you have to cover and what has to be introduced or what has to be solid before they really go on to the first grade, just kind of making sure that you fit all that in over the course of the year. And with all the different children at different levels, some you may have doing one activity or one objective you may have done back in February and you know they have mastered that. Whereas one child, you are still working on it because they are still not getting it.

I: Looking at the report card. You have lots of objectives covering a variety of subject matter areas. But on the report card it is much more narrow. And mostly academic kinds of things. There is lots of talk in the philosophy and the general goals about the whole child and social development and stuff like that, but not much mention about that on the report card. I'm wondering, what gets the focus in your classroom, the stuff on the report card or the stuff in the curriculum guide or is that . . . ?

T: Well, this is personal opinion because I . . . the report card that I work with, I mean, I use it. There is one whole side that is social skills. Listen[s] attentively, completes tasks, and things like that. What I will do is mark a lot of those, and yet in my comments, maybe stress a little bit more what that child needs to do socially to be able to be ready. He needs to stay on task longer or concentrate on taking responsibility to finish his own work or things like that. So you can stretch that out in the comments. As far as the academic part goes, I have also added to that, I will write in there a lot of different skills that we do that are in our curriculum guide that is not included as a specific skill on the report card. For instance, when math is very general, and where I think they should be able to build sets of objects matched to numbers . . . that is not even listed in the math, and I think that is an important skill, and I will write that in where there is room provided.

I: For each child or particular children?

T: Most of those things I do put in for each. But as far as the reading, I have individualized it according to what that child is reading because I have had several kids who were reading at the first-grade level and some just beginning at the first-grade level, some that still haven't gotten all the letters. So there are so many different levels that I have kind of individualized the reading aspect of the report card.

I: Do you think . . . or do you know if other teachers in this system are doing this same kind of adaption that . . . the kinds of things you are doing?

T: I don't know for sure that all of them . . . I know a few do. And I think you almost have to.

I: Tell me why you have to?

T: Because the philosophy of the school system is an individualized approach, which would mean that either you have to show and provide for that child and what they are doing and let them know if they are progressing or if they are at satisfactory level. It is no set grade—needs help or progressing or satisfactory. And then if you give them an *N* for needs help, explain why and what kind of help they need. Then that is when you provide that for them.

I: A couple of times you have mentioned something called the "big book." Can you tell me what that is?

T: Right. That is the Houghton Mifflin reading program. It comes with two big books teaching you letters and sounds. It's just simply a huge book that you set on the table, and the children sit on the floor and work with the big book. They also have what we call a "practice book." It's a workbook that goes along with the page, but it is not the one that has the exact same page on it, so they are not reinforced with the exact same page. It's the same skill, but it is different pictures and everything on it so that they are using that skill that they just did at the big book and transferring it over into something concrete with . . . at their seat or with the group.

I: Can you think of a particular example of how a lesson might go and what the reinforcement might be?

T: Say they are teaching the letter *B*. They have what is the magic picture. They have the letter *B* printed over the black and white picture of a boot. Because *B* begins with boot. They would have to take their crayons . . . at the big book, we talk about the big book page first, and they'll have that *B*, boot there and there will be five or six things, some will begin with *B*, and some don't. And then the children will have to listen to the sentences and find out what makes sense with what I say and begins with *B*. And then we find those pictures on the page. Well, then they would go back . . .

I: Then there would be several choices?

T: Right. There would be some that begin with *B* and some that would not. Then we go back to our seats, and sometimes we do it in a group. They would have to just look at that page. It also has the magic picture B up in the corner. But all the other pictures would be different pictures. So that they would have to look at their own book and name all these other pictures and find what begins with B and mark those. Because they would be totally different pictures than what were on the big book. So they would be practicing the sound itself.

I: So you might spend one period on B or several periods on B and then revisit B later?

T: Right. I will reinforce that besides what we do in the big book. Like the job at the work time the next day might be a worksheet on the letter B—cutting and pasting worksheet. Or it might be a group project where they take a poster board and write down a letter B on the top, and they have to cut out of magazines all the things that begin with B and paste them on. Different projects like that.

I: We're starting to hear now of children failing kindergarten. How do you respond when you hear that phrase: *failing kindergarten*?

T: We don't hear that too much. I do have several that need to be retained or we are suggesting that be retained. We don't enforce that. We let the parents have the final decision. I think a lot of it, too, and that is just speaking from our area, a lot of these students go to nursery school, and they have been in nursery school one or two years, and they come to kindergarten, and they have been working on papers for so long, and those students who don't have that advantage of having been to nursery school are . . . come in behind the others. Now they are at a level where they are just ready to begin, but because they have not had all these extra experiences before, they are found to be behind the others. And it seems that if they come in behind, they stay behind all year long. If I think of one example I have been concerned with now, I find that is the same way. This child has had absolutely no experiences before this except television and has not worked or played with groups of kids before he came to kindergarten. And this has been just such a stimulating environment for him and more in tune to the active social part of it than any academics, and now he is really far behind academically. He didn't have a nursery school to practice letters and numbers and didn't have the practice at home with family members to do that with them. So now we are finding out he is really far behind, but before he can go on to our first-grade program, because of the way it is set up, it is being suggested that he be retained a year.

I: "It's being suggested" means that you are suggesting it? And is the principal involved in that?

T: Yes. Yes he is.

I: Is there a conference with the parent?

T: Several times through the course of the year, we have had conferences. Especially after report card with the mother explaining to her where he stands and what needs to be done, and now we'll have this last confer-ence, which will be today and how . . . we're making this strong sugges-tion. She has another one coming up, and we don't know what her deci-sion will be.

I: What do you predict, though?

T: Well, she's half sounded like she doesn't want to keep him home. In fact, this is one child I suggested at the beginning of the year . . . wait a year before coming. Don't stay in kindergarten. And she simply said, if I take him out, he'll only sit and watch T.V., so why should I? And I said, in that case, you are right that he will get the social skills that he needs here for a year. But then you have to prepare them for the fact that there is the possibility of retention because another year might just be what he needs to pick up all those academics and then start next year being able to pick up on those other important things. Constant conferencing throughout the year.

I: Maybe you have already answered this. Let me ask again. If you . . . think about this child you have just described whose . . . has been unsuccessful, can you compare what is different about—is this a little boy?

T: Yes.

I: Can you compare what is different about this little boy and another child who has been very successful in your class? What are the differences between those two kids?

T: Probably the social skills and getting along with others would be one. Whereas the child who should be retained is still so socially more aggres-sive, more on the active things, doesn't like to sit down and do.

I: He would rather be up throwing airplanes. [I observed this earlier, while she was teaching.]

T: Right. Rather than sitting down at the table and completing something. Maybe after one whole worksheet, he is exhausted and can't go on any-more. Physically can't do it or just mentally is done. Whereas another child who is successful, you can see the progress. Maybe at the beginning of the year, it was easier for them to maybe do two jobs before they would have to get up and move or do any kind of moving activity. Or sitting in a group, listening attentively instead of focusing their attention on me and what I'm doing in the story, they are playing with little things on the floor or drawing lines or strings on the carpet or things like that. Their attention span is a lot shorter for the unsuccessful child. And the progress made during the course of the year would be slower. Instead of in a couple of months in school to be able to stay on task more and needing less of the active type of thing, at this point in time still needing the active moving around.

I: What is it about the child that makes him need that?

T: I think a lot of it is experience. I know a lot of it, too, is age. A lot of the younger children are like that when they come in. I can't say that as a general rule because I have seen the exceptions to that. Where it is the young child who comes in and happens to be ready, has had more experience, more reactive in being able to do lots of different types of things. Not the kind of child that has been put outside to play all day and that is it. Has had experience with books, with maybe sitting down with other children at a table and coloring together. Or things like that that they have had more experience at.

I: OK. Let me shift gears here. Think in broad terms about functions of kindergarten. Why do you think we have kindergarten? What is the purpose of kindergarten?

T: What is . . . as I see it now or what I think it is? . . . should be?

I: Both. What do you think it is, first?

T: I think the purpose is to prepare for first grade. Getting ready to be able to handle the work load, because that is so important, like right here in our system. Getting that child ready and used to the fact that they are going to have to share with other kids. They are going to have to keep within a time frame, which is very difficult for these little ones to do. Keep in a time frame to do their certain jobs, or even today I discovered in keeping in a time frame to eat their lunch. You can't sit and talk all the time. You have to eat your lunch and get it done with. And that kind of thing, keeping within a time frame, building responsibility to be able to take care of themselves and follow through on a lot of things on their own without constant teacher guidance, working in large group situations. A lot of times they have not been exposed to that. Where they are just 1 of 25 instead of being just 1 of 3 in the family. That type of thing. Here, in _____ , it is very much that. I think a lot of it is academics, too, getting them learning the basics, the letters, the sounds, the basics of math, the numbers, the simple addition, getting ready for that first-grade program, which is going to start them out pretty quickly. So I think that is basically what it is for, to get them ready.

I: What should it be?

T: Well, I'm an old fan . . . think the kids need some time to play. I think that although you can fit academics in and do a lot of this stuff, you need to also leave them time to be free, to have the free time to enjoy the other activities that there are. Otherwise there would be no sense in having blocks in the kindergarten or the playhouse. They need some free time to be able to work and play socially with other children in small group situations where they could choose the people they want to be with and choose what they want to play with. And then I also think the academics are important. Maybe not quite as far as we go except maybe for those children who are ready for it. Maybe, there might be a handfull of five or eight kids in a class that need to go on in math because they are so ready for it, but if they don't, it is not good to hold them back. So you should be allowed to time the opportunity to let those kids go on with their simple addition or whatever. But to try to make that something that everybody learns, I'm not sure that is right either. The skill levels between . . . in one kindergarten class is so broad, like from two to seven year old. That is a lot.

I: Sounds like it. You've been involved with kindergartens for eight years, you say. Could you characterize the changes you have seen in kindergarten programs you have seen in that period of time?

T: A lot more publicity as far as getting children ready. There [are] always articles out, and a lot of topics and speakers are presented about readiness and what is really readiness and when is a child ready. And how do you deal with that? A lot more preschool programs as far as maybe going into all-day kindergartens and those types of things. Whether a school system should or shouldn't. And I've seen people on both sides of the fences for that. Teachers who have taught and teachers who haven't taught it and who have real strict ideas about it. A lot more about the nursery schools. A lot more around here, the nursery schools are cooperating with the public schools, finding out what kind of printing we teach in order to teach printing that way for their students. That type of thing.

I: What about the experience for kids? What's different for kids this year as compared to the first year you taught? Are there differences?

T: You mean the experiences they come to?

I: Yea. What happens to them during the day? Is that about the same now as then?

T: I think there [are] more of the students who come from many years in day-care centers. I have a lot of students that are bussed back and forth between day-care centers, have working families, very professional families, mothers and fathers both involved in a lot of work, long hours. And there is not as much family activity going on as there used to be, I don't think. I had a lot more families and mothers and fathers involved in the classroom before. Now because they are working here or they're working there or they belong to this club that meets on Tuesday's and they can't come that day. That type of thing. There is not as much family involvement as there used to be.

I: The curriculum, how has that changed?

T: When we wrote the curriculum a couple of years back, there really hadn't been one previously to that. There had not been anything set on paper with what kindergarten was teaching. It was just kind of understood. So we sat down and wrote that curriculum. We sat down, this group of kindergarten teachers, and decided what types of things in each area needed to be covered. It tried to cover all the different areas. Then when they transferred over to these new courses of study that are being written, I don't see a whole lot of change. I think that they have included all that needs to be included, stretching that whole gamut of skills.

I: What do you think . . . if you project down the road . . . what do you think is going to happen to kindergartens in say five years?

T: I see more of the all-day kindergartens. I see kindergarten turning into more of the academic atmosphere. If you think back, they talk about how kindergarten is not what it used to be. It used to be all just play, and now it is so much academic. Down the road, it could be very well it could end up being more of a first-grade program, an accelerated program, especially in an area like this one where there are a lot of professional people, and these students have more experience knowing about NASA and the space program. That kind of thing.

I: How do you feel about that more academic side of . . .

T: I think it is a little too much pressure on the child. I really do. Right away the first questions you are getting in September are, "Do they have to read? When will they be reading?" It's like, slow down, let them be kids. They are only five years old, and while I can see what their concern is and yet I keep trying to tell myself, he'll do it when he is ready. And yet as a parent you want your child to be going on and doing the next thing. I can understand their point of view. But I think there is a lot of pressure on those little ones to keep up with everybody else. And I think it is very hard for them.

I: One more different kind of question. Just one more. You're doing great, too. OK. What qualities do you see as important for kindergarten teachers? What makes a good kindergarten teacher?

T: First of all, you have to love a small child. You have to be able to look at that child and have to understand that they are just a child. They are not a small adult. I think that is important. I think you have to understand the development of a small child because if you don't know how a child develops and in what stages they do certain things, then you really have a hard time keying into where they are at and what they are able to accomplish. You have to have a lot of patience, which I tell my husband now with our little one. You have to have the patience to understand that if that is something they are not ready to do right now, you are not going to force them to do it at that time. And you have to be able to share in their excitement when they do do something that they have been trying for weeks, like tying their shoes— a simple thing like that. A lot of the teachers in the upper grades say, "How can you teach it? I can't stand that. Buttoning and zipping their coats for them." That kind of thing. But I think you have to have that kind of patience because they are just tiny children, and I think you have to understand that. Kind of remember that no matter what you are doing with them.

I: If you were making a comparison between kindergarten teachers as a group, if that is possible, and fourth-grade teachers, what are the differences between those two. Are there differences?

T: Probably in the dealings with the children, I would say kindergarten teachers are more actively involved with each child, step by step on how they do things. Whether it is learning how to share with somebody else, they have to be involved in that. Whereas fourth-grade teachers maybe assume more of giving a child direction, and they will carry through on their own. More responsible for themself. Whereas I think kindergarten teachers have to realize that these kids aren't quite responsible for themselves. They have to be guided more, and they have to be given the opportunity to explore more different areas. And I think those teachers know, the teachers of older children know that and kind of build on the child's independence. I don't know. I've never taught fourth grade. I imagine that to be the difference.

I: That's great! Thanks for talking with me. Like I said, I'll be sending you a copy of what we find out once all the interviews are done. Anything else you want to add before I turn off the machine?

T: No, I think that about covers it.

I: Thanks again.

Master Outline for Dissertation Findings

(Hatch, 1984, pp. 145–46)

Social Goals

A. Affiliation Goal Domain
    1. Ways to Make Contact
        a. Direct Requests
        b. Conversation Openers
        c. Nonverbal Entry
    2. Ways to Check on Standings with Peers
        a. Direct Requests
        b. Indirect Requests
    3. Ways to Express Feelings of Affection and Belonging
        a. Direct Expressions
        b. Effusive Expressions
        c. Cooperative Expressions
        d. Expressions of Loyalty and Sympathy
        e. Physical Expressions

B. Competence Goal Domain
    1. Ways to Request Evaluation
        a. Direct Requests
        b. Indirect Requests

    2. Ways to Respond to Evaluation
       a. Offensive Responses
       b. Laughing It Off Responses
       c. Disclaiming Responses
       d. Denial Responses
       e. Avoidance Responses
       f. Acceptance Reponses

C. Status Goal Domain
    1. Ways to Practice Self-Promotion
       a. Personal Superiority Promotions
       b. Associative Superiority Promotions
    2. Ways to Respond to Self-Promotions
       a. One-upsmanship Strategies
       b. Bandwagon Strategies
       c. Challenging Strategies
       d. Ignoring Strategies
       e. Accepting Strategies
    3. Ways to Put Others Down
       a. Pointing Out Inadequacies
       b. Expressing Condescension
       c. Name Calling
       d. Ordering
       e. Threatening
       f. Intimidating
       g. Rubbing It In
    4. Ways to Respond to Put-Downs
       a. Denial Strategies
       b. Logical Strategies
       c. Offensive Strategies
       d. Covering Strategies
       e. Ignoring Strategies
       f. Sympathy-Seeking Strategies

REFERENCES

Agar, M. H. (1980). *The professional stranger: In informal introduction to ethnography.* New York: Academic Press.

Anderson, J. A. (1987). *Communication research: Issues and methods.* New York: McGraw-Hill.

Ashworth, P. (1999). "Bracketing" in phenomenology: Renouncing assumptions in hearing about student cheating. *Qualitative Studies in Education, 12,* 707–721.

Atkinson, P. (1990). *The ethnographic imagination: Textual constructions of reality.* New York: Routledge.

———. (1992). *Understanding ethnographic texts.* Newbury Park, CA: Sage.

Barone, T. (1983). Things of use and things of beauty: The story of the Swain County arts program. *Daedalus, 112,* 1–28.

Becker, H. S. (1963). *Outsiders: Studies in the sociology of deviance.* New York: Free Press.

———. (1986). *Writing for social scientists: How to start and finish your thesis, book, or article.* Chicago: University of Chicago Press.

Becker, H. S., & Geer, B. (1957). Participant observation and interviewing: A comparison. *Human Organization, 16,* 28–32.

Behar, R., & Gordon, D. A. (Eds.). (1995). *Women writing culture.* Berkeley: University of California Press.

Belenky, M., Clincy, B., Goldberger, N., & Tarule, J. (1987). *Women's ways of knowing.* New York: Basic Books.

Berg, B. L. (1998). *Qualitative research methods for the social sciences.* Boston: Allyn & Bacon.

Berger, P. L., & Kellner, H. (1981). *Sociology reinterpreted: An essay on method and vocation.* Garden City, NY: Anchor Books.

Bernard, H. R. (1994). *Research methods in anthropology: Qualitative and quantitative approaches*. Thousand Oaks, CA: Sage.

Bloom, L. R., & Munro, P. (1995). Conflicts of selves: Nonunitary subjectivity in women administrators' life history narratives. In J. A. Hatch & R. Wisniewski (Eds.), *Life history and narrative* (pp. 99–112). London: Falmer.

Blumer, H. (1969). *Symbolic interactionism: Perspective and method*. Berkeley, CA: University of California Press.

Bogdan, R. C., & Biklen, S. K. (1992). *Qualitative research for education: An introduction to theory and methods*. Boston: Allyn & Bacon.

Bogdan, R. C., Taylor, S. J. (1975). *Introduction to qualitative methods: A phenomenological approach to the social sciences*. New York: Wiley.

Bondy, E. (1983). *Children's talk in and out of school: Contextual influences on oral language*. Unpublished paper, University of Florida.

Bremme, D. W., & Erickson, F. (1977). Relationships between verbal and non-verbal classroom behaviors. *Theory and Practice, 16*, 153–161.

Britzman, D. P. (1991). *Practice makes practice: A critical study of learning to teach*. Albany: State University of New York Press.

Bruner, E. M. (1984). The opening up of anthropology. In E. M. Bruner (Ed.), *Text, play, and story: The construction and reconstruction of self and society* (pp. 1–18). Washington DC: The American Ethological Society.

Bruner, J. (1986). *Actual minds, possible worlds*. Cambridge, MA: Harvard University Press.

Byers, P. Y., & Wilcox, J. R. (1991). Focus groups: A qualitative opportunity for researchers. *Journal of Business Communications, 28*, 63–77.

Cannella, G. S. (1997). *Deconstructing early childhood education: Social justice and revolution*. New York: Peter Lang.

Cannella, G. S., & Bailey, C. (1999). Postmodern research in early childhood education. *Early Education and Day Care, 10*, 3–39.

Carr, W. (1995). *For education: Towards critical educational inquiry*. Buckingham, UK: Open University Press.

Carr, W., & Kemmis, S. (1986). *Becoming critical: Education, knowledge, and action research*. London: Falmer.

Casey, K. (1993). *I answer with my life: Life histories of women teachers working for social change*. New York: Teachers College Press.

Ceglowski, D. (1994). Conversations about Head Start salaries: A feminist analysis. *Early Childhood Research Quarterly, 9*, 367–386.

———. (2000). Research as relationship. *Qualitative Inquiry, 6*, 88–103.

Charon, J. M. (1998). *Symbolic interactionism: An introduction, an interpretation, an integration*. Upper Saddle River, NJ: Prentice Hall.

Chiseri-Strater, E., & Sunstein, B. S. (1997). *Fieldworking: Reading and writing research*. Upper Saddle River, NJ: Prentice Hall.

Clandinin, D. J., & Connelly, F. M. (1994). Personal experience methods. In N. K. Denzin & Y. S. Lincoln (Eds.), *Handbook of qualitative research* (pp. 413–427). Thousand Oaks, CA: Sage.

Clifford, G. J. (1989). Man/woman/teacher: Gender, family, and career in American educational history. In D. Warren (Ed.), *American teachers: Histories of a profession at work* (pp. 293–343). New York: Macmillan.

Clifford, J. (1988). *The predicament of culture: Twentieth-century ethnography, literature, and art*. Cambridge, MA: Harvard University Press.

———. (1990). Notes on (field) notes. In R. Sanjek (Ed.), *Fieldnotes: The making of anthropology* (pp. 47–71). Ithaca, NY: Cornell University Press.

Clifford, J., & Marcus, G. (1986). *Writing culture*. Berkeley: University of California Press.

Clough, P. T. (1998). *The end(s) of ethnography: From realism to social criticism*. New York: Peter Lang.

Cochran-Smith, M., & Lytle, S. (1993). *Inside/outside: Teacher research and knowledge*. New York: Teachers College Press.

Coffey, A., & Atkinson, P. A. (1996). *Making sense of qualitative data*. Thousand Oaks, CA: Sage.

Cohen, R. M. (1991). *A lifetime of teaching: Portraits of five veteran high school teachers*. New York: Teachers College Press.

Collins, W. A. (Ed.) (1979). *Children's language and communication*. Hillsdale, NJ: Earlbaum.

Cook, T., & Campbell, D. T. (1979). Quasi-experimentation: Design and analysis issues for field settings. Chicago: Rand McNally.

Corsaro, W. A. (1985). *Friendship and peer culture in the early years*. Norwood, NJ: Ablex.

Creswell, J. W. (1998). *Qualitative inquiry and research design: Choosing among the five traditions*. Thousand Oaks, CA: Sage.

Curry, T. J. (1993). A little pain never hurt anyone: Athletic career socialization and the normalization of sports injury. *Symbolic Interaction, 16*, 273–290.

Dean, J. P., Eichhorn, R. L., & Dean, L. R. (1969). Establishing field relations. In G. J. McCall & J. Simmons (Eds.), *Issues in participant observation: A text and reader* (pp. 68–70). Reading, MA: Addison-Wesley.

Delamont, S, Coffey, A., & Atkinson, P. (2000). The twilight years? Educational ethnography and the five moments model. *Qualitative Studies in Education, 13*, 223–238.

deLone, R. H. (1979). *Small futures: Children, inequality, and the limits of liberal reform*. New York: Harcourt Brace Jovanovich.

278 *References*

Denzin, N. K. (1978). *The research act.* Chicago: Aldine.

———. (1989a). *Interpretive biography.* Newbury Park, CA: Sage.

———. (1989b). *Interpretive interactionism.* Newbury Park, CA: Sage.

———. (1994). The art and politics of interpretation. In N. K. Denzin & Y. S. Lincoln (Eds.), *Handbook of qualitative research* (pp. 500–515). Thousand Oaks, CA: Sage.

———. (1997). *Interpretive ethnography: Ethnographic practices for the 21st century.* Thousand Oaks, CA: Sage.

Denzin, N. K., & Lincoln, Y. S. (1994). Introduction: Entering the field of qualitative research. In N. K. Denzin & Y. S. Lincoln (Eds.), *Handbook of qualitative research* (pp. 1–18). Thousand Oaks, CA: Sage.

Derrida, J. (1981). *Dissemination.* (B. Johnson, Trans.). Chicago: University of Chicago Press.

DeVault, M. L. (1990). Talking and listening from women's standpoints: Feminist strategies for interviewing and analysis. *Social Problems, 37,* 96–116.

Eichelberger, R. T. (1989). *Disciplined inquiry: Understanding and doing educational research.* White Plains, NY: Longman.

Eisenberg, M. E., Wagenaar, A., & Neumark-Sztainer, D. (1997). Viewpoints of Minnesota students on school-based sexuality education. *Journal of School Health, 67,* 322–326.

Eisner, E. W. (1991). *The enlightened eye: Qualitative inquiry and the enhancement of educational practice.* New York: Macmillan.

Ellis, C., & Bochner, A. P. (Eds.). (1996). *Composing ethnography: Alternative forms of qualitative writing.* Walnut Creek, CA: AltaMira.

Ely, M., Anzul, M., Friedman, T., Garner, D., & Steinmetz, A. M. (1991). *Doing qualitative research: Circles within circles.* London: Falmer.

Emerson, R. M., Fretz, R. I., & Shaw, L. L. (1995). *Writing ethnographic fieldnotes.* Chicago: University of Chicago Press.

Emig, J. (1977). Writing as a model of learning. *College Composition and Communication, 28,* 122–128.

Erickson, F. (1977). Some approaches to inquiry in school-community ethnography. *Anthropology and Education Quarterly, 8,* 58–69.

———. (1986). Qualitative methods in research on teaching. In M. C. Wittrock (Ed.). *Handbook of research on teaching* (3rd ed.; pp. 119–161). New York: Macmillan.

Erickson, F., & Mohatt, G. (1982). The cultural organization of participation structures in two classrooms of Indian students. In G. Spindler (Ed.), *Doing the ethnography of schooling* (pp. 132–174). New York: Holt, Rinehart, & Winston.

Erickson, F., & Wilson, J. (1982). *Sights and sounds of life in school: A resource guide to film and videotape for research and education.* Ann Arbor: Institute for Research on Teaching of the College of Education at Michigan State University.

Fielding, N, & Lee, R. M. (1998). *Computer analysis and qualitative research.* London: Sage.

Finch, J. (1984). "It's great to have someone to talk to": The ethics and politics of interviewing women. In C. Bell and H. Roberts (Eds.), *Social researching* (pp. 70–87). London: Routledge & Kegan Paul.

Fine, M. (1991). *Framing dropouts: Notes on the politics of an urban public high school.* Albany: State University of New York Press.

Fisher, M. (1997). *Qualitative computing: Using software for qualitative data analysis.* Brookfield, VT: Ashgate.

Flax, J. (1990). *Thinking fragments: Psychoanalysis, feminism, and postmodernism in the contemporary West.* Berkeley: University of California Press.

Fontana, A., & Frey, J. H. (1984). Interviewing: The art of science. In N. K. Denzin & Y. S. Lincoln (Eds.), *Handbook of qualitative research* (pp. 361–376). Thousand Oaks, CA: Sage.

Foucault, M. (1972). *The archeology of knowledge.* (A. M. S. Smith, Trans.). New York: Pantheon.

———. (1977). *Discipline and punish: The birth of the prison.* New York: Pantheon.

Freeman, E. B., & Hatch, J. A. (1989). What schools expect young children to know and do: An analysis of kindergarten report cards. *Elementary School Journal, 89,* 595–605.

Freeman, M. P. (1993). *Rewriting the self: History, memory, narrative.* New York: Routledge.

Fulwiler, T. (Ed.). (1987). *The journal book.* Upper Montclair, NJ: Boynton/Cook.

Garrick, J. (1999). Doubting the philosophical assumptions of interpretive research. *Qualitative Studies in Education, 12,* 147–156.

Geertz, C. (1973). *The interpretation of cultures.* New York: Basic Books.

Giddens, A. (1971). *Capitalism and modern social theory: An analysis of the writings of Marx, Durkheim, and Max Weber.* New York: Cambridge University Press.

Giorgi, A. (1985). *Phenomenology and psychological research.* Pittsburgh: Duquesne University Press.

Giroux, H. (1988). *Schooling and the struggle for public life: Critical pedagogy in the modern age.* Minneapolis: University of Minnesota Press.

Gitlin, A., & Margonis, F. (1995). The political aspects of reform: Teacher resistance as good sense. *American Journal of Education, 103,* 377–405.

Glaser, B. G., & Strauss, A. L. (1967). *The discovery of grounded theory: Strategies for qualitative research.* Mill Valley, CA: Sociology Press.

Glesne, C., & Peshkin, A. (1992). *Becoming qualitative researchers: An introduction.* White Plains, NY: Longman.

Goetz, J. P., & LeCompte, M. D. (1984). *Ethnography and qualitative design in educational research.* New York: Academic Press.

Goffman, E. (1959). *The presentation of self in everyday life.* Garden City, NY: Anchor.

———. (1963). *Stigma.* Englewood Cliffs, NJ: Prentice-Hall.

———. (1967). *Interaction ritual: Essays on face-to-face behavior.* New York: Pantheon.

———. (1974). *Frame analysis.* New York: Harper & Row.

Golden-Biddle, K., & Locke, K. D. (1997). *Composing qualitative research.* Thousand Oaks, CA: Sage.

Goodall, H. L. (2000). *Writing the new ethnography.* Lanham, MD: AltaMira.

Grace, D. J., & Tobin, J. (1997). Carnival in the classroom: Elementary students making videos. In J. Tobin (Ed.), *Making a place for pleasure in early childhood education* (pp. 159–187). New Haven, CT: Yale University Press.

Graham, D., Doherty, J., & Malek, M. (1992). Introduction: The context and language of postmodernism. In J. Doherty, E. Graham, & M. Malek (Eds.), *Postmodernism and the social sciences* (pp. 1–23). New York: St. Martin's Press.

Graue, M. E. (1993). *Ready for what? Constructing meanings of readiness for kindergarten.* Albany: State University of New York Press.

Graue, M. E., & Walsh, D. J. (1995). Children in context: Interpreting the here and now of children's lives. In J. A. Hatch (Ed.), *Qualitative research in early childhood settings* (pp. 135–154). Westport, CT: Praeger.

———. (1998). *Studying children in context: Theories, methods, and ethics.* Thousand Oaks, CA: Sage.

Greenbaum, T. L. (1998). *The handbook for focus group research* (2nd ed.). Thousand Oaks, CA: Sage.

Guba, E. G., & Lincoln, Y. S. (1994). Competing paradigms in qualitative research. In N. K. Denzin & Y. S. Lincoln (Eds.), *Handbook of qualitative research* (pp. 105–117). Thousand Oaks, CA: Sage.

Gubrium, J. F., & Holstein, J. A. (1997). *The new language of qualitative method.* New York: Oxford University Press.

Hamilton, D. (1994). Traditions, preferences, and postures in applied qualitative research. In N. K. Denzin & Y. S. Lincoln (Eds.), *Handbook of qualitative research* (pp. 60–69). Thousand Oaks, CA: Sage.

Hammersley, M., & Atkinson, P. (1983). *Ethnography: Principles and practices.* London: Tavistock.

Harding, S. (1987). Introduction: Is there a feminist method? In S. Harding (Ed.), *Feminism and methodology.* Bloomington: Indiana University Press.

Hargreaves, D. H. (1967). *Social relations in a secondary school.* London: Routledge & Kegan Paul.

Hatch, J. A. (1984). *The social goals of children: A naturalistic study of child-to-child interaction in a kindergarten.* Doctoral dissertation, University of Florida, Gainesville.

———. (1985). The quantoids versus the smooshes: Struggling with methodological rapprochement. *Issues in Education, 3,* 158–167.

———. (1988). Learning to be an outsider: Peer stigmatization in kindergarten. *Urban Review, 20,* 59–72.

———. (1995a). Introduction: Qualitative research in early childhood settings. In J. A. Hatch (Ed.), *Qualitative research in early childhood settings* (pp. xi–xvii). Westport, CT: Praeger.

———. (1995b). Ethical conflicts in classroom research. In J. A. Hatch (Ed.), *Qualitative research in early childhood settings* (pp. 213–222). Westport, CT: Praeger.

———. (1995c). Studying childhood as a cultural invention: A rationale and framework. In J. A. Hatch (Ed.), *Qualitative research in early childhood settings* (pp. 117–133). Westport, CT: Praeger.

———. (1998). Qualitative research in early childhood education. In B. Spodek, O. Saracho, & A. Pellegrini (Eds.), *Yearbook in early childhood education: Issues in early childhood educational research* (pp. 49–75). New York: Teachers College Press.

———. (1999). Introducing postmodern thought in a thoroughly modern university. In L. D. Soto (Ed.). *The politics of early childhood education.* (pp. 179–196). New York: Peter Lang.

Hatch, J. A., & Bondy, E. (1984). A double dose of the same medicine: Implications from a naturalistic study of summer school reading instruction. *Urban Education, 19,* 29–38.

———. (1986). The researcher-teacher relationship: Observations and implications from naturalistic studies in classrooms. *The Journal of Research and Development in Education, 19,* 48–56.

Hatch, J. A., & Freeman, E. B. (1988). Kindergarten philosophies and practices: Perspectives of teachers, principals, and supervisors. *Early Childhood Research Quarterly, 3,* 151–166.

Hatch, J. A., & Wisniewski, R. (1995). Life history and narrative: Questions, issues, and exemplary works. In J. A. Hatch & R. Wisniewski (Eds.), *Life history and narrative* (pp. 113–136). London: Falmer.

Hawkesworth, M. E. (1989). Knowers, knowing, known: Feminist theory and claims of truth. In M. R. Malson, J. F. O'Barr, S. Westphal Wihl, & M. Wyer (Eds.), *Feminist theory in practice and process* (pp. 327–351). Chicago: University of Chicago Press.

Henry, J. (1965). *Culture against man.* New York: Random House.

Henry, M. E. (1992). School rituals as educational contexts: Symbolizing the world, others, and self in Waldorf and college prep schools. *Qualitative Studies in Education, 5,* 295–309.

Hill, M. R. (1993). *Archival strategies and techniques*. Newbury Park, CA: Sage.

Hillebrandt, I. S. (1979). Focus group research: Behind the one-way mirror. *Public Relations Journal, 35*, 17–33.

Hitchcock, G., & Hughes, D. (1995). *Research and the teacher: A qualitative introduction to school-based research*. London: Routledge.

Hodder, I. (1994). The interpretation of documents and material culture. In N. K. Denzin & Y. S. Lincoln (Eds.), *Handbook of qualitative research* (pp. 393–402). Thousand Oaks, CA: Sage.

Hoffman, D. (1999). Turning power inside out: Reflections on resistance from the (anthropological) field. *Qualitative Studies in Education, 12*, 671–687.

Holmes, M., & Weiss, B. J. (Eds.). (1995). *Lives of women public schoolteachers: Scenes from American educational history*. New York: Garland.

Holmes, R. M. (1995). *How young children perceive race*. Thousand Oaks, CA: Sage.

Howard, D. C. P. (1994). Human-computer interactions: A phenomenological examination of the adult first-time computer experience. *Qualitative Studies in Education, 7*, 33–49.

Husserl, E. (1913). *Ideas*. London: George Allen & Unwin.

Hymes, D. (1982). What is ethnography? In P. Gilmore & A. A. Glatthorn (Eds.), *Children in and out of school: Ethnography and education* (pp. 22–32). Washington, DC: Center for Applied Linguistics.

Jackson, P. (1968). *Life in classrooms*. New York: Holt, Rinehart, & Winston.

Jacob, E. (1987). Qualitative research traditions: A review. *Review of Educational Research, 57*, 1–50.

———. (1988). Clarifying qualitative research: A focus on traditions. *Educational Researcher, 17*, 16–24.

Janesick, V. J. (1998). *Stretching exercises for qualitative researchers*. Thousand Oaks, CA: Sage.

Johnson, J. M. (1975). *Doing field research*. Beverly Hills, CA; Sage.

Johnson, L. G., & Hatch, J. A. (1990). A descriptive study of the creative and social behavior of four highly original young children. *Journal of Creative Behavior, 24*, 205–224.

Johnstone, A. C. (1994). *Uses for journal keeping: An ethnography of writing in a university science class*. Norwood, NJ: Ablex.

Kelle, E. (Ed.). (1995). *Computer-aided qualitative data analysis*. Thousand Oaks, CA: Sage.

Kincheloe, J. L. (1991). *Teachers as researchers: Qualitative inquiry as a path to empowerment*. London: Falmer.

Kirk, J., & Miller, M. L. (1986). *Reliability and validity in qualitative research*. Beverly Hills, CA: Sage.

Kluckhohn, F. (1940). The participant observer technique in small communities. *American Journal of Sociology, 46*, 331–343.

Krueger, R. A. (1994). *Focus groups: A practical guide for applied research.* Thousand Oaks, CA: Sage.

Kuhn, T. S. (1970). *The structure of scientific revolutions.* Chicago: University of Chicago Press.

Kvale, S. (1996). *InterViews: An introduction to qualitative research interviewing.* Thousand Oaks, CA: Sage.

Labov, W. (1972). *Sociolinguistic patterns.* Philadelphia: University of Pennsylvania Press.

Ladson-Billings, G. (1994). *The dreamkeepers: Successful teachers of African-American children.* San Francisco: Jossey-Bass.

Langer, J. (1992, January 6). 18 ways to say "shut up!" *Marketing News, 2,* 15.

Lapadat, A., & Lindsay, A. (1999). Transcription in research and practice: From standardization of technique to interpretive positionings. *Qualitative Inquiry, 5,* 64–86.

Lather, P. (1988). Feminist perspectives on empowering research methodologies. *Womens Studies International Forum, 11,* 569–581.

———. (1991a). *Feminist research in education: Within/against.* Geelong: Deakin University Press.

———. (1991b). *Getting smart: Feminist research and pedagogy with/in the postmodern.* New York: Routledge.

Lather, P., & Smithies, C. (1997). *Troubling the angels: Women living with AIDS/HIV.* Boulder, CO: Westview.

LeCompte, M. D., & Preissle, J. (1993). *Ethnography and qualitative design in educational research* (2nd ed.). San Diego, CA: Academic Press.

LeCompte, M. D., & Schensul, J. J. (1999). *Analyzing and interpreting ethnographic data.* Walnut Creek, CA: AltaMira.

Leedy, P. D. (1997). *Practical research: Planning and design.* Upper Saddle River, NJ: Merrill.

Lewin, K. (1952). *Field theory in social science.* London: Tavistock.

Lightfoot, S. L. (1983). *The good high school.* New York: Basic Books.

Lincoln, Y. S. (1995). Emerging criteria for quality in qualitative and interpretive inquiry. *Qualitative Inquiry, 1,* 275–289.

Lincoln, Y. S., & Guba, E. G. (1985). *Naturalistic inquiry.* Beverly Hills, CA: Sage.

Lindesmith, A. R. (1952). Comment on W. S. Robinson's The Logical Structure of Analytic Induction. *American Sociological Review, 17,* 493–494.

Loftland, J., & Loftland, L. H. (1984). *Analyzing social settings.* Belmont, CA: Wadsworth.

Lynd, R. S., & Lynd, H. M. (1937). *Middletown in transition*. New York: Harcourt, Brace and Company.

Malinowski, B. (1922). *Argonauts of the Western Pacific*. London: Routledge.

Manning, K. (1995). Rituals and rescission: Building community in hard times. *Journal of College Student Development, 35,* 275–281.

Marcus, G., & Fischer, M. (1986). *Anthropology as cultural critique: An experimental moment in the human sciences*. Chicago: University of Chicago Press.

Marshall, C., & Rossman, G. B. (1995). *Designing qualitative research*. Thousand Oaks, CA: Sage.

Maxwell, J. A. (1996). *Qualitative research design: An interactive approach*. Thousand Oaks, CA: Sage.

McBeth, D. (1994). Resuming: The final contingency of reproach. *Qualitative Studies in Education, 7,* 135–154.

McCall, G. J., & Simmons, J. L. (Eds.). (1969). *Issues in participant observation: A text and reader*. Reading, MA: Addison-Wesley.

McDermott, R. (1976). *Kids make sense: An ethnographic account of the interactional management of success and failure in one first grade classroom*. Unpublished doctoral dissertation, Stanford University.

McLaren, P., & Farahmandpur, R. (2000). Reconsidering Marx in post-Marxist times: A requiem for postmodernism? *Educational Researcher, 29,* 25–33.

Meadmore, D., Hatcher, C., & McWilliam, E. (2000). Getting tense about genealogy. *Qualitative Studies in Education, 13,* 463–476.

Measor, L., & Sikes, P. (1992). Visiting lives: Ethics and methodology in life history. In I. F. Goodson (Ed.), *Studying teachers' lives*. New York: Teachers College Press.

Meloy, J. M. (1994). *Writing the qualitative dissertation: Understanding by doing*. Hillsdale, NJ: Lawrence Erlbaum.

Merriam, S. B. (1988). *Case study research in education: A qualitative approach*. San Francisco: Jossey-Bass.

Merton, R. K., Fiske, M., & Kendall, P. L. (1990). *The focused interview* (2nd ed.). New York: Free Press.

Merton, R. K., & Kendall, P. L. (1946). The focused interview. *American Journal of Sociology, 51,* 541–557.

Metz, M. H. (2001). Intellectual boarder crossing in graduate education: A report from the field. *Educational Researcher, 30,* 12–18.

Miles, M. B., & Huberman, A. M. (1994). *Qualitative data analysis: A sourcebook of new methods*. Newbury Park, CA: Sage.

Mishler, E. G. (1986). *Research interviewing: Context and narrative*. Cambridge, MA: Harvard University Press.

Moore-Gilbert, B. J. (1997). *Postcolonial theory: Contexts, practices, politics*. New York: Verso.

Morgan, D. L. (Ed.). (1993). *Successful focus groups: Advancing the state of the art.* Newbury Park, CA: Sage.

———. (1997). *Focus groups as qualitative research* (2nd ed.). Newbury Park, CA: Sage.

Morris, M. B. (1977). *An excursion into creative sociology.* New York: Columbia University Press.

Morrow, R. A., & Brown, D. D. (1994). *Critical theory and methodology.* Thousand Oaks, CA: Sage.

Murray, D. (1986). One writer's secrets. *College Composition and Communication, 37,* 146–153.

National Commission for the Protection of Human Subjects of Biomedical and Behavioral Research. (1979). *The Belmont report: Ethical principals and guidelines for the protection of human subjects of research.* Washington DC: Department of Health, Education and Welfare.

Newman, J. (Ed.). (1998). *Tensions of teaching: Beyond tips to critical reflection.* New York: Teachers College Press.

Olesen, V. (1994). Feminisms and models of qualitative research. In N. K. Denzin & Y. S. Lincoln (Eds.), *Handbook of qualitative research* (pp. 158–174). Thousand Oaks, CA: Sage.

Opler, M. E. (1945). Themes as dynamic forces in culture. *American Journal of Sociology, 53,* 198–206.

Orr, L. (1991). *A dictionary of critical theory.* New York: Greenwood.

Pallas, A. M. (2001). Preparing education doctoral students for epistemological diversity. *Educational Researcher, 30,* 6–11.

Parker, L., Deyhle, D., Villenas, S., & Nebeker, K. C. (1998). Guest editors' introduction: Critical race theory and qualitative studies in education. *Qualitative Studies in Education, 11,* 5–6.

Patton, M. Q. (1980). *Qualitative evaluation methods.* Newbury Park, CA: Sage.

———. (1990). *Qualitative research and evaluation methods.* Newbury Park, CA: Sage.

Peshkin, A. (1986). *God's choice: The total world of a fundamentalist Christian school.* Chicago: University of Chicago Press.

———. (1988). Understanding complexity: A gift of qualitative inquiry. *Anthropology and Education Quarterly, 19,* 416–424.

———. (1991). *The color of strangers, the color of friends: The play of ethnicity in school and community.* Chicago: University of Chicago Press.

———. (1997). *Places of memory: Whiteman's schools and Native American communities.* Mahwah, NJ: Lawrence Erlbaum.

Peters, M. (Ed.). (1999). *After the disciplines: The emergence of cultural studies.* Westport, CT: Bergin & Garvey.

Pfuhl, E. H. (1980). *The deviance process.* New York: Van Norstrand Reinhold.

Phelan, P. (1993). *The unmarked: The politics of performance.* London: Routledge.

Polakow, V. (1993). *Lives on the edge: Single mothers and their children in the other America.* Chicago: University of Chicago Press.

Polkinghorne, D. E. (1995). Narrative configuration and qualitative analysis. In J. A. Hatch & R. Wisniewski (Eds.), *Life history and narrative* (pp. 5–24). London: Falmer.

Potter, W. J. (1996). *An analysis of thinking and research about qualitative methods.* Mahwah, NJ: Lawrence Erlbaum.

Prawat, R. S. (2000). Responding to the reviews: What's an author to do? *American Educational Research Journal, 37,* 307–314.

Prosser, J. (Ed.) (1998). *Image-based research: A sourcebook for qualitative researchers.* London: Falmer.

Reinharz, S. (1979). *On becoming a social scientist.* San Francisco: Jossey-Bass.

———. (1992). *Feminist methods in social research.* New York: Oxford University Press.

Richardson, L. (1994). Writing: A method of inquiry. In N. K. Denzin & Y. S. Lincoln (Eds.), *Handbook of qualitative research* (pp. 516–529). Thousand Oaks, CA: Sage.

———. (2000). Evaluating ethnography. *Qualitative Inquiry, 6,* 253–255.

———. (2001). Getting personal: Writing stories. *Qualitative Studies in Education, 14,* 33–38.

Rist, R. C. (1980). Blitzkrieg ethnography: On the transformation of a method into a movement. *Educational Researcher, 9,* 8–10.

Robinson, W. S. (1951). The logical structure of analytic induction. *American Sociological Review, 16,* 812–818.

Roman, L. G. (1992). The political significance of other ways of narrating ethnography: A feminist materialist approach. In M. D. LeCompte, W. L. Millroy, & J. Preissle (Eds.), *The handbook of qualitative research in education* (pp. 555–594). New York: Academic Press.

Rosaldo, R. (1989). *Culture and truth: The remaking of social analysis.* Boston: Beacon.

Rubin, H. J., & Rubin, I. S. (1995). *Qualitative interviewing: The art of hearing data.* Thousand Oaks, CA: Sage.

Ryan, W. (1976). *Blaming the victim.* New York: Pantheon Books.

Salkind, N. J. (1991). *Exploring research.* New York: Macmillan.

Sanjek, R. (Ed.) (1990). *Fieldnotes: The making of anthropology.* Ithaca, NY: Cornell University Press.

Sarap, M. (1993). *An introductory guide to poststructuralism and postmodernism.* Athens, GA: University of Georgia Press.

Sartre, J-P. (1964). *Nausea.* Norfolk, CT: New Directions. (Original published in 1938).

Schatzman, L., & Strauss, A. L. (1973). *Field research: Strategies for natural sociology.* Englewood Cliffs, NJ: Prentice-Hall.

Schickedanz, J. A., York, M. E., Stewart, I. S., & White, S. (1983). *Strategies for teaching young children* (2nd ed.). Englewood Cliffs, NJ: Prentice-Hall.

Schwartz, H., & Jacobs, J. (1979). *Qualitative sociology.* New York: Free Press.

Schwartz, M. S., & Schwartz, C. G. (1955). Problems in participant observation. *American Journal of Sociology, 60,* 343–353.

Scott, J. (1990). *A matter of record: Documentary sources in social research.* Cambridge, UK: Polity Press.

Seidman, I. (1998). *Interviewing as qualitative research: A guide for researchers in education and the social sciences.* New York: Teachers College Press.

Sherman, R. (1993). Reflections on the editing experience: Writing qualitative research. *Qualitative Studies in Education, 6,* 233–239.

Shor, I., & Friere, P. (1987). *A pedagogy for liberation.* South Hadley, MA: Bergin & Garvey.

Shultz, J., & Florio, S. (1979). Stop and freeze: The negotiation of social and physical space in a kindergarten/first grade classroom. *Anthropology and Education Quarterly, 10,* 166–181.

Shultz, J., Florio, S., & Erickson, F. (1982). Where's the floor? Aspects of the cultural organization of social relationships in communication at home and at school. In P. Gilmore & A. Glatthorn (Eds.), *Ethnography and education: Children in and out of school* (pp. 88–123). Washington DC: Center for Applied Linguistics.

Silvers, R. J. (1977). Appearances: A videographic study of children's culture. In P. Woods & M. Hammersley (Eds.), *School Experience* (pp. 129–162). London: Croom Helm.

Smith, L. M. (1979). An evolving logic of participant observation, educational ethnography, and other case studies. *Review of Research in Education, 6,* 316–377.

Smith, L. M., & Geoffrey, W. (1968). *The complexities of an urban classroom: An analysis toward a general theory of teaching.* New York: Holt, Rinehart, & Winston.

Smith, M. L. (1989). Teachers' beliefs about retention. In L. A. Shepard & M. L. Smith (Eds.), *Flunking grades: Research and policies on retention* (pp. 132–150). London: Falmer.

Smulyan, L. (2000a). *Balancing acts: Women principals at work.* Albany: State University of New York Press.

———. (2000b). Feminist cases of nonfeminist subjects: Case studies of women principals. *Qualitative Studies in Education, 13,* 589–609.

Spindler, G. (Ed.). (1955). *Education and anthropology.* Stanford, CA: Stanford University Press.

———. (Ed.). (1982). *Doing the ethnography of schooling: Educational ethnography in action*. New York: Holt, Rinehart, & Winston.

Spradley, J. P. (1979). *The ethnographic interview*. New York: Holt, Rinehart & Winston.

———. (1980). *Participant observation*. New York: Holt, Rinehart & Winston.

Stake, R. E. (1994). Case studies. In N. K. Denzin & Y. S. Lincoln (Eds.), *Handbook of qualitative research* (pp. 236–247). Thousand Oaks, CA: Sage.

Stanfield, J. H. (1994). Ethnic modeling in qualitative research. In N. K. Denzin & Y. S. Lincoln (Eds.), *Handbook of qualitative research* (pp. 175–188). Thousand Oaks, CA: Sage.

Stenhouse, L. (1975). *An introduction to curriculum research and development*. London: Heinemann.

Stewart, A. J. (1994). Toward a feminist strategy for studying women's lives. In C. E. Franz & A. J. Steward (Eds.), *Women creating lives: Identities, resilience and resistance* (pp. 11–35). Boulder, CO: Westview.

Stewart, D. W., & Shamdasani, P. N. (1990). *Focus groups: Theory and practice*. Newbury Park, CA: Sage.

St. Pierre, E. A. (2000). Poststructural feminism in education. *Qualitative Studies in Education, 13*, 477–515.

Strauss, A. L. (1987). *Qualitative analysis for social scientists*. Cambridge: Cambridge University Press.

Strauss, A. L., & Corbin, J. (1990). *Basics of qualitative research: Grounded theory procedures and techniques*. Newberry Park, CA: Sage.

———. (1998). *Basics of qualitative research: Techniques and procedures for developing grounded theory*. Thousand Oaks, CA: Sage.

Stringer, E. T. (1999). *Action research*. Thousand Oaks, CA: Sage.

Strunk, W., & White, E. B. (1972). *Elements of style* (2nd Edition). New York: Macmillan.

Tesch, R. (1990). *Qualitative research: Analysis types and software tools*. London: Falmer.

Thomas, J. (1993). *Doing critical ethnography*. Newbury Park, CA: Sage.

Tierney, W. G. (1993a). Self and identity in a postmodern world: A life story. In D. McLaughlin & W. G. Tierney (Eds.), *Naming silenced lives: Personal narratives and the process of educational change* (pp. 119–134). New York: Routledge.

———. (1993b). The cedar closet. *Qualitative Studies in Education, 6*, 303–314.

Tierney, W. G., & Lincoln, Y. S. (Eds.). (1997). *Representation and the text: Re-framing the narrative voice*. Albany: State University of New York Press.

Tobin, J. (1995). Post-structural research in early childhood education. In J. A. Hatch (Ed.), *Qualitative research in early childhood settings* (pp. 223–243). Westport, CT: Praeger.

———. (1997). Playing doctor in two cultures: The United States and Ireland. In J. Tobin (Ed.), *Making a place for pleasure in early childhood education* (pp. 119–158). New Haven, CT: Yale University Press.

Tobin, J. J., Wu, D. Y., & Davidson, D. H. (1989). *Preschool in three cultures: Japan, China, and the United States.* New Haven, CT: Yale University Press.

Tripp, D. (1994). Teachers' lives, critical incidents, and professional practice. *Qualitative Studies in Education, 3,* 271–284.

University of Tennessee Institutional Review Board. (1999). *Instruction guide for faculty, staff, and students.* Knoxville: University of Tennessee.

Van Maanen, J. (1988). *Tales of the field: On writing ethnography.* Chicago: University of Chicago Press.

Van Manen, M. (1990). *Researching lived experience: Human science for an action sensitive pedagogy.* Albany: State University of New York Press.

Vaughn, S., Schumm, J. S., & Sinagub, J. (1996). *Focus group interviews in education and psychology.* Thousand Oaks, CA; Sage.

Vidich, A. J., & Lyman, S. M. (1994). Qualitative methods: Their history in sociology and anthropology. In N. K. Denzin & Y. S. Lincoln (Eds.), *Handbook of qualitative research* (pp. 1–18). Thousand Oaks, CA: Sage.

Walsh, D. J., Tobin, J. J., Graue, M. E. (1993). The interpretive voice: Qualitative research in early childhood education. In B. Spodek (Ed.), *Handbook of research on the education of young children* (pp. 464–476). New York: Macmillan.

Warner, M. (Ed.). (1993). *Fear of a queer planet.* Minneapolis: University of Minnesota Press.

Webb, E., Campbell, D., Schwartz, R., Sechrest, L., & Grove, J. B. (1981). *Nonreactive measures in the social sciences.* Boston: Houghton Mifflin.

Weiler, K. (1992). Remembering and representing life choices: A critical perspective on teachers' oral history narratives. *Qualitative Studies in Education, 5,* 39–50.

Weitzman, E. A., & Miles, M. B. (1995). *Computer programs for qualitative data analysis.* Thousand Oaks, CA: Sage.

Wesley, P. W., Buysse, V., & Tyndall, S. (1997). Family and professional perspectives on early intervention: An exploration using focus groups. *Topics in Early Childhood Special Education, 17,* 435–456.

Wilkinson, L. C. (Ed.) (1982). *Communicating in the classroom.* New York: Academic Press.

Wolcott, H. F. (1973). *The man in the principal's office: An ethnography.* New York: Holt, Rinehart, & Winston.

———. (1982). Differing styles on on-site research, or, "If it isn't ethnography, what is it?" *Review Journal of Philosophy and Social Science, 7,* 154–169.

———. (1988). Ethnographic research in education. In R. M. Jaeger (Ed.), *Complimentary methods for research in education.* Washington, DC: American Educational Research Association.

———. (1990). *Writing up qualitative research*. Newbury Park, CA: Sage.

———. (1992). Posturing in qualitative inquiry. In M. D. Le Compte, W. L. Millroy, & J. Preissle (Eds.), *The handbook of qualitative research in education* (pp. 3–52). San Diego: Academic Press.

———. (1994). *Transforming qualitative data: Description, analysis, and interpretation*. Thousand Oaks, CA: Sage.

———. (1995). *The art of fieldwork*. Walnut Creek, CA: AltaMira.

Wolf, R. L., & Tymitz, B. (1978). *Whatever happened to the giant wombat: An investigation of the impact of the Ice Age Mammals and Emergence of Man Exhibit*. Washington, DC: Smithsonian Institutes.

Woods, P. (1986). *Inside schools: Ethnography in educational research*. London: Routledge & Kegan Paul.

———. (1999). *Successful writing for qualitative researchers*. London: Routledge.

Yin, R. K. (1994). *Case study research: Design and methods*. Thousand Oaks, CA: Sage.

Yow, V. R. (1994). *Recording oral history: A practical guide for social scientists*. Thousand Oaks, CA: Sage.

Zeller, N. (1995). Narrative strategies for case reports. In J. A. Hatch & R. Wisniewski (Eds.), *Life history and narrative* (pp. 75–88). London: Falmer.

Zigo, D. (2001). Rethinking reciprocity: Collaboration in labor as a path toward equalizing power in classroom studies. *Qualitative Studies in Education, 14,* 351–365.

AUTHOR INDEX

SUBJECT INDEX